The Presidencies of
JAMES A. GARFIELD
&
CHESTER A. ARTHUR

The Presidencies of
JAMES A. GARFIELD
&
CHESTER A. ARTHUR

Justus D. Doenecke

UNIVERSITY PRESS OF KANSAS

Published by the University Press of Kansas (Lawrence, Kansas 66045),
which was organized by the Kansas Board of Regents and is
operated and funded by Emporia State University, Fort Hays State
University, Kansas State University, Pittsburg State University,
the University of Kansas, and Wichita State University

Library of Congress Cataloging in Publication Data

Doenecke, Justus D.
The Presidencies of James A. Garfield & Chester A. Arthur.

(American Presidency series)
Includes bibliographical references and index.
1. United States—Politics and government—1881-1885.
2. Garfield, James Abram, Pres., U. S., 1831-1881.
3. Arthur, Chester Alan, Pres., U. S., 1830-1886.
         I. Title.   II. Series.
E686.D63   973.8′4   80-18957
          ISBN 0-7006-0208-9

Printed in the United States of America

To
Laszlo

CONTENTS

FOREWORD

The aim of the American Presidency Series is to present historians and the general reading public with interesting, scholarly assessments of the various presidential administrations. These interpretive surveys are intended to cover the broad ground between biographies, specialized monographs, and journalistic accounts. As such, each will be a comprehensive, synthetic work which will draw upon the best in pertinent secondary literature, yet leave room for the author's own analysis and interpretation.

Volumes in the series will present the data essential to understanding the administration under consideration. Particularly, each book will treat the then current problems facing the United States and its people and how the president and his associates felt about, thought about, and worked to cope with these problems. Attention will be given to how the office developed and operated during the president's tenure. Equally important will be consideration of the vital relationships between the president, his staff, the executive officers, Congress, foreign representatives, the judiciary, state officials, the public, political parties, the press, and influential private citizens. The series will also be concerned with how this unique American institution—the presidency—was viewed by the presidents, and with what results.

All this will be set, insofar as possible, in the context not only of contemporary politics but also of economics, international relations, law, morals, public administration, religion, and thought. Such a broad approach is necessary to understanding, for a presidential administration is more than the elected and appointed officers composing it, since its work so often reflects the major problems, anxieties, and glories of the nation. In short, the authors in the series will strive to recount and evaluate the record of each administration and to identify its distinctiveness and relationships to the past, its own time, and the future.

The General Editors

PREFACE

American historians, more often than not, have found the Gilded Age something of an embarrassment. In the 1930s, such writers as Charles A. Beard and Vernon L. Parrington portrayed the era as a "great barbecue," involving a "saturnalia of plunder." Even today, most general surveys race through the period, finding it an unfortunate hiatus between the noble crusades embodied in the War for the Union and the progressive movement. Seldom have personalities and issues been taken on their own terms.

Little wonder that the presidents of this time have suffered from much neglect. Usually portrayed as colorless and opinionless men of portly bearing and drab countenance, they were more often subject to quips than to analysis. Novelist Thomas Wolfe undoubtedly represented the attitudes of many of his countrymen when he referred to them as "the lost Americans: their gravely vacant and bewhiskered faces mixed, melted, swam together. . . . Which had the whiskers, which the burnsides: which was which?" Chester Alan Arthur was a particularly obscure chief executive, a man who added to the sense of mystery surrounding him by burning all his personal papers the day before he died.

Currently, however, presidents of the Gilded Age and their administrations are coming under renewed examination. This volume, part of a series that stresses the synthesis of recent scholarly work, has benefited from a host of new explorations, ranging from fresh and massive biographies of Garfield and Arthur to detailed articles covering crises in Ireland, Korea, and Madagascar. No historian ever confesses to an overabundance of sources. Yet we are now blessed with many dissertations, monographs, and articles on various aspects of political life and public policy, particularly on such topics as southern politics, Indian policy, and civil-service reform.

In some ways, this renewed interest in the Gilded Age is inevitable. The events of the past twenty years have forced historians to focus upon the consequences of presidential assassination, corruption in high places, setbacks overseas, economic recession, the predicament of the South, and the plight of blacks and Native Americans. In addition, we are learning afresh how deeply American society was transformed by the technological revolution of the era, a transformation that particularly influenced American foreign policy.

Some readers will find this book quite revisionist, for it presents a renewed appreciation of both Garfield and Arthur. Both men were far more than cynical spoilsmen or naïve incompetents, individuals whose presidencies provide studies in ineptitude. Rather, they possessed considerable ability. Arthur, in particular, pioneered in the development of the navy, sought foreign markets for American surpluses, fostered civil-service reform, and pressed for a scientific tariff. More important, both chief executives sought, often successfully, to keep Congress from making inroads on their prerogatives and power. The battle over the collectorship of the New York Customhouse, for example, might appear trivial to later generations, but for those who had to wage it, it was a necessary holding action.

The book is revisionist in another sense; that is, in its treatment of foreign policy. It takes advantage of a host of new studies and, by so doing, challenges the long-held view that the nation was withdrawn and insular. Instead, this work stresses the many involvements of American policy makers, whose attention was focused upon such distant areas as Peru, Indochina, Hawaii, and the Congo. During the presidencies of Garfield and Arthur, the United States attempted to intervene in a war between Chile and Peru, sought to turn Nicaragua into a protectorate, supplied leading advisers to Madagascar and Korea, and took a major part in the Congo conference of 1884. Yet all revisionism has its limits, and this book emphasizes uncoordinated statescraft and inept diplomacy more than Open Door imperialism or grand designs for world markets.

In a more important way as well—that dealing with the presidency as an institution—this study is tempered. The book offers few candidates for canonization. Garfield died less than six months after he entered office, making his presidency something of a question mark. He had yet to be tested on major issues of public policy. Arthur was ill prepared to be chief executive, lethargic while he occupied the White House. Much of the time in poor health, he was probably never meant to be cast in a heroic mold. His most prominent exercise of presidential powers lay in his use of the veto.

In short, we might best see the two men as transitional figures, way stations on the road leading from the weak leadership of Andrew Johnson to the forceful direction of Theodore Roosevelt. But transitional figures, as well as transitional administrations, can be significant in their own right, giving the reader a unique chance to see how institutions operate under stress. And in the early 1880s, one could find stress aplenty.

Other scholars have given most generously of their time, and at no little personal sacrifice, to make this book a reality. Vincent P. De Santis, Ellen McDonald, Forrest McDonald, James G. Moseley, and Hans L. Trefousse have read the entire manuscript with the greatest of care. So too have the three editors of this series: Donald R. McCoy, Clifford S. Griffin, and Homer E. Socolofsky. Thomas C. Reeves has unsparingly criticized my treatment of Arthur's domestic policy, as has Allan Peskin concerning Garfield. As both scholars were engaged in projects that in part overlapped this one, their friendship and kindness is something that will never be forgotten. The same altruism is revealed by R. Hal Williams, now writing a life of James G. Blaine. Various scholars have read material on the following topics: Raymond G. O'Connor on the navy, David Evans on Asia, Anna Macias on Latin America, and Richard N. Ellis on Indians. Robert Knox has freely shared his mastery of prose style and of American literature as well. When I first began this project, my general inquiries were graciously answered by Allan G. Bogue, Leslie E. Decker, David Herbert Donald, Paul Goodman, Ray Ginger, James Tice Moore, Morton Rothstein, Ari Hoogenboom, Robert H. Wiebe, Paul S. Holbo, Edward C. Kirkland, and C. Vann Woodward. The rich world of the Gilded Age was opened to me first by Charles Ray Wilson, then by David Herbert Donald. All interpretations arc mine alone, and I take full responsibility for any possible errors.

Other individuals, although not directly related to this project, have gone out of their way to be encouraging. Here I must mention Arthur S. Link, Eugene Lewis, and Laszlo Deme. Pat Bryant, reference librarian at New College of the University of South Florida, deserves special mention, for she has come to my aid on countless occasions and on quite short notice. The Institute for Humane Studies has generously supported research on this project over several years, and in this connection I particularly want to thank its former vice-president, Kenneth S. Templeton, Jr., and Leonard P. Liggio, now its president.

Most of all I want to thank my wife, Carol, who has labored with me along every step of this project.

Justus D. Doenecke

Bradenton, Florida

1

★ ★ ★ ★ ★

INSTITUTIONS IN TRANSITION

"Life is that of the squirrel in his revolving cage," observed James Bryce in 1883, when he visited the United States.[1] The British journalist was hardly exaggerating. Americans were engaging in a frenzy of activity, from taming a continent to absorbing massive numbers of immigrants. A nation that had relatively recently finished the bloodiest war of the century was beginning the most comprehensive industrialization in all history.

By 1880, a technological revolution was altering the entire framework of American society. The linchpin of this revolution lay in railroads: miles of track created mass markets, bound together the continent's resources, stimulated production, and fostered a host of inventions. Demands for steel rails resulted in devising the Bessemer process for converting pig iron into steel; the development of such industries as steel, iron, and coal created a desire for the Corliss steam engine.

Yet, if in many ways the technological revolution was bringing the country closer together, both modernizing the nation and binding it, there was a price to pay. Farmers were often troubled, for lighter work loads and greater output could not always compensate for inadequate financing and for incomplete systems of transportation. Wheat and cotton prices, in particular, could fluctuate wildly. The cities were facing even greater dislocation, with traditional neighborhoods being forced to absorb a burgeoning factory system. They lacked such essentials as sewers and fresh water. If, in the United States, jobs were far more plentiful and wages far higher than they were overseas, many workers—both native and foreign—could not help but feel dehumanized. The eighties witnessed the ascendancy of the factory system, staffed by masses of unskilled and semiskilled laborers. The average industrial worker still did not earn enough to support his family. Grinding toil, frequent wage cuts and layoffs, fourteen-hour days, and seven-day weeks were all part of the norm.

Intellectually too the nation was experiencing a transformation. The early 1880s marked significant breakthroughs in what historian Eric Goldman has called "the steel chain of ideas."[2] Darwinism was assaulting an entire world of fixed truths; in its most radical form, it denied that the individual was a free moral agent and that God had determined the fate of each of his children.

In social thought the ideology of laissez faire was taking quite a different form, with Yale sociologist William Graham Sumner seeking to apply Darwinism to a world that far transcended biology. In a series of tracts, he condemned reformism, protectionism, socialism, and other forms of government intervention: all, he said, were attempts to deny the invariable struggle for existence. A misunderstood man, in his own time and ours, Sumner feared plutocrats as much as he feared proletarians. His hero was "the forgotten man," the independent middle-class producer who quietly provided for his family without making exorbitant demands upon the state. "What do social classes owe each other?" he asked in 1883 and answered, "Nothing."

True, most businessmen probably did not accept Social Darwinism as a general philosophy, finding its teachings too abstruse. As historian Edward Chase Kirkland notes, "Darwinism may have done no more for the business community than to furnish a terminology for old ideas"—said ideas being the "natural" laws of trade and the canons of self-help.[3] When, for example, economist Henry Wood wrote *Natural Law in the Business World* (1884), he went back to Adam Smith in order to propagate the ideas of the free market, the law of supply and demand, and the proposition that self-interest is the mainspring of human action.

Of course, not all science contained such controversial implications as did Darwinism. In fact, much of the American scientific enterprise was concerned with application, not theory, for abstract discovery possessed a low status within the nation. When compared to Europe, the United States was usually outclassed.

There were significant exceptions, however. In the field of pure science, Josiah Willard Gibbs of Yale was discovering principles in mathematical physics that would help to revolutionize the discipline. Even though his findings were too technical to be featured in *Harper's* or *Popular Science Monthly*, Gibbs was praised by his peers as an individual of the highest genius. And Gibbs did not stand alone. One also saw Henry A. Rowland, in spectrum analysis; Albert A. Michelson, in physics; and Simon Newcomb, in astronomy. Yet, all such research was *terra incognita* for most Americans, to whom "science" simply meant the evolution controversy.

With the passage of time, that dispute itself became muted. Some theorists, less agnostic than Sumner, attempted to harmonize Darwin and Jesus: for example, essayist John Fiske found that God was the ultimate impetus behind natural selection. Many Americans, quite understandably, held fast to Genesis I and II and supported such revivalists as Dwight L. Moody, but a "new theology" began to take hold. Based upon the theme of God's imminence in both the world and in human nature, the new belief system not only embraced Darwinism but even went so far as to find all religious expression—including Christianity—culturally conditioned. To Theodore Munger, possibly the most literate of the new theologians, natural law was not antithetical to any kingdom of faith but was the agent of its fulfillment. Indeed, some liberals presented God as more of a cosmic partner than a divine father.

Darwinism was creating other kinds of debate as well, for Lester Frank Ward was advancing a reformist interpretation of this philosophy. Henry George's *Progress and Poverty* (1879) might have been the first major broadside against Social Darwinism, but paleontologist Ward was able to use Charles Darwin's own data in such a way as to suggest that man could mold his own environment and thereby direct the very course of evolution. In his first major work, *Dynamic Sociology* (1883), Ward claimed that the rise of civilization was neither automatic nor mechanical. Rather, it was based upon one's ability to harness the blind forces of nature.

In the field of jurisprudence a revolution was also in the offing, spearheaded by the Boston attorney Oliver Wendell Holmes. In *The Common Law* (1881), Holmes claimed that the law was based neither upon abstraction nor upon precedent. Indeed, it was not a fixed body of received and conjectural rules divorced from policy. Instead, it was a product of prevailing moral and political theories, even of the prejudices of the judges. In one of the most widely quoted sentences ever penned by a legal scholar, Holmes wrote, "The life of the law has not been logic: it has been experience."[4]

All of the nation's intellectual life was not marked by innovation. The arts were still dominated by what critic George Santayana has called the genteel tradition. In literature, this tradition included a vague romanticism, a structured narrative, a plot with clear ethical choices, and an affirmation of middle-class values. The horrors of industrialism were usually avoided; so were celebrations of sexual passion. Stress was on the passive, the decorative, the delicate. Santayana's comments concerning genteel poetry could apply to other forms of American literature as well: it was "simple, sweet, humane, Protestant literature, grandmotherly in that sedate spectacled wonder with which it gazed at this terrible world and said how beautiful and how interesting it all was."[5] From General Lew Wallace's *Ben Hur* (1880), with its sentimental glorification of early Christianity, to James Whitcomb Riley's "The Old Swimmin'-Hole" (1882), with its unrealistic eulogy of rural life, most writing centered on the traditional and the familiar.

Admittedly, some popular fiction contained iconoclastic themes. For example, Rhoda Broughton's *Belinda* (1883), one of the popular novels among American women, portrayed a wife so starved for affection that she sought to abandon her husband. Yet, for the most part, traditionalism stood triumphant.

A realistic school, however, was making a breakthrough. Henry James's *Portrait of a Lady* (1881) revealed psychological processes with accuracy, while Mark Twain's *Life on the Mississippi* (1883) depicted the ruggedness of frontier life. If William Dean Howells's *A Modern Instance* (1882) came down on the side of the familiar virtues, it conveyed more earthly passions as well.

Other arts were less innovative. In painting, Thomas Eakins and Winslow Homer were beginning a new realism; yet the impressionism so much the vogue in Europe had still to make its impact on this side of the Atlantic. In architecture, a Romanesque revival was under way, but the foundations of anything truly pioneering still had to be laid.

Despite the variety of economic and intellectual currents, astute foreign visitors, such as Bryce, saw the basis of American society lying, not in economic institutions, but in political ones—and here parties were of primary importance. Indeed, the voting public welcomed the picnics, rallies, and torchlight parades with much the same gusto as a later generation of sport fans would root for a favorite team or as an earlier generation of the pious would have attended a revival. So popular was this form of entertainment that proportionately more people went to the polls in presidential elections than had ever done so before or would do so again during "the age of reform." In the national elections of the 1880s, 80 percent of the electorate voted, and this participation involved a genuine cross section of the public, as poor whites, rural people, and blacks cast their ballots alongside their wealthier countrymen. Richard Jensen claims that "the electorate followed political developments, recognized politicians, and understood the issues."[6] They could sit through hours of speeches without a break, absorbing minute details concerning the tariff, currency, industrial policy, and prohibition.

Even given the disorientation of the Gilded Age, however, it remains doubtful whether such fascination reflected any serious belief that government could solve the nation's problems. The economy, so most educated people thought, was self-regulating, and natural laws controlled the forces of the market. Reasons for mass participation were different. With social dislocation so pronounced and with direct ties between nation and citizens so rare, party identification gave one a sense of a group identity and national attachment. Parties, in other words, implied certainty amid uncertainty, the one area where the individual could find links to the bucolic eden sought by the Jacksonians or the sacred conflict to preserve the Union. Note, for example, that the nickname Grand Old Party was given to the Republicans less than twenty-five years after their birth.

The politicos, of course, had their own interest in fostering the hoopla, for the balance of power was most precarious. The period was not, contrary to stereotype, a "Republican era"; rather, it was marked by party instability. Throughout the Gilded Age, major parties seldom received a solid mandate. Majorities continually fluctuated: for instance, the Democrats won the House in 1874, lost it in 1880, regained it in 1882, lost it again in 1888, and recaptured it in 1890. Turnovers in Congress were frequent, and the majority of representatives were always first-termers. Between 1875 and 1895, there were only two times when the Republicans were able to organize the House and the Democrats powerful enough to control the Senate. No president saw his party control both houses for a full term. During the eighties, the GOP never won a majority of the popular vote; only once, in 1880, did it receive a plurality, and this of less than one-tenth of 1 percent. Yet such shifting domination of the presidency and the Congress did not result from major changes in the sentiments of the voters. Instead, a highly delicate balance permitted minor changes to tip party control in one direction or the other, and a quick slump in the economy or the sudden entry of a new and charismatic figure could change this balance quickly indeed.

Such a precariousness made party leaders—many of whom had learned their mobilization experiences during the Civil War—apt in conceiving of the party organization as an army, with the various troops (or voters) fighting on the battlefield (or the polls). As Jensen notes, even the language of politics was cast in military terms:

> From the *opening gun* of the *campaign* the *standard bearer*, along with other *war-horses fielded* by the party, *rallied* the *rank and file* around the party *standard*, the *bloody shirt*, and other *slogans*. *Precinct captains aligned* their *phalanxes shoulder-to-shoulder* to mobilize votes for the *Old Guard*. Meanwhile the *Mugwumps* warned that the *palace troops* sought to *plunder* the treasury; their *strategy* was to *crusade* against the *myrmidons* of corruption. Even a *man on horseback* could not have saved the *lost cause* with

5

his *jingoism*. But party *headquarters* changed *tactics* and emptied its *war chest* to buy *mercenaries* and *Hessians*. Finally the *well-drilled fugelmen* in the *last ditch* closed *ranks*, overwhelmed the enemy *camp*, and divided the *spoils* of victory.[7]

Localism and the issues that it generated often held the key to political success. Members of the House were subject to election every two years; the choice of senators depended upon state legislatures. And as for the national party, it was—in a very real sense—a confederation, organized from the bottom up. It consisted of the city, district, and county clubs, where political influence first resided, since they sent delegates to the state convention. The state group in turn, once every four years, sent representatives to the national convention, where presidential candidates and a platform were chosen. Otherwise, the national assemblage served little function.

True, each convention established a national committee, supposedly to provide the party with some continuity. Although this body usually included a leader from each state, it was often ignored. In 1880, as Robert D. Marcus notes, the Republican National Committee remained "an ancillary to the state committees, with no power over the action of the national convention, little central direction, scant control of the way the funds it raised were spent, and hardly any organizational continuity."[8] Political leaders preferred to work through the traditional alliances of bosses and local leaders and to devote themselves to pleasing state, not national, constituencies. Most of the time, a politico's fate depended little on the success of a presidential campaign. Win or lose, he would continue to hold his office and thereby wield the power he sought.

The voters might find politics a spectator sport or an ideological battle, but to professional politicians it was a business. Bryce called politics "a livelihood," "a gainful profession, like advocacy, stockbroking, the dry goods trade, or the setting up of companies."[9] To the politicos, the machine was a corporation; the electorate, stockholders; the voters, profits; the favors, dividends; and themselves, management. The sheer number of elections made professional administration important, as did the filling of patronage positions in the federal bureaucracy, a number that reached one hundred thousand by 1881. An ambitious politician, as John G. Sproat has noted, worked "hard at his job and relied on ability, perseverance, and luck to move him to the top. He crippled his competitors, took what profits the market would yield, and entrenched himself in power with a tight, efficient organization."[10] Such motives were particularly important in the early 1880s, because the ideological conflicts surrounding the Civil War and Reconstruction were waning, while many of the issues produced by the new industrialism had yet to come to the fore. Hence, more than ever, the maintenance of party organization, not the advancement of specific public policies, lay at the base of political life.

Each state party had its own local units. At their weakest, they were organizations; at their strongest, machines. In New York City, for example, the classic Democratic machine was the Irish-based Tammany Hall, which had a host of positions ranging from ward heeler to city boss and was thus able to supply many welfare tasks. Within the city, Tammany was rivaled by Irving Hall; outside, by various upstate enclaves. When united, the New York unit could supply the bulk of leadership and funds for the national party, with money that came from real estate, commerce, and investment banking.

In rural regions, perhaps because fewer dollars and positions were involved, one-party rule was relatively more relaxed. In New Hampshire, for instance, Republicans did not always fight Democrats; they often fought each other. The rival party factions were headed by two competing railroads, the Concord and the Boston and Maine. The latter road supported William E. Chandler, who led the state party—at times with difficulty—until the turn of the century.

The South was another single-party area, this one governed by the Democrats. Here too debates were internal and factional, and states often sent members of both new and old elites to Congress. For example, Alabama's Senator John Tyler Morgan represented old-line conservatives, whereas James L. Pugh advanced the cause of the state's burgeoning steel industry.

Ethnic or religious identity often determined the character of an area. English and Welsh usually voted Republican, although to different degrees. Similarly, many Irish Catholics were Democrats, although the percentage fluctuated from year to year and city to city. Irish Protestants tended to be Republican, as did Canadian Protestants. French-Canadians were usually Democrats. Norwegian Lutherans were strongly anti-Democratic; Swedish Lutherans, even more so. Old French, Poles, and Bohemian Catholics were ardent Democrats. Affiliations of "native" whites in the Old Northwest varied, with Methodists, Quakers, Free-Will Baptists, Congregationalists, and Presbyterians providing many anti-Democratic votes.

Germans were far from homogeneous: they varied according to place of origin and religion. Pomeranians were strong Democrats; Württembergers, weak ones. German Catholics were Democrats. German Lutherans were split; only those who came between 1839 and 1845 stood steadfast in the Democracy. Such German sectarian groups as the United

Brethren, the Evangelical Association, and the German Methodist Episcopal Church supported the Grand Old Party.

Such group identification could be more important than either class or occupation in determining party affiliation. For example, in major urban areas of Michigan, Ohio, and Wisconsin, the proportion of each party that was working class differed little. Rural areas did not go overwhelmingly Republican; or cities, Democratic. Consistently throughout the 1880s the GOP carried such metropolises as Chicago, Philadelphia, Cleveland, and Cincinnati. Indeed, it captured over half the cities that had a population of fifty thousand or more. Later historians might talk of real and nonreal issues, but for those who lived in the Gilded Age, appeals to class would have been disruptive rather than reinforcing.

It was, it should be stressed, local attachments, not national issues, that determined most elections. About two-thirds of the voters did not split their ticket, and an additional 10 percent usually leaned towards one party. Hence, politicians could pinpoint the swing regions and could therefore exert attention there proportionately. Some midwestern states, such as Ohio, Illinois, and Indiana, were in this category—Democrats were strong in the southern half of each of them; Republicans, in the northern. It is no accident that only twice between 1860 and 1912 did the Republicans fail to select a presidential candidate from one of these states.

Several eastern states—New York, New Jersey, Connecticut, Massachusetts—could, at times, decide an election. Here, in contrast to the Middle West, the rural-urban split was quite pronounced. Democrats would often hold sway in industrial areas, gaining contributions from conservative businessmen and free traders known as Bourbons. Republicans frequently dominated rural regions, but there were also many urban big businessmen and industrialists who gave to the GOP. Such states were likely to shift their allegiance when the economy was declining, and the large proportion of independent voters in them made these areas unpredictable.

Ideologically as well as geographically, the parties were fragmented. The Democrats in particular were prone to fissure. Yet the tone of the Democracy was often set by the Bourbon wing, which adhered firmly to laissez faire and maintained that society functioned according to immutable natural laws. Government, so such Bourbons as Senator Thomas Francis Bayard of Delaware maintained, played no positive function whatsoever; its primary task was to remove those man-made obstacles that could hinder these laws from operating smoothly. Together with laissez faire went states' rights and decentralization. The party looked back to a Jacksonian golden age of national leadership; it recalled with bitterness how the GOP had attempted to centralize federal authority during and after the War between the States. For many party leaders, a low tariff, "sound" currency, and administrative economy summarized their own ideology as much as it had Jefferson's.

Some Democrats dissented. Party factions in the South and West backed antimonopoly and inflationary movements; those in northeastern cities sought federal subsidies and appropriations. Even the tariff began to be a divisive issue. Such congressmen as Samuel J. Randall of Pennsylvania and about forty of his followers opposed any significant reduction. Southerners too would silently back Republican efforts to keep levels high in return for internal improvements.

Despite its disunity, the Democratic party often possessed a winning strategy. Otherwise, less than a decade after Appomattox, it could never have gained control of the House, much less maintained this control for sixteen of the next twenty years. Nor could it have received the plurality of popular votes in four of the five presidential elections held between 1876 and 1892. In each such election, the party began with the Solid South and the border states, then attempted to capture the urban Northeast, California, and Nevada, and finally tried to gain such middle-western swing states as Indiana and Ohio. (Some territories—such as Arizona, Idaho, and Montana—sent nonvoting Democratic delegates to Congress, but in a presidential race, their sentiment did little good.)

Certain Democratic principles—retrenchment and reform, for example —could well be a drawing card, because most Americans—except in an emergency—wanted to leave well enough alone. In its diffuse constituency —composed of farmers, factory workers, immigrants, small businessmen, merchants, and railroad magnates—some groups in particular would appreciate the Democratic ideology. For example, southern whites, who feared black rule, and Irish Catholics, opposed to prohibition, would find the Democratic stress upon laissez faire most attractive.

Democratic prospects were aided by Republican weakness. By 1877, the GOP was in trouble: the House was usually beyond its reach; its hold on state governments was diminishing. Party strength was confined to the Northeast and Midwest, and as the sacred causes of antislavery and moral reform ebbed, popular support declined notably in the latter region. The effort of President Rutherford B. Hayes to conciliate the South had backfired; therefore, by 1880, any serious chances of establishing a viable organization below the Mason-Dixon line had diminished greatly. Only in upper New England could the GOP count on victory.

The party's Unionist ideology had become increasing irrelevant with the end of the Civil War. True, the cause of the blacks necessitated federal action, but the needed measures would far exceed party resources and could not, in any case, evoke the public commitment. The Grant scandals and Hayes's fights with selected spoilsmen did little for the GOP's ethical image;

furthermore, they divided the party's leadership. At the same time, it was still doubtful whether a wholehearted effort to establish civil service could attract converts to the party. The public was simply not that interested.

In some ways, the party's heritage was a most ambivalent one. On the one hand, it had inherited the Whig tradition of a weak presidency, said tradition one in which the duties of chief executive were limited to approving cabinet decisions and enforcing laws passed by Congress. On the other hand, it retained the doctrine of an active state; and voters needed no reminding that it was the GOP that had centralized banking, issued massive grants to railroads, passed a protective tariff, divided the South into five military districts, and confiscated millions of dollars worth of property in the form of slaves. This kind of activism, if it involved temperance and Sabbatarianism on a local level, could alienate such immigrant groups as German Lutherans. Failure to act, however, could antagonize varied pietists who often composed the base of the party.

As was the case with the Democrats, Republican strategy was based upon a diverse constituency, one that drew upon farmers, businessmen, professional people, skilled laborers, substantial wage earners, Union veterans, and blacks. To win, one had to adopt the Democratic strategy in reverse: start with southern New England, the upper part of the Old Northwest, and much of the Great Plains, basing your strength on the realization that a host of states—Colorado, Kansas, Nebraska, Iowa, and Minnesota—were safely Republican. The GOP then had to capture Nevada and California, the industrial East, and such swing states as Indiana. An occasional southern state, such as Virginia, was not written off.

Given the chaotic nature of the economy and given the precarious party system, it is little wonder that Leonard D. White observed that "the federal system from Grant through McKinley was generally undistinguished." "Executive talent," he continued, "tended to be drained off into railways, steel, manufacturing, and urban utilities."[11]

It was the states, not the federal government, that citizens came in contact with most directly and that did nearly all of the governing. State legislatures, for example, performed the crucial task of chartering corporations, while city and county administrators issued local licenses. "An American may," reported Bryce, "through a long life, never be reminded of the Federal Government, except when he votes at presidential and congressional elections, lodges a complaint against the post-office, and opens his trunks for a custom-house official on the pier at New York when he returns from a tour in Europe."[12]

Not that state and municipal government was either strong or efficient.

Beginning in the 1870s, state governments had entered into what Morton Keller calls a period of atrophy, one in which fewer laws were passed, budgets declined, and taxes were reduced.[13] Power was usually divided into three parts. All legislatures were bicameral, and the governor was even weaker than his federal counterpart. And when a state did attempt to exert positive powers, its efforts could be destructive. State regulation of corporations, whose operations were interstate in scope, effected no meaningful change; rather, it impeded legitimate business activity, thereby forcing businessmen into convoluted and extralegal schemes in order to carry on quite acceptable pursuits.

In large cities the mayor, and in counties a single elected board, ran the government. Even though, to use the phrasing of Loren P. Beth, the Gilded Age marked "the heyday of the elected official," terms of office were usually short, in some cases lasting only a year. Voters believed that they were acting on the assumption that "where annual elections end, tyranny begins."[14] At both local and state levels, however, irresponsible and petty tyranny was enhanced, inefficiency fostered. Machine politicians might realize, at least better than reformers, that cities were amalgams of neighborhoods, classes, and interests. By no means, however, could such politicos cope with pressing needs in education, sanitation, and safety.

To talk of national policy was itself an illusion, because Washington administrators had neither the will nor the apparatus to supervise policy continually. They would simply pass a law, then perhaps check a few of its results later on. After Congress had acted, power went back to the recipients, and even when government intervention appeared needed, Americans managed to muddle along without it. Congressman James A. Garfield undoubtedly reflected much popular sentiment when, in the midst of depression, he spoke against appropriations for public-works measures. The proposal of President Ulysses S. Grant, Garfield said in 1874, was a "foolish notion"; it was "not part of the functions of the national government to find employment for people—and if we were to appropriate a hundred millions for this purpose, we should be taxing forty millions of people to keep a few thousand employed."[15]

If the national government had one central responsibility, it centered on the surplus in the treasury. From 1866 to 1893, the Treasury Department was collecting more than it was spending, and during the 1880s, the surplus averaged over $100 million a year. The situation was far more dangerous than it looked, for it kept large sums out of circulation when an expanding economy most needed them. Some Americans wanted to give the surplus away, either by directly distributing it to the states, reducing the debt, offering pensions to veterans, or passing pork-barrel bills. Others recommended cutting income, by which they often meant lowering the tariff.

11

The disposal of the surplus and other decisions made by the federal government were likely to rest with Congress. Woodrow Wilson, commenting on the early eighties, claimed that the legislative branch "has virtually taken into its own hands all the substantial powers of government"; administration was merely its "clerical part."[16] The future president was hardly exaggerating. Congress had the authority to make appropriations, set salaries for federal employees, and pass on certain appointments. The chief executive, in fact, was not consulted on the preparation of budget estimates, and the secretary of the treasury was more a compiler than a minister of finance.

By any reasonable definition of efficiency, however, the Congress was plainly incompetent. "Effective statesmanship," as White notes, "requires concentration of decision-making authority, steadiness of long-range goals, a national outlook, a capacity to reach timely decisions, a sense of responsibility, and an organization designed to facilitate action by securing adequate information, opportunity for open discussion, and certainty in ultimate conclusion."[17] In all of these characteristics, Congress was distinctly lacking.

Part of the problem lay in the fractionalization of the major parties. Part lay in the extremely close party balances that could turn any factional dispute into a crisis. And part lay in the fact that individual senators might be so politically insecure that they felt forced to concentrate upon fence-mending in their constituencies rather than upon their legislative responsibilities. Indeed, state and party chieftains often considered national policy-making irrelevant.

The Senate, in a sense, was a federation of state bosses, in which—as George Frisbie Hoar (Rep., Mass.) commented in 1877—each member "kept his own orbit and shone in his sphere, within which he tolerated no intrusion from the President or from anybody else."[18] Here indeed were the brokers of patronage and power. A Senate seat was particularly attractive, because it gave state party leaders control over much federal patronage.

Foremost among the Republican senators was Roscoe Conkling of New York State. Beginning his career as district attorney of Oneida County and as mayor of Utica, Conkling served in the House from 1859 to 1863 and again from 1865 to 1867. Elected to the Senate in 1867, he gained the reputation of being a staunch Radical. He once summed up his political philosophy in a single sentence: "I do not know how to belong to a party a little."[19] As if to offer proof of this, in 1873 he declined the post of chief justice of the United States Supreme Court, doing so in order to continue his political involvements. Tall, vain, and dressed like a dandy, he tyrannized subordinates and suspected all men's motives but his own. Congressman

12

Garfield appraised Conkling as "a great fighter, inspired more by his hates than his loves," and he was correct.[20]

By 1872, Conkling was enjoying a privileged status in the Senate. His followers usually dominated the Committee on Committees, which in turn staffed the working committees; therefore, support for the New York senator could be rewarded with positions on the Railroad, Judiciary, or Finance committees. By 1880, his faction had become known as the Stalwarts; it centered on hostility to the South and allegiance to Ulysses S. Grant.

Conkling's power was organizational, not legislative; he never controlled Senate procedure. His personality was too overbearing, his temper too short, to dictate general policy. In addition, his hold on the New York machine became increasingly shaky, particularly as President Hayes had deposed Conkling's chief lieutenant, Chester Alan Arthur, from the collectorship of the New York Customhouse.

The Grant wing of the Senate Republicans possessed other powerful figures, including J. Donald Cameron of Pennsylvania and John A. Logan of Illinois. Cameron had inherited the Republican machinery from his father, Simon, who had been Lincoln's secretary of war and minister to Russia. Himself briefly secretary of war under Grant, the young Cameron was senator from 1877 to 1897. Although urbane enough to cultivate such intellectuals as Henry Adams and John Hay, he was the most stubborn of partisans, a posture that paid off in January 1880 when he became chairman of the Republican National Committee.

A far less sophisticated man was "Black Jack" Logan, originally a Democratic congressman, who had fought in the Civil War as a Union general. He had then helped to organize Washington's most powerful lobby, the Grand Army of the Republic, which rewarded him three times by making him its president. To be sure, Logan—with his long black hair, bristling moustache, and bad grammar—was a noisy and disagreeable man, but he ran Illinois as if it were a feudal fief. Senator from 1871 to 1877 and again from 1879 until his death in 1886, he was continually pushing for army pensions and for internal improvements and warning against a predatory South.

Senate Republicans were divided, however, with the Stalwarts being opposed by the tall, vigorous James G. Blaine of Maine. Charming as he was ambitious, Blaine combined a quick, shrewd mind with a genial and confident manner. As Speaker of the House from 1869 to 1875 and as senator thereafter, he called for black enfranchisement and always opposed abandoning the Republican party in the South. Marcus notes, "He supported Lincoln, stayed a shade behind the Radicals, satisfied both the Liberals and the GAR in the early seventies, played with civil service reform, and found the precise eye of every storm over the currency."[21]

Blaine openly sought the presidency in 1876, but a railroad-bond scandal helped cost him the nomination. "When I want a thing, I want it dreadfully," he once said, and his emotional intensity could border on hysteria.[22]

Blaine had his drawbacks, however, which included a suspicious nature, a bent towards intrigue, a barren legislative record, and—as one senator noted—an inexhaustible capacity for making enemies. Foremost among these enemies was Roscoe Conkling, whom Blaine had publicly insulted. By 1881, the Stalwarts had dubbed his followers "Half-Breeds," implying that they were deficient in GOP loyalty, but in reality the partisanship of the Blaine wing was just as strong. One could argue that the Half-Breeds, who increasingly put emphasis upon the tariff, were the more forward-looking of the two factions, but in day-to-day operations, there was no substantive issue dividing the two groups. Both, for example, were vehement in their opposition to reforms in the civil service.

But if the Senate Republicans were split, the Senate Democrats were even more disunited. Usually a minority, and thereby not in control, they could neither determine the order of debate nor the chairmanship of committees. The party did not control the presidency, so it often lacked access to federal patronage. Even in 1879, when the Democrats did gain control of the Senate, the party lacked firm and united leadership. It conducted what little business it had most informally, since its southern members in particular usually knew each other before they came to Congress. Textbook stereotypes of party factions break down, because no neat divisions existed between the so-called Bourbon senators, who supposedly favored corporations, and those who opposed them.

Senate organization, however, added to the weakness of that body. Measures were considered without reference to any guiding program. No one controlled senatorial caucuses closely, and voting fluctuated according to the discussion at hand. If parties could, at times, show surprising cohesion, the young political scientist Woodrow Wilson found little coherence concerning either legislation or debates: "To attend to such discussions is uninteresting; to be instructed by them is impossible."[23]

The House was, if anything, more chaotic. Business was conducted haphazardly: members conversed privately, wrote letters, read newspapers, and strutted noisily—in fact, did practically everything but attend to matters at hand. When members desired to hear a speaker, they had to crowd closely around him. No one controlled the order of debate; minorities could obstruct legislation by refusing to answer the roll or filibustering at will. Hundreds of measures were rushed through without serious deliberation. Few proposals were launched by party organizations, and parties caucused infrequently. The Speaker was expected to act in a partisan manner, but such partisanship usually had personal, not party, overtones. As far as

14

legislation went, he was powerless. In 1880, the House voted to modernize its rules slightly, but little improvement resulted.

Many congressmen had little standing outside of their own districts, causing Bryce to comment that "a simple member of the House of Representatives is nobody."[24] More than one-third of their time was spent on patronage matters, as the average congressman dealt with over a thousand applications. Indeed, it was only because the local machine screened prospective civil servants that a congressman could ever free himself from such activity.

Of all the major branches of government, the executive was the weakest. The president played a peripheral role, and when he presented items for congressional consideration, he did so with diffidence. Congress correctly interpreted his annual message as containing mere suggestions. And unlike his successors of later generations, the president often found foreign policy too unimportant to warrant executive action.

The function of the executive was indeed limited. Wilson declared that "the President is no greater than his prerogative of veto makes him," and Bryce agreed: "A President need not be a man of brilliant intellectual gifts. . . . Four-fifths of his work is the same in kind as that which devolves on the chairman of a commercial company or the manager of a railway."[25] Since his tasks were primarily administrative, the chief executive acted as a tenured civil servant. Partisan and administrative matters—many of a trivial nature—occupied a major share of his time, and he seldom found relief possible. Ironically, although the president was head of the administrative machine, the machine itself had the power of self-propulsion and usually did not need the aid of the occupant of the White House.

If the chief executive did not usually initiate major domestic and foreign policies, he still exercised certain administrative functions, particularly ones centering on the power of appointment. As the party leader, the president was responsible for filling over one hundred thousand posts in the federal bureaucracy. Many positions were subject to confirmation by the Senate, but the majority evaded that hurdle. His appointments were made on three levels: first, cabinet members and immediate advisers whom the president, in consultation with party leaders, chose by himself; second, relatively obscure but powerful positions that helped to build up his personal power base; and, third, lesser appointments, executed in consultation with party politicos and in particular with the senior senator from the appointee's state. On this third level—one that included postmasters and tax collectors—he almost always rubber-stamped the choice made by local political leaders.

15

Presidents used spoils and appointments to keep party ranks firm. Rutherford B. Hayes, for example, in 1878 tapped Republican officeholders for "voluntary contributions." Only an unusually strong chief executive could survive the blackmail of a state machine, for if powerful, the machine could survive, independent of presidential assistance. And if located in a swing state, it could force the chief executive to bestow patronage by threatening to withdraw support.

For the president to play any positive role, that role usually had to be symbolic. Several chief executives attempted to serve as moral leader of the nation, exemplifying public decency, honest administration, and what Robert H. Wiebe has called "an almost ostentatious propriety."[26] In this sense, his power of veto could make him the keeper of the federal conscience, perhaps the test of a truly moral man.

There were several reasons for the weakness of the executive, one being historical. The battle between Andrew Johnson and Congress had resulted in such a one-sided victory that, by the time that Grant became president, the position held little power. Hayes, in fact, attempted to regain lost privileges, as he defied senatorial leadership and vetoed House appropriation bills containing riders.

A second reason was ideological. While the Democrats adhered to the abstract doctrine of laissez faire, Republican political thought drew much from the experience of the Whigs. From the time of their battles with "King Andrew" Jackson, the Whig party had fought executive power. The president, so Whig doctrine dictated, should "execute," not "make," laws, and he should not "meddle" in legislative affairs. Even Lincoln, aside from his frequent use of emergency war powers, has been aptly called "a Whig in the White House."

A third factor was inherent in the American political system. As we have seen, party organizations lacked discipline, and a chief executive often did not possess a majority in Congress. The presidential candidate was seldom chosen for firmness of executive grasp or for clarity of national vision, but rather because he could appeal to conflicting voting blocs. "What a party wants," Bryce commented, "is not a good President but a good candidate." And undoubtedly, Bryce had the nomination of James Abram Garfield in mind.[27]

2

★ ★ ★ ★ ★

THE UNEASY VICTORY

From the standpoint of any serious Republican politico, the presidency of Rutherford B. Hayes had been far from successful. By removing Chester A. Arthur as collector of the New York Customhouse, he challenged the Stalwart machine. And by appointing patrician William M. Evarts as secretary of state and reformer Carl Schurz as secretary of the interior, he alienated such party regulars as Blaine. Because of the peculiar circumstances of his election, he was sometimes referred to as "His Fraudulency." He realized that public pressure demanded the removal of federal troops from the South; however, because much of that region remained uncooperative, almost all Republicans deemed his policy there a failure. When Pittsburgh saw a major labor outbreak in 1877, Hayes ordered federal troops to suppress railroad strikers there. He opposed the Bland-Allison Silver Purchase Act, a proposal that was particularly appealing to the Midwest. To the president the gold standard was the only sound economic doctrine. Hayes had other problems as well, such as the refusal of a Democratic Congress to pass army appropriations as long as federal marshals remained in the South. Towards the end of Hayes's presidency, party wheelhorse Robert G. Ingersoll concluded that Hayes could not be reelected, and as far as party leaders were concerned, Ingersoll was dead right.

Hayes had announced in 1876 that he would not seek another term, and Republicans were delighted to take him at his word. Realizing that, at any rate, he could not be nominated again, he threw his support to Secretary of the Treasury John Sherman of Ohio. At age fifty-seven, Sherman had already served six years in the House, sixteen in the Senate, and four in the cabinet. Some Americans credited him with the signs of prosperity, believing that it had resulted from his resumption of specie payments. A colorless but cagey man, he was not able to arouse much personal loyalty; nevertheless, he hoped that individuals who distrusted each other might, if deadlocked, be willing to trust him.

Sherman was not without his weaknesses. Because of his part in Arthur's removal from the New York Customhouse, he had incurred Conkling's enmity. In addition, he had to face charges of pro-Catholicism, an ironic accusation in light of his defense of the public-school system. However, to Republicans of "substance," Sherman's platform was eminently sensible: tariff protection; national aid to education; avoidance of the bloody shirt; moderation in the South, with local rule accepted if federal law prevailed; and an "honest dollar." His manipulation of treasury patronage assured him of some hundred delegates, mainly from the rotten boroughs of the South, and he used the treasury contingency fund to cover some campaign expenses.

The Stalwart triumvirate of Conkling, Cameron, and Logan had its own candidate, Ulysses Simpson Grant. If reformers recalled the Whiskey Ring and the Indian frauds, the masses still remembered Appomattox. True, as H. Wayne Morgan notes, he was "short, stout, and unexciting," but he was still "first citizen to most Americans."[1] Having just returned from a world tour in the fall of 1879, the former president was met by huge crowds everywhere. In Philadelphia, for example, some sixty thousand people participated in a procession twelve miles long. John Hay found no more chance of halting Grant's campaign than of stopping yellow fever with a brass band, and the diplomat's view was shared by many. While Grant never once mentioned his own candidacy, he had enjoyed being president, considered himself rather a strong one, and desired the nomination. Such newspapers as the *Chicago Tribune*, the *Boston Advertiser*, the *New York Times*, and the *Providence Journal* sought a third term for him.

For all three members of the triumvirate, another Grant presidency could mean a new lease on life, and they hoped to stampede the convention on his behalf. Far from possessing the power usually ascribed to them, they had a most uncertain hold on their states. Logan had been defeated for reelection in 1877; he had reentered the Senate two years later with difficulty. By 1880, anti-Grant Republicans had captured the Cook County Republican Convention, and some downstaters favored James G. Blaine. Cameron's organization had lost control of the Pennsylvania Legislature in 1879, and a railroad scandal had led to the conviction of several important figures in his organization.

Conkling, for all his bluster, was probably in the most trouble of all: his choice for Speaker of the New York House had passed the state GOP caucus by only nine votes; his candidate for governor had barely squeaked through the state convention. The scandal linking the senator to the beautiful and ambitious Kate Chase Sprague did little to enhance Conkling's prestige. Yet if Grant were elected, such worries would be over. Conkling would be the most powerful man in the country; he might even inherit the presidency in four years. Furthermore, the New Yorker genuinely admired Grant—inasmuch, that is, as he admired anyone not in his own mirror!

The triumvirate, however, was anxious concerning its chances, and it had good reason to be so. Certain events in particular justified its fears. First, the Grant boom started too early, alerting opponents and giving them a chance to organize. Grant needed 379 delegates to win; by convention time he had somewhere between 310 and 360. His managers, realizing that his return was wearing thin, had him visit Mexico and Cuba, then the South, but the decrease in enthusiasm continued.

Second, what was called the "unit rule" might be challenged. If New York, Pennsylvania, and Illinois were to cast their votes unanimously for Grant, those three states together could give him 170 out of the needed 379 delegates. Then if, in turn, this 170 were combined with 176 sure votes from the South, it would be well nigh impossible to stop him. Yet there was a catch, and it was an important one. Grant could begin with a base of 170 only if the respective state conventions were unified, but according to precedent, the delegates were under no obligation to unite. His fortunes, therefore, depended on whether the convention would adopt the unit format. The scheme was a clever one, but—in the words of Robert D. Marcus—"doubtless far too clever to succeed."[2]

Besides, there was still the power of James G. Blaine to reckon with, and that of a few dark horses as well. Possessing just under three hundred delegates as the convention opened, the Maine senator did not openly declare himself, but claimed to put his fate in the hands of his friends. At best, he hoped that a deadlocked convention would draft him; at worst, the meeting would nominate a candidate pledged to his views. And in addition to Blaine, there was the austere and gruff Vermont senator George F. Edmunds, famous only for his efforts to outlaw polygamy in Utah and fund the debts of the Union Pacific railroad; Elihu B. Washburne, minister to France during the Franco-Prussian War and a former Grant sponsor; Senator William Windom, a moderate agrarian from Minnesota; Hamilton Fish, Grant's secretary of state—and Senator James A. Garfield of Ohio, ostensibly in the Sherman camp and serving as his campaign manager. A deadlock could bring any one of them to the fore, and given the relative strength of the leading contenders, such a deadlock was quite possible.

19

On Wednesday, June 2, 1880, when the GOP convention formally opened in Chicago, a stalemate was clearly in the offing. Four days before, Garfield had written his wife: "I find the city boiling over with politics. Everything is in the vague of vastness and uncertainty."[3] Within a day, however, after the convention gathered, the triumvirate had lost all the major battles. It only took three hours, in fact, for the Half-Breeds to capture the nomination machinery. Senator George F. Hoar of Massachusetts, nominally an Edmunds man, became temporary, then permanent, chairman, thereby ending Stalwart hopes of controlling that position. William E. Chandler of New Hampshire, an official in the Treasury Department from 1865 to 1867 and now leader of the Blaine forces, headed the Credentials Committee.

Garfield was particularly prominent in the convention battles. He chaired the Rules Committee, which had the task of drafting a platform. He privately convinced Blaine and Sherman to back Hoar for permanent chairman. He was instrumental in the convention's rejection of the unit rule, the means by which the triumvirate had sought to create a Grant bandwagon. When Conkling sought to eject delegates who would not pledge in advance to support any nominee whom the convention chose, Garfield protested so skillfully that the New York senator was forced to withdraw the motion. Conkling immediately sent Garfield a message, congratulating him on being "Ohio's real candidate and dark horse."[4] During this period, Garfield always made a point of entering the convention late, making it easy for Wharton Barker, a Pennsylvania banker who had long been his booster, to orchestrate an ovation. Then Garfield obtained new visibility when he nominated Sherman in a moving address, one that appealed to party unity while making little reference to Sherman's candidacy. One dark horse was becoming a bit less dark.

Once the balloting had begun, it became readily apparent that neither Grant, Blaine, nor Sherman had enough strength to be nominated. Finally, on the thirty-fourth ballot, the Wisconsin delegation threw 16 crucial votes to Garfield, a move that first brought silence, then cheers from the convention. On the next ballot, 35 Indiana delegates, led by Benjamin Harrison, lined up for Garfield, and on the thirty-sixth ballot the stampede really began. Connecticut, Illinois, Iowa, Maine, Ohio—all switched to him, and soon he was over the top. He sat, sober and pale, while ten thousand voices sang "Rally Round the Flag." Conkling, whose "Old Guard" of 306 had remained steadfast for Grant, moved to make the nomination unanimous.

There was still the matter of the vice-presidential nominee. Both logic and tradition deemed that the slot should go to the defeated faction, and Garfield realized this. Using Ohio governor William Dennison as his intermediary, he first asked Levi P. Morton to be his running mate. Morton was a prominent New York banker who later became Harrison's vice-president. He was also one of Garfield's personal friends, had previously been mentioned as a vice-presidential candidate, and possessed an eminent reputation. Yet as a member of the Old Guard, he let Conkling veto the bid.

Despite Morton's refusal, the New York delegation still had the right to name Garfield's running mate. Some Conkling lieutenants, without the knowledge of their boss, sounded out former customhouse chief Chester A. Arthur, who replied that, if asked, he would accept the nomination. Arthur's latest biographer suggests that he might have seen running on the national ticket a vindication of his conduct as collector of the Port of New York.[5] In addition, it might well boost his status among the highly factionalized Stalwarts of New York and compensate for Conkling's decline in stature in both the Senate and the state. When Arthur told Conkling about the Ohio feelers, the latter commented: "Well, sir, you should drop it as you would a red hot shoe from the forge." Garfield, said Conkling, was bound to be defeated at the polls. Arthur refused to be dissuaded, declaring that "the office of the Vice-President is a greater honor than I ever dreamed of attaining."[6] Garfield had not authorized Dennison's overture and in fact turned pale when he first heard of the bid, but he realized that any successful candidacy needed the Stalwarts' cooperation.

Arthur was soon chosen. He received Stalwart blessing in a session chaired by Conkling, and then the convention's as well. On the only ballot conducted, he won 468 of 611 cast. Washburne, his nearest competitor, polled 103. Publicly, Garfield appeared pleased; privately, he regretted that Morton had not run. The reformist *Nation* was relieved, finding "no place in which [Arthur's] powers of mischief will be so small as in the Vice-Presidency. . . . It is true General Garfield, if elected, may die during his term of office, but this is too unlikely a contingency to be worth making extraordinary provisions for."[7]

The Republicans chose well. Now in the prime of his life, James Abram Garfield was both tall and handsome, possessing a full beard, bright grey eyes, and dark brown hair with patches of red. He stood erect, his expression usually firm.

His personal history, as Thomas C. Reeves notes, was "a campaign manager's dream."[8] He was born in 1831 in a rude hut near Orange, Ohio, in the heart of the Western Reserve. The son of an impoverished young widow, who was splitting logs within days of her husband's funeral. Garfield spent his youth working on his mother's farm. His six-weeks' stint as a barge driver provided Horatio Alger with the title for the campaign biography *From Canal Boy to President*, although Garfield later lamented his humble origins. The turning point of his life came at the age of eighteen, when he was baptized into the Disciples of Christ, for now the hitherto lackadaisical lad saw himself an instrument of God's destiny. He attended his denomination's newly organized Western Reserve Eclectic Institute (later Hiram College) in Hiram, Ohio, then completed his education at Williams College. After graduating, he returned to the Eclectic, first as teacher, then as president. Finding the faculty's bickering intolerable, he ran for the Ohio Legislature, in 1859 becoming its youngest member.

His early career marked him as a staunch Unionist, a position that he never abandoned. An ardent Republican, he canvassed for Fremont, admired John Brown, called slavery "this giant Evil," and opposed all efforts at sectional compromise. "The sin of slavery is one," so wrote a man immured in Protestant pietism, "of which it may be said that 'without the shedding of blood there is no remission.'"[9] And once war came, he helped to organize the Forty-second Ohio Infantry. Rising from lieutenant colonel to major general, he fought at Middle Creek, Shiloh, and Chickamauga and was chief of staff to General William S. Rosecrans. In 1862, the strongly abolitionist Western Reserve sent him to Congress, and here the youngest member in the House served as a staunch Radical. To Garfield, President Lincoln was a "second rate Illinois lawyer," George B. McClellan a "weakly and wickedly conservative" general, and the Democrats "the cowardly peace party."[10] After April 15, 1865, however, he matched any spellbinder in singing the praises of the Great Emancipator.

After the war, Garfield rose steadily through party ranks. At first his pedantic demeanor made him extremely unpopular with his House colleagues, but by 1871 he was part of the group that ruled the chamber. He was fascinated by finance and statistics, ultimately heading the Appropriations Committee. And as Allan Peskin notes, Garfield committed himself "to the hard-money cause with a single-mindedness bordering on monomania."[11] At the height of the Greenback agitation, he was the only western Congressman to oppose inflation, and he claimed that he would never vote "against the truth of the multiplication table."[12] On Reconstruction issues, he followed the lead of the congressional Radicals. Immediately after the Civil War, he waved the bloody shirt, supported the Freedman's Bureau and civil-rights bills, and favored the impeachment of Andrew Johnson.

Usually, however, Garfield was a strong believer in laissez faire, even defending its tenets in time of depression. He once said that "the chief duty of government is to keep the peace and stand out of the sunshine of the people."[13] He endorsed low tariffs and mild civil-service reform, and as early as 1868, he sought amnesty for the South. (There were lapses in his fervor for good government: once, when in a tight spot, he was cold-blooded in his use of patronage; at another time he pushed for a high tariff on pig iron, an important industry in his district.) He suspected the Granger movement of being a disguised form of communism, opposed labor unions, and found an eight-hour day for federal employees an unwarrantable interference in the rights of labor. Strikes, he thought, should be met by federal troops. The "industrial revolution"—a term he used thirty years before it became popular—was something to be welcomed, not resisted. Garfield was suspicious of immigrants from eastern Europe, believing that they were tied to municipal corruption, and in 1874, he favored imposing property qualifications for voters. Mobs, he maintained, could be fickle, though he thought education could make most people act responsibly. He also opposed woman suffrage, asserting that this "aetheistic" movement would annihilate marriage and the family.

Garfield, however, was not quite the political counterpart of your ordinary "robber baron." He endorsed federal regulation of railroads but opposed both monopoly and government aid to corporations. And in a sense, Garfield never left the classroom. A national Department of Education, the Smithsonian Institution, a federal census, the Coast and Geodetic Survey, studies in astronomy, new court procedures—all these were causes that appealed to a scholar in politics.

Yet scholar though he was, Garfield had a chance to prove his partisanship while serving on the fifteen-member Electoral Commission of 1876, which Congress had established to decide the Hayes-Tilden election. Here he loyally cast his vote for the Republican candidate. And though he saw the need for new issues during Grant's administration, the president left office with Garfield's blessing. "No American," Garfield said, "has carried greater fame out of the White House than this silent man who leaves it today."[14]

By the time he was elected senator in 1880, Garfield had long held the respect of his fellow legislators. Few congressmen worked as hard, and few were as intelligent. Though he may not have been a particularly profound man, he read widely and well. Drawing upon his 3,000-volume library, he could wade through seven volumes of Froude's history of England, translate Horace's odes, and find genuine enjoyment in Goethe, Shakespeare, and, above all, Tennyson. Working long hours to prepare for debate, he was an able speaker; and although skilled in argument, he avoided personalities. His general knowledge of the governmental process was unparalleled. "One of the most useful men ever in the lower house," commented a contemporary; and he was not wrong.[15]

Garfield possessed two quite disparate traits—a belief in himself as a child of destiny and a sense of inadequacy. Hence, he often passed up coveted opportunities, leaving the initiative to others. It would not be fair to see Garfield as a restless man, obsessed by ambition. True, he wanted to be president, but he did not hunger for the office. Throughout most of his congressional career, he desired nothing more than the speakership of the House.

Even Garfield's "betrayal" of John Sherman at the Chicago convention does not necessarily reveal ruthlessness. In 1875, he had concluded that "few men in our history have ever obtained the Presidency by planning to obtain it," and he acted in accordance with that belief.[16] He had no real personal liking for Sherman (particularly because of Sherman's flirtation with silver), did not see him as a serious contender for the presidency, and did not believe that he was the best man for the post. Sherman, by insisting that his forces be led by Garfield at the convention, was acting most unfairly.

Nor would it be correct to see Garfield as a calculating trimmer, one whom expediency could turn into a perennial weather vane. His steadfastness on antislavery, hard money, and the sanctity of the Union reveals how firm he could be when he saw a fundamental issue at stake. Rather, he was a "reasonable" man, a moderate by instinct. During the stormy Hayes administration, he sought, but without success, to be the pacifier of a party that appeared to be bent on cannibalization. Even in something as highly personal as religious doctrine, Garfield, a former lay preacher, readily accepted the teachings of Darwin and moved towards a form of universalism.

The Republican candidate had problems little known to the outside world. In his early life, Garfield had not only been an irresolute man but a morbid one as well. Within two years after he was married, he was on the brink of emotional collapse. Actually, he later fell in love with his wife, Lucretia, who bore him seven children. As Peskin notes, "His capacity for detachment and self-doubt at times paralyzed his will" and rendered him "incapable of any emotion stronger than sentimentality." In fact, writes Peskin, it was probably just as well that he never achieved his ambition of becoming Speaker of the House, for he lacked the will power needed to tame that unruly body.[17]

A greater problem involved a certain sanctimoniousness. Garfield could imply that his fellow congressmen were in the pockets of the railroads while ignoring his own indelicate efforts on behalf of Pennsylvania oilmen. Although he was not really guilty of corruption in the Crédit Mobilier scandal of 1873, his testimony could have been much franker. And in defending himself in a paving scandal, where he was obviously trading on his chairmanship of the Appropriations Committee, he acted most obtusely.

Despite such drawbacks, however, Garfield in 1880 obviously had more strengths than weaknesses, and he needed everyone of them in what was bound to be a close race. In fact, it was doubtful whether any other Republican candidate could win. All the rest had too many enemies.

The Democrats made life no easier. Meeting in Cincinnati late in June, they nominated General Winfield Scott Hancock of Pennsylvania for president and chose William H. English—War Democrat, banker, and former congressman from Indiana—as his running mate. Hancock had commanded a Union corps at Gettysburg, a task that the party hoped might endear him to northern voters. At the same time, his moderate administration of Louisiana and Texas during Reconstruction, when he was military commander there, might solidify southern support. Reeves writes, "Without any political experience, he was without enemies."[18] In a party so split and parochial, Hancock's relative obscurity was an asset. English was even less known, having played no part in politics since the Civil War. His one claim to fame was the English bill, an effort to bribe Kansas into accepting the notorious Lecompton Constitution by promising large land grants.

In part the Democratic platform was equivocal, as it evaded the silver issue, called for southern "home rule" without defining it, and promised "a general and thorough reform of the civil service" without saying what the substance of the reform would be. In part, the platform offered standard Democratic fare, condemning centralization, endorsing a free ballot (though blacks were not mentioned), and calling for restrictions on Chinese immigration and for a tariff for revenue only.

The Greenbackers also nominated a Union general, James B. Weaver, whose wartime service included action at Fort Donelson, Shiloh, and Corinth. After the conflict, Weaver became a district attorney and internal-revenue collector in Iowa. Although he originally had been a Republican, his desire for an expanded currency made him persona non grata to the GOP, and in 1878, he had been elected to Congress as a Greenbacker. In addition to seeking inflation, his party called for prohibition of "Chinese servile laborers," reservation of the public domain for actual settlers, federally enforced labor standards, an eight-hour day, a graduated income tax, and federal regulation of railroads. The candidate of the Prohibitionist party was Neal Dow, a Civil War general who privately backed Garfield.

The Republican platform differed little from that of 1876. The party endorsed the record of the Hayes administration, claimed to have "transformed 4,000,000 human beings from the likeness of things to the rank of citizens," and called for a tariff that would "discriminate as to favor American Labor." It also promised to pay pensions to veterans, demanded that Congress improve seacoasts and harbors, and opposed polygamy, unlimited immigration of Chinese, and further land grants to railroads and corporations. Sometimes it boasted about things that were only remotely connected to party policy, such as the 51,000 miles of railroad track that

25

had been constructed between 1860 and 1874. The civil-service plank, stating that "fitness, ascertained by proper practical tests, shall admit to the public service," was obviously ambivalent. When a Massachusetts man sought "thorough, radical, and complete" reform, one Texas delegate to the Chicago convention retorted, "What are we up here for? I mean that members of the Republican party are entitled to office, and if we are victorious we will have office."[19]

As the race began, Garfield retreated to his homestead at Mentor, Ohio, a village some twenty miles northeast of Cleveland. He honored tradition by not making any speeches, yet his private correspondence revealed much about his conservatism. To alleviate anxieties of railroad leaders over the Granger cases, for example, Garfield assured Whitelaw Reid, editor of the New York Tribune, that his appointments to Supreme Court posts would be based "upon evidence . . . satisfactory to you as well as to me," hence giving Reid and the railroad leaders a tacit veto over the highest court.[20]

Such comments might reveal Garfield's own predilections, but they had little to do with getting mass support; therefore, as the GOP convention ended, party leaders were discouraged. Blaine doubted whether the ticket could win; Conkling remained contemptuous. Garfield hoped to keep peace in the party family through his bland letter of acceptance, a document that, given the political customs of the Gilded Age, was bound to receive widespread publicity. Here he endorsed sound money, moderate protection, a free ballot, pensions for veterans, and a treaty that could end the unrestricted Chinese immigration permitted by the Burlingame agreement of 1868. His position on the civil service was a weak one, promising to consider merit, on the one hand, and pledging to consult with local party leaders on the other. Garfield indeed went so far as to repudiate Hayes's order banning federal officeholders from engaging in political activity. In a private letter to his close friend Burke Aaron Hinsdale, Garfield suggested that there be fixed terms for appointees to minor offices but not to policy-making ones.

Arthur's letter of acceptance was more partisan, as one would expect from a person in a secondary position. He supported the free ballot, praised Hayes's vetoes of army bills, and lauded executive firmness in general while opposing civil-service examinations in particular. As with past public statements, he claimed to stand for merit appointments and for established tenure of office.

Problems still remained with the Stalwarts. At first, Garfield hoped that his civil-service policy would mollify Conkling. So too, he hoped, would the appointment of a Grant protégé and Arkansas carpetbagger, former senator Stephen W. Dorsey, as secretary of the Republican National

Committee. He soon learned, however, that more was necessary. Chandler, Arthur, and Dorsey urged Garfield to travel to New York City, there to deal with the Stalwarts directly, and the candidate reluctantly agreed to do so. After making some twenty-five innocuous speeches en route, Garfield met on August 5 with all factions of GOP leadership at the fashionable Fifth Avenue Hotel. Conkling refused to appear, perhaps because he did not want to be in the presence of certain reformers, perhaps because Blaine was present. "It was," Peskin notes, "like a wedding party without the bride," as Stalwart bargaining authority passed to New York party leader Thomas C. Platt, banker Levi P. Morton, and Chester A. Arthur.[21]

No one knows exactly what transpired at this summit meeting, or what the specific terms were. Garfield was deliberately ambiguous, merely noting in his diary, "No trades, no shackles and as well fitted for defeat or victory as ever."[22] Nonetheless, one thing was clear: he had promised to recognize every wing of the party when crucial appointments were made, with a particular—if unspecified—plum for Morton.

Historians place different emphases on the "Treaty of Fifth Avenue." Peskin finds the conference "a personal triumph for Garfield." Reeves, noting that the Stalwarts were both shrewd and cynical, claims that "only the most positive and unequivocal assurances" could have prompted them to enter vigorously into the campaign.[23] Obviously each faction needed the other, and the day of reckoning could always be postponed.

Cooperation from the Stalwarts was not long in coming. Morton assumed the task of raising money. Grant and Conkling campaigned through the doubtful states of Ohio and Indiana. On September 28, in fact, they were part of a party of two hundred that visited Garfield at Mentor. Conkling later claimed that Garfield called him the savior of the campaign and promised to allow him to make all federal appointments in New York State. Yet, in reality, all conversation was limited to pleasantries.

Arthur played a crucial role in the campaign. As chairman of New York's state committee, he coordinated scores of rallies and meetings. In addition, he was perhaps the first "advance man" in American history, taking personal charge of campaign tours for Grant and Conkling through the doubtful states of Ohio and Indiana. He assessed a score of public servants—ranging from federal judges to lighthouse keepers—for party contributions, with the request being routinely pegged at 3 percent of one's salary. And although such commitments were made in the form of an appeal not a threat, noncontributors soon saw their names forwarded to party supervisors on the federal payroll. Not a phase of these operations escaped Arthur's attention, and he could well have raised $125,000 by this method.

In addition, Arthur, along with Morton, canvassed New York businessmen for a secret fund to be used in Indiana. Like Ohio, the Hoosier

State held elections in October. Richard Jensen notes that "a variety of conflicts and rivalries raged fiercely there: Southerners distrusted Yankees, the southern part of the state resented the northern part, Methodists feared Catholics, hard-money men ridiculed inflationists, natives denounced immigrants."[24] A doubtful state, Indiana in 1876 and 1878 had been carried by Democrats, who—so rumor had it—would import nonresidents to vote and intimidate the state's black population. After polling Indiana voters extensively, Dorsey sent what might have been as much as $70,000 to bolster campaign efforts. Garfield was fully aware of the fund and the use to which it was put; he wrote Dorsey at one point: "Don't relax any grip anywhere."[25]

Garfield may, in fact, have retained the public image of civic virtue; nevertheless, he was deeply concerned with the collection of assessments. He privately sought all possible aid from Thomas J. Brady, second assistant postmaster general, then involved in canvassing Republican officeholders. At one point, Garfield wrote to the chairman of the Finance Committee of the Congressional Campaign Committee: "Please tell me how the Departments generally are doing."[26] Until the fall, business contributions to the Democrats far exceeded those to the Republicans. Indeed, only in September did the GOP receive its major contributions from officeholders. The loss of the governorship of Maine, an event that took place in September, caused Blaine to instruct party workers to discard the bloody shirt and to shift to protection. Garfield concurred; he noted that the Republicans had lost votes in Maine's shipping towns but had gained in manufacturing ones, two facts that perhaps revealed that the tariff was an issue. With prosperity returning and with the Great Lakes states becoming industrialized, a tariff appeal might carry Indiana, Ohio, and the Old Northwest and also New York and some Middle Atlantic States.

Suddenly the Democrats played into the Republicans' hands, as Hancock called the tariff a local matter. Hancock was not a free trader; Garfield had said the same thing a number of times. Yet, in trying to explain himself, the Democratic front runner only dug his hole deeper. Businessmen promptly started giving generously to Republican coffers. When the Republicans safely—and honestly—carried Ohio and Indiana late in October, Democratic leaders conceded that the tariff argument had made the difference.

As with most Gilded Age campaigns, mudslinging and chicanery were by no means absent. True, Hancock ran a modest campaign, staying at a military base on Governor's Island and remaining content to endorse his party's platform. And true, there was much banality in the various campaign biographies. At one point, for example, Garfield supposedly said,

"The American people have done much for the locomotive, and the locomotive has done much for them."[27]

But there was more. The Democrats revived the issues regarding the Crédit Mobilier and the Washington paving company; in addition, they accused Garfield of refusing to pay a laundry bill, spurning a poor soldier who asked for relief, and stealing bedding from a widow in the South. Republicans charged that during the Civil War, Hancock had plotted to march on Washington and depose Lincoln. Furthermore, the Democratic nominee had assumedly directed a swindle in the oil industry, hauled down the American flag while entertaining General P. G. T. Beauregard, and issued fraudulent bonds in Louisiana.

The most damaging accusation centered on Garfield's supposed acquiescence in unlimited Chinese immigration. On October 20, a penny newspaper in New York City entitled *Truth* printed a letter that it claimed had been written by Garfield on House stationery. The letter, addressed to one H. L. Morey of Lynn, Massachusetts, opposed Chinese restriction and reaffirmed the Burlingame Treaty of 1868, an agreement giving the Chinese the right to settle freely in the United States. Furthermore, it implied that labor was a commodity and that employers possessed the right to hire it as cheaply as possible. From one perspective, Garfield was merely stressing, as the Constitution states, that treaties are "the supreme law of the land" and that the Burlingame Treaty probably should not be abrogated until corporations had obtained the labor they needed. From another perspective, however, Garfield appeared to be insulting the whites of California, Oregon, and Nevada, where restrictionist sentiments ran high. The Democrats played it for all it was worth, even though a week before the election, the Republicans proved that the letter had been a forgery. Garfield might have gained, not lost, from such a crude attempt, but it did cost the Republicans a Senate seat in California.

The Morey letter notwithstanding, by midnight of November 2, Garfield appeared to have been safely elected. At seven the next morning, when Hancock's wife told him that the results were "a complete Waterloo," he replied: "That is all right, I can stand it," and went back to sleep.[28] Democrats talked of contesting New York State; but Hancock, fearing disorders, wanted no more disputed elections. He went to his grave thinking that he had been the legitimately elected president.

As far as the popular vote was concerned, the 1880 election was the closest one in American history, with a margin of less than one-tenth of one percent. Yet, amid the 9.2 million individuals tallied, the buckeye politician received only some 7,368 more popular votes than Hancock had. The electoral college was safely in Garfield's hands by the margin of 214 to 155. New York, as had been expected, was the pivotal state, for, had its 35 electoral votes gone to Hancock, he would have won the election. The election not only solidified the South; it showed that the GOP could win without that region and that, therefore, the fate of the southern black was incidental to Republican victory. Democrats had yet to shake their parochial image, much less overcome northern and western distrust. The Republicans regained control of the House by 147 to 135. If the Senate was deadlocked, Arthur could still, as vice-president, cast the deciding vote. The Greenbackers, despite their broadly reformist platform, pulled just over 300,000 votes, mainly in the Midwest.

Amid the general Republican rejoicing, only Garfield was distressed. He confided to his diary less than a week after the election, "There is a tone of sadness running through this triumph which I can hardly explain."[29] He had every reason to be anxious.

As soon as he arrived in Washington in late November, Garfield found himself in a quandary. He had hoped to spend most of his time moving out of his residence on I Street, but he quickly became entangled in the spoils system at its highest levels. Reformer Carl Schurz told Garfield, "Your real troubles will now begin." This was, if anything, an understatement, for, as H. Wayne Morgan notes, "Cabinet-making was as elaborately political as in any European state, colorful and intricate like the peacock's mating dance."[30] Yet if Garfield were to win another term, harmony in GOP ranks would be absolutely essential; and to achieve such harmony, he would have to balance his appointments among the various factions.

It took the Stalwarts little time to confront the president-elect. On November 27, Levi P. Morton, who had raised large sums for the campaign war chest, met with Garfield. Morton told him—on the basis of conversation with others—that, according to the "Treaty of Fifth Avenue," he, Morton, was due to become secretary of the treasury. Conkling would have been particularly pleased if the banker were appointed, because this would eliminate Morton from an already crowded Senate race. Garfield, denying that he had made any such promise, turned Morton down. Although he shared Morton's deflationary views, he replied that the appointment "would be a congestion of financial power at the money centre and would create jealousy at the West."[31] Morton's closeness to the controversial financier Jay Gould would particularly arouse protest. In addition, the law prohibited anyone who sold government securities from holding the treasury post. Then the president-elect went further, denying that he had made any binding commitment to the Stalwarts.

What Garfield did not say, but what is crucial in understanding his attitude, was the there were some fifteen hundred patronage positions in the

Treasury Department, and he did not think that he could cope with a secretary who might be a tool of the Stalwarts. In fact, because of its functions, the Treasury Department was the most important federal agency of all. Its tasks ranged from collecting revenue to regulating the currency, and it daily enforced laws dealing with specie resumption, war debts, and the tariff. Within its jurisdiction lay the collectorship of the Customhouse of New York, a most important patronage position, because that city's harbor handled more imports and collected more revenue than all other ports of entry combined. It dealt with up to 75 percent of the nation's customs receipts, and $840 million passed through the collector's office during a single year. The collector could receive remuneration of almost $100,000 annually. President Hayes had removed Chester A. Arthur from the post in 1877; so the Stalwarts now wanted the position back, and wanted it badly.

Garfield soon returned to Mentor, hoping that the isolation of northern Ohio would afford the advantage of distance. He spoke little, listened much, and greeted the continual stream of visitors with little more than a smile. Although he realized that stormy relations with the Stalwarts lay ahead, he decided upon Blaine for the State Department, a bid that was accepted on December 20. Blaine undoubtedly realized that the new position would not only make him Garfield's heir apparent; it would save him from a bitter reelection contest in Maine and permit him to lead the social life he loved. Stalwarts, reformers, and former President Hayes were all opposed: they were afraid of Blaine's recklessness, detected a payoff, and, in some ways, saw a "prime ministership" being created. The choice, in one sense, however, was quite rational: "Blainiacs" had delivered the great bulk of Garfield's votes in Chicago, and Blaine was both the most important Republican in the nation and personally close to the president-elect.

Their relations had not always been so cordial. In 1868, Garfield had been bitter, as Blaine, who had just been chosen Speaker of the House, had passed him over in selecting the chairman of the Ways and Means Committee. By 1871, however, the two men were friendly, and in 1876, Garfield claimed that his Maine colleague would make a good president. In April 1880, he confided to his diary, "I like Blaine, always have, and yet there is an element in him which I distrust."[32] Peskin, on the other hand, finds Garfield, "bewitched" by Blaine's magnetism, remaining under the man's "spell for the rest of his life."[33]

The appointment of Blaine only embittered Conkling further, for the Stalwart leader thought that his faction deserved to possess as much power as the Half-Breeds. Blaine's continual intrigue just made the New York boss all the more angry. On December 30, Blaine journeyed to New York City, where, using Garfield's name, he convinced Vanderbilt attorney Chauncey Depew to run for the Senate against several rival Stalwart candidates. Since three Conkling followers—Levi P. Morton, Thomas C. Platt of Owego, and Richard Crowley of Buffalo—were all vying for one Senate seat, the Empire State Half-Breeds held the balance of power.

Suddenly, on January 12, 1881, Half-Breed leader William H. Robertson, president pro tem of the New York Senate, shifted his forces from Depew to Platt. Platt, who was president of the United States Express Company, had sat in the House for two terms. He had long been a Stalwart, but his hunger for a Senate seat made him amenable to bargaining. Hence he pledged to Robertson that he would not deprive those New York delegates who had backed Garfield at Chicago of their share of patronage. Indeed, Platt said that he would even support Robertson for a post in the cabinet. As a result of Platt's maneuver, Conkling saw his machine being split in two, with the second Senate slot evading his grasp. His chances for securing strong representation in the cabinet already seemed to have weakened, and now it appeared certain that the Half-Breeds would reap some New York spoils.

Just a little over a week before, as if in warning, Blaine wrote an "anonymous" editorial in the January 3 issue of Whitelaw Reid's *New York Tribune*. Stating that he was writing "by authority," the author promised that Garfield would reward those New York Half-Breeds who had supported him at the convention. Not only had Garfield not seen the statement beforehand; Reid had also assured him that the piece only indicated that the president-elect would not "meddle" in the Senate race. Nevertheless, Conkling was furious. He asked, "What was the meaning of that article, but that the men who had voted faithfully for Grant need expect no quarter from the administration, while the men who had basely violated their pledges by abandoning Grant for Garfield were to be rewarded for their treachery?"[34]

Almost as if to confirm Conkling's fears, Blaine besieged Garfield with advice, so much so that some of it could not be ignored. Loving conspiracy for its own sake, Blaine went so far as to mark letters with a code that he promptly forgot. If he could match his control of the State Department with that of the treasury, his domination of the new administration would be well-nigh complete. He went so far as to oppose any Stalwart representation in the cabinet, calling the Old Guard "all the desperate bad men of the party."[35] When Garfield mentioned William Windom for the treasury, a move that was approved by Hayes and Sherman, Blaine claimed that Windom was too ignorant, that he was too much of a spendthrift, and that he had "the Presidential bee in his bonnet *terribly*."[36] Blaine had his own candidate for the position: William B. Allison. The Iowa senator was an old friend of Garfield's and during the campaign had served as a confidential agent for him. For the present, however, Garfield fended off the suggestion, fearing opposition from high-tariff and hard-money Republicans of the East.

On January 18, 1881, the *New York Times* noted that "if all reports are true, President Garfield's Cabinet will contain about one hundred and twenty-five persons."[37] Although he was still holding off on the strategic treasury position, the president-elect had narrowed down a good many choices. At one point, Garfield considered choosing Conkling himself for the State Department and moving Blaine to treasury. Blaine himself had first suggested the idea, but—upon more sober reflection—wrote Garfield that the appointment of Conkling "would act like strychnine upon your administration—first, bring contortions and then be followed by death."[38]

Conkling remained depressed; once he was so disheartened that he believed that Arthur, his most loyal lieutenant, had turned against him. The vice-president-elect, who shared a Washington apartment with Conkling, had no intention of abandoning him. But he could do Conkling little good: he lacked Garfield's ear, was anathema to Blaine, and gave a tactless speech at Delmonico's fashionable New York restaurant, in which he implied, undoubtedly aided by some libation, that Dorsey and the Republican National Committee had purchased the votes needed to win Indiana.

At one point it appeared as if the conflict could be resolved. On February 16, Conkling arrived at Mentor to see "this man Garfield." The visit lasted eight hours, but, as in the case of the "Treaty of Fifth Avenue" episode, participants read the situation differently. To Garfield, Conkling appeared "frank and friendly," a man whose "judgment is sound." In summarizing the conversation, Garfield wrote to his intimate friend Hinsdale: "On one side, information, suggestions and argument, but no demands; on the other, listening, questioning, comparison of views but no promises."[39] Garfield asked Conkling about the ability of Charles J. Folger, the respected chief justice of the New York Supreme Court. Conkling misread the situation, thinking that Folger was being considered to direct the coveted treasury post. Instead, although Conkling did not know it, Garfield wanted Folger to head the Justice Department.

Conkling soon felt betrayed, as Folger was called to Mentor and there was offered the post of attorney general. Garfield dropped the hint that, "in a contingency," Folger might be asked to head the Treasury Department. For a quite different reason, Blaine was apprehensive. He feared that the Stalwarts might eventually control the Treasury Department, and on this point, such figures as Sherman and Hayes agreed with him. Folger, out of his element, could not face such varied opposition; therefore, ten days before the inauguration, he bowed out.

Soon after Folger declined, Garfield was able to fill a few administration slots. On February 26, Morton deserted Conkling, indicating that he was available for almost any administration appointment. He was offered the Navy Department, which he accepted two days later. It was hoped that the problem of New York representation in the cabinet had been solved.

Then Garfield found that the rising Chicago lawyer Robert Todd Lincoln was willing to head the War Department. "Black Jack" Logan seems to have originated the idea, although Senator J. Donald Cameron and Illinois' Governor Shelby M. Cullom may have reached Garfield first. The appointment assured a form of apostolic succession to the martyred president. In addition, young Lincoln had been a Grant booster in 1880, hence offering more Stalwart representation. On the same day, Wayne MacVeagh, a Philadelphia lawyer, accepted the offer of attorney general. Although he was part of the anti-Grant movement, MacVeagh was boosted by people as disparate as Cameron and Schurz.

On February 28, Garfield, confident that his cabinet was nearly completed, left Mentor for Washington. His assurance, however, was short-lived. Within four days, Morton had withdrawn from the navy post. A Stalwart congressman had called him out of his sick bed early one morning and whisked him to "the Morgue," the name given to Conkling's home. There, both Conkling and Garfield's own running mate denounced Morton's "betrayal" of the Stalwarts and convinced him to resign.

Yet Garfield continued to seek representation for Conkling's machine, this time offering the position of postmaster general. He had long toyed with the name of Thomas L. James, an unusually competent postmaster of New York; but because of James's ties to the New York machine, the president-elect needed assurance of his loyalty. And just in case James would not accept, Garfield had Louisiana judge William Henry Hunt committed to the position.

On March 3, Whitelaw Reid secretly brought James to Washington, where he was first smuggled into Blaine's residence and then into Garfield's hotel. According to Reid, James "pledged loyalty in the strongest fashion."[40] Thus, Conkling was denied control of post-office patronage. Blaine, who had at first opposed James, so hoped that Allison would accept the treasury position that he acquiesced in what he saw as a lesser post. Platt seemed to imply that the James appointment would appease the Stalwarts. When, however, Platt told Arthur and Conkling about Garfield's move, all three rushed to the Riggs House, where the president-elect was staying. Conkling railed at Garfield for an hour, asserting that the office of postmaster general was not big enough for his state. Garfield sat on the side of his bed, making no reply, undoubtedly smiling inwardly in the realization that James was committed to his administration.

On that very day, Garfield had another reason to be confident, because Allison had just accepted the coveted treasury position. In February, Garfield had settled upon Windom, but by early March, Blaine had talked him out of making that appointment. The president-elect would have been far less sanguine had he known that, at 8:30 the next morning, Allison would withdraw his acceptance. Contrary to myth, Allison did not withdraw because of Stalwart pressure. Rather, his wife was mentally ill and hence was in no condition to handle the publicity that would come with being the spouse of a cabinet member. In addition, Allison wanted to be chairman of the Senate Appropriations Committee, and he wanted to save Iowa the chaos involved in a new Senate race. As Garfield was entering the presidency, his cabinet was not yet complete.

The inaugural address, delivered on March 4, had been finished at 2:30 that morning. Although Garfield had read previous inaugurals for inspiration, it had done him little good. His speech, as Morgan notes, was "a collection of platitudes."[41] The hoarse Garfield promised an end to sectionalism, committed himself to bimetallism, called for the education of southern blacks, and promised a civil-service law. As he bucked the Washington frost, he was indeed a tired man giving a tired speech.

By that evening, Garfield could breathe a bit more easily. He had reverted back to Windom for secretary of the treasury, and as he returned to the White House from the inaugural ball, he found the Minnesota senator willing to accept. On the following day, the sixty-seven-year-old Samuel J. Kirkwood, who had been Iowa's wartime governor, accepted the Interior Department post; and thus Hunt could be moved to the Navy Department. "The result is better than I expected," Garfield wrote in his journal, "Though not an ideal cabinet, it is a good combination of *esse and videre.*"[42]

It would be easy to argue that the president-elect had blundered greatly. At Chicago, Garfield had inherited a divided party; his activities during the interregnum obviously had split it further. He had, to all appearances, violated two cardinal rules of the working politician: breaking his word and interfering with the livelihood of other politicos. His sponsorship of Blaine did not necessarily show discretion, for given the blatant use of the spoils system by both factions, serious reformers would be hard put to make any serious distinction between the Stalwarts and the Half-Breeds.

In some ways, however, Garfield's cabinet was remarkably balanced. In fact, it would be difficult to find a cabinet that represented so many disparate wings of the party. There was hardly a faction or party leader that was excluded. Hayes had fostered Hunt (who also represented a sop to the South); Logan, Lincoln (also an overture to the Midwest); Cameron, his relative MacVeagh. The Kirkwood appointment pleased Allison. James, who took a cabinet seat after Morton and Folger had turned one down, represented the Stalwarts. And as if to show that there were no hard feelings, Morton was appointed minister to France.

Yet there were still problems. The Stalwarts were dissatisfied, because they did not get the crucial treasury slot. Indeed, from Conkling's personal standpoint, Vice-President Arthur alone was truly reliable. Then, there was the still-anxious Blaine, the only Half-Breed in the cabinet. Blaine's protégé Allison had rejected the treasury post, and another of his protégés, Walter Q. Gresham of Indiana, never received a bid. Instead, individuals whom Blaine had opposed, such as Windom and, initially, James, had been given cabinet positions.

Hence the showdown between the Stalwarts and the Half-Breeds was still to come. And if Garfield had rejected as many suggestions from the Maine politician as he had accepted, he had put James G. Blaine, not Roscoe Conkling, in the strategic spot when trouble came. It would come soon.

3

★ ★ ★ ★ ★

A TROUBLED PRESIDENT

Upon assuming office, Garfield quickly established a routine. Up at seven, he first read the morning papers, then, after breakfast, began a voluminous correspondence. By 10:00 A.M., he was available to the public. The White House staff, a small one, consisted of six clerks. Headed by the twenty-four-year-old Joseph Stanley Brown, it clipped newspapers, organized correspondence, and arranged the president's schedule. The rest of his day was spent in meeting office seekers.

Then, there was the cabinet. Blaine, in his funeral eulogy, noted that Garfield conducted its meetings skillfully, disposing of business with order and dispatch. Blaine did not point out, however, that Garfield usually consulted in secret with him beforehand, then reentered the meeting with other members.

Of course, Garfield had little time to show his skills as an administrator, although he was able to accomplish one thing worthy of acclaim: the successful refunding of the national debt. He instructed Windom to call in all the 6 percent bonds, giving owners the option of holding them at 3½ percent. Most holders chose this option, thereby saving the taxpayers over $10 million.

The new president paid little attention to ceremony, but the press gave him good treatment, stressing his homespun qualities. Garfield was blessed with boisterous children, a gracious wife, and an attractive mother. The life of fourteen-year-old Mollie focused upon piano lessons and luncheons for her girl friends; that of ten-year-old Irvin, upon riding his bicycle indoors. The younger Abram, like Irvin, was personally instructed by a classmate of

Garfield's, brought from Montana Territory, while the two older teenagers, Harry and Jim, were being tutored to prepare them for Williams in the fall. A special schoolroom was established in the White House for the latter two brothers. The president's handsome wife, Lucretia, had formerly been rather withdrawn, yet she managed to perform the tasks of First Lady with dignity and grace. She was counseled by the forceful wife of James G. Blaine, who told her to ignore busybodies and take command personally. Garfield's mother, Eliza, who was close to eighty, often remained in her room, from which she emerged at mealtime, dressed in black taffeta and escorted to dinner by her son.

Garfield himself was not too dignified to wrestle in the Executive Mansion with his sons; nor was his spouse, "Crete," above patching chairs and putting tables over worn spots in the carpets (Congress had refused to renovate the decaying White House). Temperance partisans continued to hound him, although Garfield skillfully adopted a suggestion made by John Sherman: serve liquor to guests as a needed formality, but announce that he and his wife would not drink.

No man could be in politics as long as Garfield had been without forming some opinions on the nature of presidential leadership, and his, by and large, were negative. Philosophically, as has been noted, he was a believer in laissez faire, and he had been suspicious of presidential power from the time when he fought Andrew Johnson. Garfield thought that the president could make recommendations to Congress but should never inflict his views on the legislature. Unlike Hayes, he did not see moral leadership as particularly important, and as noted, Garfield ended the temperance restrictions imposed by his predecessor.

Garfield was a man of principle regarding the causes most dear to him; nevertheless, he was more conciliator than leader. He never entered a fight if he could avoid it, thus causing critics to accuse him of "lacking sand." "I love to deal with doctrines and events," he wrote soon after he assumed the presidency. "The contests of men about men I greatly dislike."[1]

If Garfield saw one area where presidential leadership must be forceful, it was in the realm of administration. Much of his vision of the office, in fact, might be summarized in three words: appoint good men. Here he would brook no interference. In particular, the practice of senatorial courtesy, whereby the senior senator passed upon major appointments from his state, was—he said—"one of the most corrupt and vicious practices of our times."[2] It would be this belief, to which he held most firmly, that would lead to one of the greatest crises a president could face.

As soon as Garfield had taken the oath of office, he was confronted by a line of job applicants that stretched down Pennsylvania Avenue. To John

Hay, the White House corridors echoed to "the sound of beasts at feeding time."[3] At one point, the president exclaimed: "My God! What is there in this place that a man should ever want to get into it?" Tossing in his bed at night, he suspected that he might be "wholly unfit" for the position. The weariness of "wasted Presidents," he maintained, would eventually lead to civil-service reform.[4]

Such reforms had long been needed. Before 1883, a civil servant had to depend upon political patronage. Personnel was often untrained; tenure, extremely insecure; and fear of early dismissal continually lowered morale. According to Ari Hoogenboom, a historian of civil-service reform, the government bureaucracy was "largely composed of misfits employed on a temporary basis."[5]

Some historians find the spoils system rather harmless. They acknowledge that it encouraged incompetence and boondoggling but find that such procedures are preferable to making covert bargains over contributions and booty with large corporations. Even at its worst, the Grant administration had not destroyed the nation, and at any rate, the federal government seldom exerted direct influence on the average citizen. Other historians find such practices both cynical and antiquated. A newly industrialized nation could ill afford to indulge itself in inefficiency, waste, and corruption; and the chief executive, in particular, should not, as Garfield confided to his diary, see his day "frittered away by the personal seeking of people, when it ought to be given to the great problem[s] which concern the whole country."[6]

Despite the publicity given to the Pendleton Act of 1883, the onslaught against the spoils system had begun over a decade earlier. Indeed, Grant was more interested in civil service, and ran a more efficient administration, than such predecessors as Abraham Lincoln, a man who had ruthlessly used patronage in the 1864 election. In addition, much of the corruption of the Grant administration had virtually disappeared with the advent of Hayes. It was, in fact, the Conkling Republican Thomas L. James who had reformed the New York Post Office, setting up examinations and rejecting unqualified applicants.

As the 1880 presidential campaign was reaching its peak, civil-service reformers were creating an effective and permanent organization. On September 17, the moribund New York Civil Service Reform Association was revived, and within a month the dynamic George William Curtis was elected its president. By the middle of 1881, similar reform groups had been organized elsewhere. Massachusetts took the lead, with associations established in Boston, Cambridge, and West Newton. In addition, organizations were formed in Cincinnati, Milwaukee, Philadelphia, Providence, and San Francisco.

The movement was essentially conservative, with a membership both wealthy and patrician. Far from wishing to revolutionize the nation, it seldom recognized how radically industrialization had transformed American society. Its leaders were often free traders in an age of growing protectionism, antimonopolists in a period of business consolidation, hard-money men in what Irwin Unger calls the Greenback Era.[7] (Reformist editor E. L. Godkin claimed never to have seen an advocate of paper money "who had not a queer look about his eyes.")[8]

The nation that emerged from the Civil War, so the reformers believed, had lost its sense of purpose. Not only were businesses corrupt, government extravagant, and taxation excessive; the "new" immigration, the growth of radicalism, and waves of strikes were ruining the land. "Politics," mourned civil-service reformer Dorman B. Eaton, "became a trade."[9] Before the days of Jackson and before the building of factories, men of reform background, status, and education had been unquestioned leaders of society. Only through civil-service reform might the country regain a sense of order, deference, and stability. Perhaps, just perhaps, civil-service reform could decentralize the state, restoring the pristine republic of virtue and creating a government staffed by people like themselves: a well-educated elite, responsible neither to grasping politicos nor to an unruly populace.

In 1880, the reformers first wanted Hayes to be renominated. Once it became clear that the president was out of the running, they gravitated towards Edmunds, one of the most contentious individuals in the Senate. Others among their favorites were Washburne and Sherman—and Senator-elect James A. Garfield of Ohio.

Reformers had mixed feelings about the incoming president. They were displeased with Garfield's acceptance letter, in which he vaguely endorsed tenure for civil servants while specifically promising to consult party leaders on major appointments. H. Wayne Morgan notes that Garfield wanted "a partisan merit service," and his unpublicized expressions of concern with assessments show just how partisan he was.[10] Several reformers, however— Schurz, Godkin, and Mark Twain among them—backed Garfield in the presidential race. Once he was elected, devotees of good government were delighted to see him choose James to head the Post Office Department and were equally pleased to see New York's Assistant Postmaster Henry G. Pearson assume James's old post.

Other activities of the new administration, however, were far less to their liking. As a group, they were most disappointed that Blaine was chosen as secretary of state. Blaine, in turn, had little use for the Independents, the "reformers by profession" whom he dubbed the "Unco Guid," declaring them to be "the worst possible political advisers, upstarts, conceited, foolish, vain, without knowledge of measures, ignorant of men."[11] The reformers realized that Kirkwood had abolished civil-service reform in the Department of the Interior, that various Conklingites were now being given governmental positions, and that a scandal concerning the mail service was brewing. Then Garfield gave so many positions to old friends that, to use Peskin's phrasing, "the civil service list read like the 42nd Regiment's muster roll or a Hiram class reunion."[12]

In addition, Garfield's inaugural displeased the reformers. It simply proposed that tenure cover all minor officeholders and be limited to an unspecified number of years, a proposal that led Godkin to comment that the president sought to subsidize those dregs in the labor market who could not keep a steady job. Hayes's outgoing remarks to Congress had called for much more change, as the retiring president wanted uniform methods of appointment, the competitive system, the revival of the Civil Service Commission, and an end to congressional interference with executive officeholders. Reformers were beginning to realize that Garfield was not yet one of them. They had yet to learn that whatever battle he would fight would center more on presidential prerogative than on the creation of a bureaucracy filled with nonpartisan experts.

At first, it was hoped that any fight over such prerogative could be avoided. On March 20, Garfield called Conkling to his office, there to confer on the topic of appointments. In the course of two and a half hours, he told the Stalwart leader that he intended to recognize "the New York protestants" who had supported him at the Chicago convention. Conkling grudgingly concurred, while trying to shunt them off to foreign posts. The president responded that they did not "deserve exile but rather a place in the affairs of their own state."[13] Conkling asked who was to head the New York Customhouse, with its staff of fifteen hundred workers. He thought that Garfield had responded with a promise to consult him about this strategic appointment. However, as was often the case when Garfield confronted hard questions, he was evasive.

The New York senator was undoubtedly pleased when, two days later, the president recommended to the Senate some five New York reappointments that Conkling had approved. The positions included two United States marshals, the United States attorney for the eastern district of New York, and the customs collector at Buffalo, New York. Stewart L. Woodford, a Union general who had given the nominating speech for Conkling at the 1876 Republican convention, was slated for the highly lucrative position of United States attorney for the Southern District.

Now Blaine had reason to be worried, for he had hoped to manipulate all patronage so as to punish his political enemies. To the new secretary of state, the appointment of a Logan protégé as marshal in Illinois meant "political suicide," whereas making one of Blaine's distant relatives postmaster of Helena was "the last chance to make Montana Republican."[14] His effort to place William E. Chandler as solicitor general caused the new attorney general to threaten to resign, and MacVeagh only withdrew his resignation when Garfield agreed to scuttle the New Hampshire politico. As soon as Blaine learned of the Stalwart nominations, he threatened to resign from the new administration; however, he agreed to stay if Garfield would reward William H. Robertson, the New York State leader of his forces as the 1880 convention, with some position equal to Woodford's post. The position he had in mind was the collectorship of the New York Customhouse.

Blaine designed an ingenious plan, one that would insult the Stalwarts at every step. It came as a series of presidential nominations that resembled a game of musical chairs. General Edwin A. Merritt, the reformist collector of the port of New York, was to become consul general in London, with Robertson scheduled as his replacement. General Adam Badeau, the present consul general in London, was slated for transfer to Copenhagen. During the Civil War, Badeau had been Grant's personal secretary, and he was court historian of Grant's presidency. If, as in the case of Merritt, the move was technically a promotion, Badeau had enjoyed the London post, and Grant had specifically insisted that Badeau be allowed to stay. The Methodist clergyman Michael J. Cramer, who was Grant's brother-in-law, was to be sent to Switzerland, there to replace Nicholas Fish, a son of Grant's secretary of state.

The appointments met with widespread criticism. To Conkling, these moves involved "perfidy without parallel"; to Grant, it was evidence that Garfield lacked "the backbone of an angle-worm."[15] Postmaster General James not only threatened Garfield with resignation, doing so in order to prove to his fellow Stalwarts that he had played no role in Robertson's nomination. He also signed a petition of protest, as did Vice-President Arthur and the New York senators. Treasury Secretary Windom too was angry, because Garfield had not told him about some changes that affected one of the most important positions in his department. Such moderate senators as Sherman and Allison, sensing that longstanding privileges were at stake, opposed Garfield; so did some of Blaine's own faction, such as Eugene Hale and William P. Frye of Maine. Reformers, of course, were far from pleased, particularly as the conscientious Merritt faced being replaced for the most partisan of reasons.

At first, Garfield reached out for compromise. Along with James, who finally agreed not to resign, he outlined a scheme that he hoped would pacify everyone. Merritt would remain as collector of the New York Customhouse. Robertson would be moved to the slot of district attorney, Grant's friends would stay in their overseas posts, and Woodford would be given a diplomatic position in a sunny climate. Conkling initially was ready to negotiate over the matter, but he abruptly changed his mind upon hearing that the governor of New York wanted him to support Robertson for the customhouse position. The request made Conkling realize how precarious his power was, and he refused to appear as a supplicant before the president.

This time it was Garfield's turn to react. The *Nation* might compare the dispute to a hypothetical "row between Gladstone and John Bright over the collectorship of Liverpool."[16] To Garfield, however, the issue would "settle the question whether the President is registering clerk of the Senate or the Executive of the United States." A more immediate question, he said, was whether America's principal port of entry would be under the administration's direction or "under the local control of a factional senator." "Robertson may be carried out of the Senate head first or feet first," he commented. "I shall never withdraw him."[17] To Whitelaw Reid, this event was "the turning point of his whole Administration—the crisis of his Fate."[18]

The president did have some misgivings, so many that, in private, he admitted that the Robertson nomination had been a mistake. But more and more in his mind, the issue was becoming one of principle. Blaine might have had his own reasons for advancing Robertson and snubbing the Stalwarts, but for Garfield the legitimate constitutional rights of the president were very much the issue. He was soon stressing that Conkling's consent was irrelevant, for the customhouse was, by its function, a national—not a state—office. He had, he maintained, consulted the Stalwarts more than anyone else in the party, and he was not to blame if they remained hostile.

Almost from the outset, Garfield was confident of victory. In his journal of March 23, he wrote, "The sensation produced by the nomination was very great but I think the Senate will approve."[19] He was widely supported in the nation's press: a tabulation showed that 125 newspapers were in favor and only 15 opposed. He remained firm, resisting all pressures to withdraw Robertson's name.

On the evening of April 14, Vice-President Arthur begged the president to give Robertson a different post. The appointment, he declared, would ruin the Stalwart machine. The press might criticize the vice-president for disloyalty, but as his biographer Thomas C. Reeves notes, "He had been a Stalwart too long to surrender an inch—much less the war—to Blaine and those he controlled. If he could not be popular, at least he could be true to his friends; and if Conkling regained his political power there would soon be admirers enough."[20]

The Stalwarts attempted blackmail, an effort that backfired. Senate Republicans, all too aware of the dangers lying in party schism, had formed a conciliation committee headed by Henry L. Dawes. Like Arthur, Dawes urged that Robertson's nomination be withdrawn; he alluded to a letter that Conkling claimed would ruin Garfield. The president assured Dawes that the letter was simply a campaign appeal to Jay Hubbell, chairman of the Republican Congressional Committee, asking that assessments be made on government workers and in particular on those in the post office. Dawes then suggested that Garfield publish the letter himself, but Blaine successfully recommended silence. When Dawes started to ask Conkling to concede, the Stalwart leader replied that capitulation would ruin him. "[I] should be burned in effigy from Buffalo to Montauk Point, and could not be elected a delegate to a county convention in Oneida County."[21] The Stalwarts published the Hubbell letter, and as the candidate had mentioned Thomas J. Brady—second assistant postmaster general, who was then under investigation—Garfield was indirectly accused of complicity in a budding post-office scandal. However aside from arousing the ire of the reformers, Conkling's maneuver backfired, doing more damage to him than to the president.

During much of this time, the Senate—which had to confirm all appointments—was deadlocked. Republicans and Democrats each had thirty-seven votes. From March 23 to May 4, the Democrats were filibustering, doing so in protest against the Republican nomination of two lieutenants of the Democratic senator from Virginia, William Mahone. Mahone was in the process of breaking from his party, and the Republicans sought to give Senate staff positions to his followers. Hence, since the GOP wanted to postpone the voting on Garfield's appointments until a compromise had been reached on the Mahone matter, it welcomed the delay. On May 4, however, the Garfield administration abandoned its efforts to try to secure jobs for the Mahone protégés, and the Democratic filibuster ended.

Action could now begin on the backlog of business. Garfield feared that the Senate might confirm the New York Stalwarts, then adjourn without taking action on Robertson. In fact, the Senate did confirm several nominations, including one of a minor Stalwart.

Hence, on May 5, Garfield withdrew all nominations but Robertson's, adopting a course of action that had been recommended by Blaine a month earlier. The *Chicago Tribune* commented aptly, "Gen. Garfield has determined to be President of the United States."[22] On the day he made his withdrawal, Garfield indicated plainly that he considered the power and prerogative of the presidency to be at stake. It was not, he confided to his diary, a mere "difference between two individuals" but an issue that affected "the independence of the executive."[23]

Garfield, who for so long had wavered, was now showing some force and a sureness of footing as well. The president, with many years of politicking in the House to his credit, was not above making promises of patronage and influence. John Sherman, for example, had originally opposed Robertson's appointment, but now he skillfully represented Garfield's cause in the Senate. Garfield was turning the contest into a test of loyalty, and senators realized that he still had far more favors to bestow than had Conkling. His opponents, the president threatened, would "henceforth require letters of introduction to the White House."[24] By May 13, administration leaders reported that they had gained enough support from the Democrats to obtain a confirmation.

It was, of all people, Thomas C. Platt who finally put an end to the controversy. Platt suggested to Conkling that they both resign from the Senate and secure reelection, thereby vindicating the Stalwart cause. Conkling at first rebuked Platt but then began to feel he had little choice. If Blaine controlled the customhouse, the Stalwarts would face ruin anyhow. Hence, on May 16, the two men tendered their resignation.

The action, predicted Garfield, would "be received with guffaws of laughter," and he was right.[25] Hayes claimed that Conkling was suffering from "monomania on the subject of his own importance"; Platt henceforth had to live with the nickname "Me Too."[26] As Morgan comments, "Lord Roscoe was now the emperor without his clothes."[27] Within two days after the resignation, all opposition to the Robertson nomination collapsed, and on May 18, he was confirmed. Garfield, commenting on his victory, wrote in his diary, "This is a great relief."[28] The news that neither Platt nor Conkling could command enough votes in the New York Legislature to be reelected was almost anticlimatic.

The showdown with Conkling had been inevitable, particularly as the New York boss persevered over appointments to the Treasury Department, then the customhouse. The president was standing up for the prerogatives of his office and, in the process, curbing the Senate's power. Future chief executives could only be grateful that a step had been made, even if a small one, to increase their control. And most important of all, Garfield's people saw him acting like a leader, a man not cowed by truculent politicos.

At the same time, Garfield had chosen a poor issue on which to wage a fight. Ousting the able Merritt in order to reward one of Conkling's foes had little to commend it. And although Garfield first showed a desire for party conciliation, at crucial junctures he was listening far too much to his devious secretary of state.

As if the dispute with Conkling were not enough, Garfield faced a budding scandal in the Post Office Department. In 1881, it was the largest government office, housing over one-half of the federal bureaucracy. Its political use matched that of the Treasury Department. The office of postmaster general was usually a party office; its occupant was entrusted with rewarding the party faithful. Here, tenure was brief; the administrative record, unimpressive. Even if he diligently transacted the daily business referred to him by his assistants, he seldom gave the impression that he was master of his department. Congress helped matters little, since it opposed regional organization and, at times, proposed questionable appointees.

Soon after Garfield had assumed the presidency, he was confronted with a major scandal known as the Star Route Affair, which centered on the contracting of mail routes. Although most mail was carried by train and steamship, in isolated areas of the West the government had established private arrangements with horse, stagecoach, and wagon agencies. The "stars" themselves were asterisks in federal contracts and stood for the words "certainty, celerity, and security." Congress generously appropriated money for these contracts, believing that the nation's population growth would soon repay the initial investment.

The procedure was legal, but supervision of it was lax. Although the Post Office Department was supposed to accept the lowest bid, it found that its difficulties were only beginning. Friendly contractors would submit bids at ridiculously low rates, then petition Congress to "improve" the service and thus receive up to three times the original bid in "compensation." By 1880, sparsely settled areas of the South and West possessed some 9,225 star routes, the cost of which had reached close to $6 million.

As early as 1872, a House committee had investigated the department, and in 1878, Stephen W. Dorsey, Republican carpetbag senator from Arkansas, was implicated in fraud. When, two years later, Congress suddenly had to make up deficits, it learned that prominent members of both parties were involved in possible scandal. However, it delayed further inquiry until the presidential election was over.

Once the returns were in, President-elect Garfield was confronted with the problem. Blaine told him that a small cabal was attempting to steal half a million dollars a year. Just five days after his inauguration, Garfield asked Postmaster General James to launch an investigation and initiate reforms. By the middle of April, Garfield had ordered an overhaul of the department, one that involved the removal of Brady as second assistant postmaster general. He confided to his diary that "the corruption and wrong-doing has been of a very gross and extensive kind."[29] Brady was permitted to resign, although the president wanted him fired. Operators of star routes attempted to retaliate, doing so by publicizing the Hubbell letter. For a while the president thought that his campaign manager, Dorsey, might be innocent, but he still persisted with the investigation. Early in June, one of Dorsey's clerks—Montfort C. Rerdell—confessed to having participated in the frauds; Rerdell implicated Dorsey, as well as Dorsey's brother and brother-in-law. Upon learning these facts, Garfield told investigators, "Go ahead regardless of where and whom you hit."[30]

Initial revelations, wrote Attorney General MacVeagh to James, went beyond anything written by Mark Twain. Although lawyers began preparing a case for the District grand jury, Garfield was impatient. Prosecutions, he believed, must begin soon.

Also needing the president's attention was a longstanding concern: the plight of the southern freedman. This group had special problems, for northerners were rapidly deserting their cause. Indeed, after 1877, many northerners believed that the racial issue could only delay national unification, trade between the sections, and good government in the South. Although at times apologetic to the South over the "excesses" of Reconstruction, they looked upon blacks as a type of peasantry, a group inferior in stamina and achievement. Even the play *Uncle Tom's Cabin* lost its bite; it was no longer a spur to racial justice but had become simply another minstrel show.

Like their white counterparts, southern blacks usually led lives that were circumscribed by farm and plantation. Lacking the capital to own land, they often worked as tenants and sharecroppers, starting each new year in debt. Indeed, Negroes of the South—over 75 percent of them remained in the South—existed almost in peonage. Only a fourth lived on the land they owned. In such states as Tennessee, Georgia, Mississippi, Louisiana, and Alabama, few blacks owned the land they worked. When blacks tried to obtain jobs in factories, white laborers began to strike, and despite the opposition of some white employers, work in cotton mills soon became reserved for whites only.

At first it appeared as if Garfield would come to the rescue. By 1878, he was criticizing Hayes's overtures to the white South, declaring that the policy of the president had "turned out to be a give-away from the beginning." In his acceptance letter, Garfield claimed that the South would only prosper when every voter could "freely and safely support the party he pleases." The presidential candidate occasionally resorted to bloody-shirt tactics. The South, he remarked, possessed a "bastard civilization," and during one rally he said, "We have seen white men betray the flag and fight to kill the Union, but in all that long, dreary war, we never saw a traitor in black skin."[31]

As far as the future of southern blacks was concerned, however, Garfield was extremely cautious. In 1865, he publicly supported Negro suffrage, believing it the only way to preserve Republican rule and therefore the sanctity of the Union. At the same time, he confessed that political equality gave him "a strong feeling of repugnance." At one point he said that he "never could get in love with [the] creatures"; at another, he hoped that they could be "colonized, sent to heaven or got rid of in any decent way"; at still another, he found Capitol Hill too "infested with negroes" to suit his taste.[32] When, in 1870, the Fifteenth Amendment was passed, Garfield believed that henceforth the blacks' fortune was "in their own hands." He commented privately in 1876 that black labor was "indispensable to the prosperity of the South" but that Negro suffrage was "a mortal offense to his late masters." Three years later, Garfield opposed movements for mass disenfranchisement. Gradually giving the vote to Negroes as they became more intelligent, he said, would have been wiser, but all dictates "of private right, of public justice, and national safety" had necessitated Negro suffrage.[33] In fact, the Republican party, so he always believed, was founded on the principle of Negro advancement.

If Garfield had any cure for the black predicament, it lay in education. Mastery of Greek and Latin had transformed him "from canal boy to president," and he found no reason why it could not elevate others. Such partisans of education as Burke Aaron Hinsdale, president of Hiram College, and Albion W. Tourgée, author of A Fool's Errand (1879), reinforced the views of the president-elect. Garfield strongly supported the provision of the 1880 Republican platform that stressed "the duty of the National Government" to aid education, maintaining during the campaign that such aid could resolve the South's difficulties. Under his schemes, the races would have similar educational opportunities, while schools receiving government assistance would remain autonomous.

As Garfield approached the presidency, he grew even more adamant on the need for black education. When a delegation of prominent southern Negroes told Garfield that they were being deprived of the ballot "by means of armed violence, fraud, and intimidation," Garfield claimed that the government should do all in its power to protect them. However, he stressed that genuine equality must come through "the native hungering and thirsting for knowledge that the Creator has planted in every child."[34] The visitors strongly endorsed Garfield's view, although a militant black journal, the New York Age, accused Garfield of simply telling Negroes to obtain "Webster's Blue Black spelling book."[35]

One-third of his inaugural focused on the Negro and the South. Here Garfield reminded southerners that "there can be no permanent disfranchized peasantry in the United States." To prohibit Negroes from voting was "a crime which, if persisted in, will destroy the Government itself." He again stressed, in an analysis closely following Tourgée's, that in education lay the permanent solution. Indeed, he pledged "all the constitutional power of the nation and of the States and all the volunteer forces of the people" to this task.[36] Late in March, addressing a delegation of fifty blacks from Louisiana, he reiterated his desire to obtain education for Negroes and his hope to see the freedmen own the land they toiled. "I am," he said, concerning southern schools, "going to keep that subject before me all the time."[37]

Garfield's solutions were not totally naïve. Seventy percent of southern blacks were illiterate, and northern states were spending three times as much on education as were southern ones. But even if the president's proposals for substantial educational programs were valid, Negroes faced economic problems that schooling alone could not alter. Moreover, it is doubtful whether the president could have mustered a national consensus behind him. During the 1880s, Senator Henry W. Blair (Rep., N.H.) frequently called for federal aid to education, but Congress always turned down his proposals. Land redistribution would probably not have helped matters, because the experience of marginal white farmers in the South showed that any small landholder faced tremendous hardships. Some prominent black educators and politicians claimed to be impressed by the new chief executive, but time did not permit a longer test of his leadership.

In the meantime, there were more practical decisions to be made. Garfield continued the Republican practice of giving certain federal offices to black politicians. Robert Elliott was made special agent of the Treasury Department; Frederick Douglass, recorder of deeds in Washington; and John Mercer Langston, minister to Haiti. Blanche K. Bruce, who had received eight votes for the vice-presidential nomination at the Chicago convention and who had been mentioned for the cabinet, was appointed registrar of the treasury.

Months before the inauguration, Garfield confided that southern Democrats would receive no more patronage. The president-elect began to reverse Hayes's policies of conciliation (a dreary failure, Garfield called it), listening to people who did not have the former president's ear. For example, Garfield was visited by former governor Daniel H. Chamberlain of South Carolina, who had lost out in the state when federal troops had departed. When Chamberlain warned against backing Democratic independents, Garfield agreed.

One effort to strengthen the Republican party in the South involved the appointment of a native white Republican, William H. Hunt, as secretary of the navy. Hunt had aligned himself with Louisiana's carpetbag government during Reconstruction; he was welcomed by southern Republicans as evidence of what Garfield meant to do in the region. Then, acting in the realization that southern Republicans were sparsely represented in Congress, Garfield promised state party chairmen that all appointments would be made on their recommendations.

Black and carpetbag coalitions did not offer Garfield a lasting solution, of course, any more than the continuation of Hayes's New Departure would have done. The South contained surprising Republican strength. In the 1880 election, for example, such states as Florida, North Carolina, Virginia, and Tennessee gave Garfield some real backing. In fact, a shift of 2 percent would have made North Carolina Republican. Yet, real victory in such states would require more white voters, individuals who were disillusioned with the Democratic establishment. In 1876, Garfield had expressed the hope that the Republicans could gain such support, doing so by means of new party alignment formed "on the great commercial and industrial questions rather than on questions of race and color."[38] One source of such backing could come from the Readjuster movement of Virginia and its leader, William Mahone.

In describing Mahone, C. Vann Woodward writes that "in the whole gallery of Southern figures of his generation, he stands out as one of the boldest and most enigmatical."[39] A dapper, full-bearded man, Mahone was under five-feet-six-inches tall and weighed less than a hundred pounds. He had been born in Southampton, Virginia, the son of a tavern keeper, and as a young man made his fortune in railroads. He was chief of the Norfolk and Petersburg Railroad at the age of twenty-six, president at thirty-one. At first, he did not dissent from southern folkways, for he owned slaves and was an ardent secessionist. During the Civil War, he rose to the rank of major general; his defense of the James River helped to make him famous. After the conflict, Mahone plunged again into railroad organization, gaining the reputation of being a "railroad Bismarck" and controlling more track than any other American railroad man. When, during the depression of the seventies, his extensive railroad system passed into receivership, he blamed this on Richmond businessmen, Conservative politicos, and the "foreign" railroads of Pennsylvania and Baltimore.

By the middle of the 1870s, Virginia itself was in difficult straits. Credit had collapsed, industry was stagnating, farms were bankrupt, and prices low. The state was truly in a depression, with its predicament compounded by the fact that its legislature had assumed full responsibility for all of Virginia's ante-bellum debt. A funding act, passed in 1871, strengthened Virginia's obligation; if honored, it would have left the state no money with which to operate its government.

In 1877, Mahone ran for governor, calling for "compromise and readjustment" of this obligation. In their campaign against the "Funders," his "Readjusters" hoped to shift a third of the debt to the relatively new state of West Virginia, sought the refunding of the remainder at low interest rates, called for money to improve state educational and charitable institutions, and demanded honest elections. Although the Readjusters were at first defeated, by 1879 they had won the legislature, and Mahone was elected to the United States Senate. Indeed, the Readjusters had become a most effective political machine. With strong black backing for their measures, they were able to create what Carl N. Degler finds to have been "the most successful political coalition of whites and blacks organized in the South between Reconstruction and the 1960's."[40]

By 1880, Mahone was seeking to become a power in national politics. He feared an old-line party battle, one that would divide white Readjusters, who were usually Democrats, from their black allies, who were usually Republican. Hence, he first wanted a fusion in which presidential electors would remain unpledged to either candidate. Such a maneuver, he believed, would retain his racial coalition; it would also provide bargaining power in a close race. When black legislators and the Republican state convention rejected the scheme, Mahone entered an independent slate of Hancock electors, one that would rival that of the Funders. Garfield, upon discovering that some Virginia Republicans considered backing the Mahone slate, cabled a loyal party worker that "no one has been authorized by me to abandon (the) fight for the Electoral vote of Virginia." Those blacks who supported Mahone, said Garfield a year before, had inflicted, "a serious if not fatal wound upon the honor and prosperity of Virginia."[41] Garfield came within a few thousand votes of carrying the Old Dominion; two Republicans were elected to the House by large majorities. Mahone's own Readjusters made a relatively poor showing and thereby realized how dependent they were upon Negro support.

Senator Mahone, however, still hoped to capture such posts as the governorship and another Senate seat, and for this effort, the support of Virginia Republicans was needed. Therefore he made overtures to George C. Gorham, Stalwart editor of the *National Republican*, who tried to intercede with Garfield, Grant, and Blaine. Before the 1880 election, prominent Republicans—including Hayes, Blaine, Sherman, and Grant—had opposed Mahone's fiscal "irresponsibility." And after the election, Garfield found his cabinet extremely distrustful of any such alliance. He himself was suspicious, first because it meant abandoning the Virginia Republican organization; second because the sheer notion of debt repudiation betrayed the sacred cause of fiscal orthodoxy. When a group of Virginia blacks sought to back the insurgent, he urged them to remain in the ranks of the GOP.

Despite Republican suspicions, Mahone realized that he was in an extremely strategic spot. The new Senate was evenly balanced, with the Democrats and Republicans each having thirty-seven members. David

Davis of Illinois, elected as an Independent, declared that he would vote as a Democrat. Yet if Mahone sided with the Republicans, Vice-President Arthur could break any tie, thereby giving the GOP control. In addition, Mahone was the only man in Virginia who could wrest the state from the Democrats, an event that might set a precedent for the entire South. Never since the days of the Redeemers had the GOP had such a dramatic opportunity of capturing a southern state.

Power always speaks its own language, and soon a variety of Republicans—including Roscoe Conkling, George Frisbie Hoar, J. Donald Cameron, and national party chairman Marshall Jewell—urged the party to support the Virginia Senator. Some white Republican leaders in Virginia also sought an alliance, including the GOP state chairman. Mahone started making his price known, and on March 23, Henry L. Dawes of Massachusetts, leader of the Senate Republican caucus, proposed five new administrative officers for that body. Mahone backer George C. Gorham was nominated for secretary of the Senate; Harrison H. Riddleberger, a Mahone associate, for sergeant-at-arms. Riddleberger was a former Confederate captain who had served as a Hancock elector in 1880; he had sponsored a measure that lay at the heart of the Readjusters' financial program, for it would scale down Virginia's debt. The Democrats blocked both nominations by not bringing them to a vote, although Mahone himself was rewarded with the chairmanship of the Senate Committee on Agriculture, in addition to positions on committees dealing with the post office, education, labor, and naval affairs.

By then, Garfield was acquiescing. If, he declared, Virginia faced genuine bankruptcy, some debt readjustment might be in order. Even more important, he found that the continued Senate deadlock justified such bargaining. "When our friends have secured all the committees by the help of Mahone," wrote Garfield to Whitelaw Reid on April 7, "they ought to stand by him until he is reasonably satisfied."[42]

Yet Garfield had misgivings. Late in May, he announced that he would not sanction any general alliance with the Readjusters at the expense of Virginia's Republicans. Though he admitted that Mahone's group was bettering the lot of the blacks, he did not intend, he said, to "remove Republicans to appoint Mahone men."[43] Behind Garfield stood Blaine, who claimed that the regular Republicans would soon be powerful enough to carry the state alone. In addition, declared Blaine, support for the Readjusters would discourage wealthy southerners whose economic views might lead them into the GOP.

Despite such uncertainties, Garfield began to work out a merger with Mahone, one that would lead towards a common ticket. In fact, it was not Chester A. Arthur but Garfield who initially altered the Republicans' southern policy. Meeting with a delegation of Virginia Republicans that included two congressmen, Garfield urged the "straight-out" Republicans to aid Mahone in every way possible. He also directed federal officials to split patronage between the two groups. In August, a convention in Lynchburg merged the Readjuster and Republican tickets, and some northern Republicans, such as Senator Cameron, raised funds for the candidates.

The new president's reluctant bargaining with the Mahone forces shows again, as in the case of Robertson, the triumph of politics over ideology. Once Arthur became president, the overtures to southern independents would be undertaken on a much more massive scale, no longer being limited to Virginia but encompassing much more south of the Mason-Dixon line.

Whatever plans Garfield had for the South would not come to fruition, for on July 2, at 9:20 A.M., the president was shot in Washington's Baltimore and Potomac Station. Garfield clutched his back, crying out "Oh, my God!" while his assassin, a disappointed office seeker named Charles Julius Guiteau, was grabbed by a policeman.

The president lingered on for several months. One bullet had lodged in his spinal column, and his physicians considered him too weak for a probe to be made. At first, the doctors had been optimistic about his chances for recovery; after each brief period of rallying, however, he grew steadily weaker. Few visitors were permitted, and the president was kept alive on a liquid diet. Even had he survived, he would have remained a cripple.

While Garfield was wasting away, the nation lacked a leader. Fortunately, Congress was not in session, and the president only had to sign one paper. Temporarily, all went smoothly. As Robert Todd Lincoln wrote, the government was "running along—every man running his own Department and thinking he is doing so well that he may be President some day."[44]

Arthur was returning from Albany to New York with Conkling when he heard that the president had been shot. The vice-president, very much shaken by the news, at first refused to go to Washington; but when Blaine telegraphed that the cabinet needed him promptly, Arthur left immediately for the capital. Conkling carried his bags to the New York depot. Blaine reportedly wanted the cabinet to declare Arthur acting president, the vice-president retaining this position until Garfield's fate had been determined. Arthur turned the proposal down, finding it improper.

Nevertheless and not surprisingly, while Garfield was dying, more and more eyes were turned upon the vice-president, and many of these eyes were apprehensive. The unsavory maneuvering that had catapulted Arthur to the top was now backfiring with a vengeance. E. L. Godkin, editor of the

Nation, noted, "It is out of this mess of filth that Mr. Arthur will go to the Presidential chair in case of the President's death." Hayes predicted that Conkling would be "the power behind the throne." Governor Charles Foster of Ohio was in a decided minority when he declared that "the people and the politicians will find that Vice-President Arthur and President Arthur are different men."[45]

Arthur's shabby behavior during some maneuvering in the Senate added to the anxiety. The resignation of Conkling and Platt had given the Democrats a majority, but Arthur, fearing that Thomas F. Bayard of Delaware would be elected president pro tem, had refused to vacate his chair. Hence, as the Senate adjourned without a president pro tem, the man who was soon to be president lacked any constitutional successor. Small wonder that Bayard wrote to Schurz, "May Heaven avert the contingency of Arthur's promotion."[46]

Arthur, however, as Senator Benjamin Harrison (Rep., Ind.) later recalled, "seemed to be overcome with the calamity." He was, Thomas C. Reeves notes, in agony: "He had never coveted the office of Chief Executive, and was overwhelmed by the prospect of filling the highest office in the land; he was stunned by the cruel circumstances that brought him to Washington and crushed by the savage attacks in the nation's press."[47] Though he might continue to consult with such Stalwarts as Grant, Conkling, and Senator John P. Jones of Nevada, Arthur still refused to assume control.

Early in September, Garfield was moved to Elberon, a village on the Jersey shore, where he died on the nineteenth. Arthur received the news, as his doorkeeper noted, with childlike sobs, and at 2:15 A.M. on the following morning a judge administered to him the oath of office. He called on Mrs. Garfield and the cabinet at Elberon; then he boarded the train for Washington. Garfield's body was placed in the rotunda of the Capitol, and during two days, some one hundred thousand countrymen filed past his remains.

On September 22, Arthur again took the presidential oath, this time before Chief Justice Morrison R. Waite. In an inaugural of only two paragraphs, Arthur referred to Garfield's "example and achievements" and to the "pathos of his death." The new chief executive noted the nation's prosperity and its "well grounded" fiscal policy. There was, he said, "no demand for speedy legislation" and hence no reason to call a special session of Congress.[48] Arthur's brief inaugural met with approval from an already mellowing press.

One saw, of course, an occasional dissenter, such as Henry Adams. Adams called the Garfield administration a "sort of *delirium tremens* vision with Blaine as the big and active snake." Now, he continued, with Arthur at the helm, "we are going to have a nasty *chopping-sea* in politics."[49]

54

4

★ ★ ★ ★ ★

MR. SECRETARY BLAINE

The death of Garfield and the subsequent accession of Arthur to the presidency did not cause any immediate shift in the nation's foreign policy. Until relatively recently, the topic itself was a neglected one, because historians tended to give the Gilded Age relatively little coverage. The United States, they claimed, was still concentrating with such fervor upon the settlement of the West and industrial expansion that it conducted little diplomacy. With statesmen warning against entanglements overseas, Congress dominated by anti-imperialists, and the public apathetic, historians have often found isolationism the unquestioned canon of the era.[1]

Such sweeping claims are rapidly being modified. Beginning in the late 1950s, a group of revisionist historians—looking at this period afresh—began to find in the Gilded Age "the roots of the American Empire." The years from Hayes to McKinley, they claimed, reveal far more than lethargy; both business and farm spokesmen continually sought to end hardship at home by means of commercial expansion overseas. Pointing to severe depressions from the seventies to the nineties, these scholars see efforts to dispose of surpluses as a central current of the nation's foreign policy.[2]

The new revisionism has contributed much to our understanding and, almost in passing, has given foreign policy a far more prominent role; nevertheless, it has not as yet succeeded in revolutionizing the traditional view. Sustained examination still reveals that the era was marked by uncoordinated diplomacy, amateurish emissaries, shallow rhetoric, and much public and congressional indifference. Pictures of bountiful markets, reciprocity networks, a thriving merchant marine, and a powerful navy might rest firmly in the minds of various policy makers, but such dreams were seldom realized. Even those members of Congress who promoted a new manifest destiny, such as Senator John T. Morgan and Congressman John A. Kasson (Rep., Iowa), found their policies too often unheeded and their vision too often unshared. Congress, the public, the press—all sought to avoid overseas entanglements and massive spending programs, and for the most part, crises in foreign affairs met with general apathy. The period 1881 to 1885, as David M. Pletcher has noted, could best be called "the awkward years," a time of transition between the internal agonies of Civil War and Reconstruction, on the one hand, and the overt imperialism of the nineties on the other.[3]

True, Garfield was genuinely interested in foreign policy, and he focused in particular upon commercial expansion. In 1876, he advocated reciprocal trade, reminding Congress that "we want all fair chances that the markets of the world can give us for selling our surplus supplies." In particular, he warned against Britain's penetration of the "great tropical world" of Latin America, an area on which the United States should place its major hopes. Garfield's horizons were not limited to this hemisphere, for—with the completion of the transcontinental railroad and the acquisition of Alaska—he saw the United States as a potent power in the Pacific, destined to become "the arbiter of that sea, the controller of its commerce and chief nation that inhabits its shores."[4]

In 1876, Garfield strongly supported the new commercial treaty with Hawaii. Economic influence, he hoped, might obviate the need for political domination. In fact, except for Canada, he repudiated territorial expansion, mentioning Cuba and the West Indies by name, and during the 1870s he backed efforts to arbitrate the *Alabama* claims and the Canadian fisheries issues. As president, Garfield continued this wide-ranging interest; at times he went so far as to tone down some of Secretary Blaine's more contentious dispatches.

The Blaine appointment, as we have seen, was primarily political. Blaine had helped Garfield gain the GOP nomination. He possessed few formal qualifications for the post of secretary of state, being neither a profound student of politics nor a great international lawyer. Indeed, he lacked diplomatic experience entirely, and while in Congress he had revealed little interest in foreign affairs. He was known to possess an intense nationalism, a strong Anglophobia, and a belief in protectionism, American commerce (in particular, shipping from the state of Maine), and hemispheric solidarity. But it was the Robertson nomination and the fight with the Conkling forces, not foreign relations, that drew most of his attention.

And even had Blaine's focus been more on a wider world, he was not blessed with an efficient department. Its pace was slow, almost purposefully so. The executive and clerical staff included only three assistants, a chief clerk, and eight bureaus, each possessing a chief and several clerks. Twenty-five ministers and five chargés d'affaires offered major representation for the nation overseas, and some three hundred consulates attempted to provide for American interests in less prominent areas. A ministerial post often served as a reward for past political favors. Garfield, in fact, was something of an exception in selecting such people as writer James Russell Lowell for Britain and Lew Wallace, novelist and Civil War general, for Turkey. (The president, who greatly admired Wallace's Ben Hur, hoped that the Ottoman Empire would provide the author with enough local color for an exciting sequel.) Most of the foreign service, however, involved second-rate personnel frequently forced to live in third-rate surroundings, a circumstance .that caused John Hay to find the vocation, "like the Catholic Church, calculated only for celibates."[5] No American diplomat held the status of ambassador, since such a title smacked of monarchy; therefore, American ministers were outranked by representatives of far less powerful and prestigious nations.

The consular service, in particular, had many drawbacks. A job in it was a tedious one; the inadequate salaries forced agents to "moonlight." Most consuls spoke only English, possessed little business or administrative experience, and were totally ignorant of international law. Even foreigners held consular positions, although they usually owed primary loyalty to their own nations. Such an inept diplomatic service could hardly manage daily business with skill, much less aid the nation in meeting crises in such regions as Latin America.

Foremost among the Latin American struggles was the War of the Pacific, a conflict that still, a hundred years later, creates bitterness among the participants. In 1874, Chile and Bolivia had drawn up a treaty dividing up a desolate area on the Pacific Coast called the Atacama Desert. The agreement had stipulated that neither government could increase taxes in the region for twenty-five years; nevertheless, in 1878, Bolivia taxed extensive Chilean nitrate developments located at Antofagasta. In February 1879, Chile denounced this tax as being a violation of the 1874 agreement, seized the port, and took direct control of the nitrate works.

Chile was in an expansionist phase, eager to imitate the great powers by adding rich territory to its domain. It was supported in its ambitions by the British, who had invested considerably in the area. On April 5, 1879, it declared war on Bolivia and also on Bolivia's ally Peru. Bolivia possessed no navy; its population was concentrated beyond the Andes and hence remained relatively insulated from the conflict. Chile concentrated increasingly upon Peru, as it was anxious to win the latter's territory of Tarapacá, an area rich in guano and nitrates. Peru's cruisers could not long hold the enemy in check; therefore, Chile moved quickly. It blockaded and shelled major ports in southern Peru, fought a naval war, occupied the disputed coastline, and in January 1881 captured the Peruvian capital of Lima. Chile then demanded that Peru cede the disputed land, but Peru refused.

If the causes of the conflict were complex, the immediate results were all too apparent. *Appletons' Annual Cyclopaedia* accurately described Peru in 1881 as "a country without a government of its own, without any regular armed force by land or by sea, and deprived of the chief sources of national income."[6] In short, the country was virtually paralyzed. In its effort to gain new territory, Chile pressured Francisco García Calderón, a wealthy attorney who headed Peru's new provisional government. Clearly, Chile was not about to brook opposition from any source.

The first phase of United States involvement began in October 1880, when it attempted to mediate the conflict. Chile refused arbitration, and the outgoing United States minister to Peru, Isaac P. Christiancy, warned Blaine that the nation must either intervene enough to establish a peace or else convert Peru into an American protectorate. Only by such means, Christiancy continued, could the United States hope to preserve any material influence in the region. Furthermore, he claimed that Calderón had little power, exercising authority only where Chilean authorities permitted. Blaine, however, recognized the Calderón government, rather than one dominated by Nicolás de Piérola, the Peruvian dictator and old revolutionary leader, who still controlled the northern mountains. Calderón, said Blaine, could best restore internal order and initiate peace negotiations.

Blaine may have genuinely hoped to resolve the conflict, but his choices for diplomats were singularly unfortunate. His new minister to Peru, Stephen A. Hurlbut, had had a checkered career as Union general, minister to Colombia, congressman from Illinois, spoilsman with the occupation army in Louisiana, and first commander in chief of the Grand Army of the Republic. Although once convicted of corruption, in 1880 he was Blaine's midwestern campaign manager. Hugh J. Kilpatrick, Blaine's minister to Chile, was undoubtedly more honest than Hurlbut but almost equally incompetent. Also a Union general, he had been a cavalry commander with General William T. Sherman on the famous march to the sea, and during the 1860s, Kilpatrick had served three years as minister to Peru. His wife, a native Chilean, was the niece of the archbishop of Santiago. Upon arriving again in Peru, Kilpatrick was stricken with Bright's disease and was therefore unable to carry out his duties.

From the outset Blaine favored Peru, and favored it strongly, and it was the secretary's insistence that Peru should not be forced to yield territory that initiated the second phase of United States involvement. For in his very first instruction to Kilpatrick, dated June 15, 1881, Blaine stressed that territorial changes should never be decided without the consent of "all the powers whose people and whose national interest are involved."[7] Peru, the secretary insisted, should be allowed to substitute a financial indemnity for a territorial one. Any boundary changes resulting from force, he feared, could only breed further war and risk foreign intervention in the entire hemisphere. He found Great Britain particularly threatening, and he would harp upon England's heavy trade with Brazil as exemplifying such a threat. To James Gillespie Blaine, prestige, peace, and economic interest were all tied together, and all implied that Chile should receive no additional territory.

Hurlbut made every effort to foster Blaine's solution, acting with such fervor that he approached a dangerous brinksmanship. On August 24, he hinted to Admiral Patricio Lynch, commander in chief of Chile's occupation forces, that the United States might not recognize any cession of territory. In addition, so Hurlbut warned Lynch, annexation would justly cause other nations to think that Chile had entered "upon the path of aggression and conquest," a comment that created much Chilean hostility towards the United States.[8] He also assured a prominent group of Peruvians, the "notables of Lima," that the United States opposed any dismemberment of their nation. Then, on September 20, acting without either instruction or permission, Hurlbut negotiated certain concessions with Calderón. Under the terms of his agreement, the United States would receive a Peruvian coaling and naval station on the Bay of Chimbote. Calderón also promised Hurlbut himself a partly built railroad to the interior, which he, in turn, could transfer to American promoters and gain a tidy profit in the process.

During this time, Hurlbut was continuing to press the State Department (which did not respond), going so far in late October as to cable that the United States should force arbitration upon the belligerents. Blaine offered no reply, perhaps because he was caught up in the assassination crisis, perhaps because he tacitly approved of the pressure that was being exerted by his representative. As Pletcher notes, "by the autumn of 1881 Hurlbut had practically committed the United States to defying Chilean plans to annex Tarapacá but without the strength to enforce this defiance."[9] For one of the more obscure and inept of American diplomats, this was heady brew indeed, and the fact that the United States warships located at Callao were not much match for Chilean ironclads did nothing to lighten it.

Kilpatrick, stationed in Santiago, attempted to repair the damage, telling the Chileans that Hurlbut was speaking without authority. Chile's secretary of state had promised Kilpatrick that his nation would allow Peru to substitute a cash indemnity in lieu of a territorial prize. Now, after Hurlbut's antics, Chile raised the ante, and even Kilpatrick's own assurances were suspect.

Hurlbut and Kilpatrick, by acting at cross-purposes, had merely succeeded in encouraging both Peruvian resistance and Chilean intransigence. On November 6, Chilean authorities arrested Calderón and his foreign minister, sending both to Santiago. The Chilean government accused Calderón of fostering foreign intervention—obviously a veiled reference to Hurlbut's diplomacy. Almost a month later, Kilpatrick dictated a rather feeble explanation of the arrest to the American State Department, but he died only a few hours after signing it. Although the Chileans gave Kilpatrick one of the most magnificent of funerals, the American consul at Valparaiso and the commander of the USS Alaska, who were stationed at that city, feared that Chile was preparing for war with the United States.

The secretary of state's hand was finally forced. On November 22, he reprimanded both diplomats. Kilpatrick, he said, should have avoided repudiating Hurlbut and should have demanded the reasons for Calderón's arrest. Hurlbut was even more severely scolded: he had had no business discussing terms with Admiral Lynch, said Blaine. In addition, Blaine believed that some annexation by Chile might be quite necessary. While thinking that an American naval station on Chimbote Bay could eventually be desirable, he found the context of Hurlbut's proposal singularly inopportune. Rear Admiral George B. Balch, commander of the United States Pacific Squadron, considered the effort premature, as the navy had not made a survey of the site.

Blaine's effort to recoup the situation did not spare him further embarrassment. In October, the Washington Post hinted that Hurlbut was serving a "ring" anxious to see the United States assume Peru's debts and thereby gain control of her guano industry. On December 11, in an effort to clear his name, the secretary released the text of his instructions to Hurlbut and Kilpatrick and thus made the public aware of his severe pressure upon Chile.

Blaine then had to face a House investigation. He had genuinely placed hopes in a scheme for marketing guano and nitrates, which had been advanced by the Société général crédit industrial et commercial, a giant French concern that was acting as a holding company for many guano bondholders in Europe. Such a plan, the secretary hoped, would meet Chile's demands, and by financing an indemnity, the company could prevent the dismemberment of Peru. However, his instructions to his ministers never involved uncritical support of foreign concerns. The House investigating committee eventually found all government officials, from Blaine on down, totally innocent, although "guano" charges haunted him throughout the campaign of

1884. In the meantime, he was clearly in trouble. And in order to extricate himself, he had to act fast.

The secretary's new diplomatic offensive began early in December, when he convinced President Arthur to send William Henry Trescot to the warring nations. Trescot, who now held the august title of envoy extraordinary and minister plenipotentiary, had been assistant secretary of state in 1860. His Confederate loyalties had prevented him from holding major diplomatic posts for two decades, although Secretary of State Evarts had appointed him as head of a delegation to China that had modified the Burlingame Treaty. Blaine's son Walker, himself third assistant secretary of state, accompanied Trescot. Here commences the third phase of American diplomacy, one that puts greater emphasis upon collective hemispheric pressure.

Yet, for a man supposedly anxious to rectify blunders, Blaine still appeared to be toying with brinksmanship. In his instructions to Trescot, he claimed that unsatisfactory explanations from Chile concerning Calderón would result in the severing of diplomatic relations. The president, Blaine said, looked upon Calderón's arrest as "an intentional and unwarranted offense."[10] He did give Chile an out, declaring that it might well have misconstrued Hurlbut's conduct. Blaine again called for a peace settlement that would be limited to financial indemnity, asserting that territorial conquest could only lead to further conflict; and he offered the good offices of the United States to resolve the dispute. If Chile proved recalcitrant, he continued, it should know that the United States would appeal to other hemispheric republics, asking them to apply pressure. Chile was being put on warning, for, as David S. Muzzey notes, Blaine's instructions were "dangerously near to the language of an ultimatum."[11]

Blaine, in fact, was already making hemispheric overtures. On November 29, he had asked all the independent Latin American nations (except the chaotic Haiti) to send representatives to a general conference. He claimed that this assemblage, scheduled in twelve months, would avoid existing controversies and focus on preventing future wars and insurrections. He obviously realized, however, that such a meeting would bolster Trescot's mission. He told Trescot to invite the three warring powers only after his plans for mediation had been solidified. Blaine also ordered him to return home by way of Argentina and Brazil; Trescot, the secretary continued, should impress upon those two powerful nations the importance of sending representatives to his forthcoming conference.

There was a method to Blaine's madness. Such a conference would be bound to overshadow Hurlbut's bungling as well as any possible failure by Trescot. In fact, it might lead to a general inter-American arbitration treaty, an event that could lessen Europe's chances of ever intervening in the New World. Most important of all, perhaps, the meeting could give Blaine—who knew that he would soon leave the State Department—the prestige he would need in the 1884 presidential race.

Yet it is hard to find more blundering statecraft. The activities of Hurlbut and Kilpatrick could only confirm the judgment made by the British minister at Lima: "The result of the interference of these untrained men in international affairs, which they did not fully understand, was a remarkable display of pretentious incapacity."[12] Blaine failed to watch his emissaries closely, foolishly stiffened Peru's intransigence, rigidly adhered to the territorial status quo when such a solution was no longer feasible, and attempted to saddle the incoming president with the most risky of policies. Although his proposal of a Pan-American conference would not ordinarily have lacked merit, its timing was bound to grate upon Latin American sensitivities, perhaps cause a boycott by leading nations, and expose its author as primarily concerned with recovering domestic prestige. President Arthur too must bear some responsibility, for he left all initiative in the hands of his secretary.

Almost equally irresponsible was Blaine's diplomacy in the boundary dispute between Mexico and Guatemala. The United States had been investing in Mexico more liberally than in Central America, and by 1880, its citizens had committed several million dollars to the area. Mexico's president Porfirio Díaz and his successor had granted to the United States the concessions for a railroad that would extend from the Rio Grande to Mexico City. Blaine, like his predecessors, was interested in all such economic opportunities, but a crisis that broke out in 1881 caused the secretary to side with Mexico's southern neighbor.

The crisis concerned the province of Chiapas, as well as the district of Soconusco, a region that faced the Pacific and that had been an object of dispute between Guatemala and Mexico for over fifty years. In 1881, both nations sent troops into the contested territories. Mexico's claim was by far the stronger, for it had long possessed the area. In the middle of June 1881, Guatemala's minister to the United States asked Blaine to intervene on behalf of its claims. Guatemala had accused Mexico of imprisoning the former's surveying and census parties in the disputed regions. In addition, so Guatemala charged, Mexico imposed its own local authorities in border areas that Guatemala held. Blaine replied in a friendly fashion, promising that the State Department would tender its good offices. Mexico denied that it had even considered using force but claimed that it could not accept United States mediation over land that had long been in its possession. Mexico also declared that the disputed boundary needed to be impartially surveyed. Although Blaine claimed to be impartial, it soon became clear that he not only favored Guatemala but favored it strongly.

Such partiality did not take place in a vacuum. Since 1871, when dictator Justo Rufino Barrios had seized power with the aid of Remington and Winchester rifles, Guatemala had relied strongly on American technology. Railroads, street-lighting, mines, telephones, farm implements—all had been developed with capital from the United States. Although a scheming tyrant, Barrios possessed considerable ability and was given to even more considerable dreams. In 1880, he told the United States minister to Guatemala, Cornelius A. Logan, that he hoped to unite his own nation to Honduras and El Salvador, and to conquer Nicaragua. He held out prospects that the United States could obtain a canal concession in Nicaragua, and he also suggested that Soconusco could serve as an ideal American naval base.

Blaine had little interest in such a base, having been told by Logan that the location would make it of little use. Yet he harbored more than a passing interest in the fate of Barrios's program. For if defeated by Mexico, Guatemala would not be able to revive the confederation of Central American nations that had been organized in 1823. Blaine believed that a Central American union might stabilize this weak and volatile area and forestall European intervention as well. Moreover, it might yield valuable canal rights. (Logan himself, fearful of German and British penetration, despaired of such a union and, in February 1881, called for an American protectorate in Guatemala.)

Blaine was soon given the opportunity to back the Guatemalan cause. Upon hearing that Mexican troops were preparing to invade Guatemala, he told the American minister to Mexico, Philip H. Morgan, that he would consider such aggression an unfriendly act. The United States, he claimed on June 21, had the right to "use its friendly offices" to discourage any movement that might "tend to disturb the balance of power." His nation, the secretary continued, fully intended to "hold up the republics of Central America in their old strength."[13] In a confidential aside, he expressed the fear that a desperate Guatemala might cede rights in Chiapas and Soconusco to a European state.

It soon became apparent that in order for Blaine's vision of Central American unity—and of an isthmian canal—to come to fruition, the United States would need to exert more pressure on Mexico. The United States, although it refused Guatemala's bid for a loan of $2 million and a military alliance, continually urged Mexico to arbitrate. During the summer of 1881, Mexico's minister for foreign affairs, Ignacio Mariscal, rejected the arbitration proposal. He declared that Mexico's claim to Chiapas and Soconusco was absolute. Mariscal also hinted that Guatemala was merely using arbitration as a ploy, first, in order to delay the establishment of a boundary commission and, second, in order to obtain United States support.

Since the United States pressure had little armed support behind it, Mexico, in the middle of September, ordered more troops to the Guatemalan border. Within days, Morgan informed Blaine that only United States intervention could prevent war. In November, Blaine again sought to arbitrate, this time limiting the issue to the boundary while acknowledging Mexico's ownership of Chiapas. In addition, he endorsed Central American unity, warning Mexico that he would construe hostility towards Guatemala as an unfriendly act.

It was in an attempt to press Mexico into arbitration (as well as to coerce Chile) that Blaine proposed his Pan-American conference. Although the conference was not to consider existing conflicts, it might abort possible efforts by Colombia and Peru to seek European arbitration of the matter. Logan believed that the proposed assembly would restrain Mexico's ambitions; and Guatemala, realizing that it was greatly favored in Blaine's eyes, strongly welcomed the meeting.

There is, however, no reason to believe that Blaine, who was to leave the State Department in December 1881, would have forced a single concession for Guatemala. True, he was anxious for a confederation of Central American states. Nevertheless, it would have indeed been difficult for him to secure as shaky a claim as that of Barrios or to promote schemes that would place other Central American states under the domination of this particular dictator. Moreover, by misleading the Guatemalan leader, he was delaying the very settlement that he sought. Here again his ambition ran ahead of wisdom.

Despite their intensity and despite their potential damage, neither the War of the Pacific nor the Mexican-border dispute involved as extended a controversy as did the issue of an isthmian canal. To understand what was at stake, some background is necessary. Two treaties, long antedating the presidencies of Garfield and Arthur, set forth the privileges and obligations of the United States. The first was a mutual-assistance treaty signed in 1846 with Colombia (then called the Republic of New Granada), a nation that ruled Panama. Under its terms, Colombia would grant free transit across the isthmus, and the United States would guarantee the neutrality of the isthmus and Colombia's sovereignty over it. Then, in 1850, when Britain and the United States were both vying over a route through Nicaragua, they signed the Clayton-Bulwer Treaty. By its provisions, each country pledged not to obtain exclusive control over any canal built through any part of

Central America and not to fortify, colonize, or assume any dominion over that area. These agreements obscured as much as they clarified, and in the early 1880s, the United States would become greatly involved in both Panama and Nicaragua.

In 1878, Colombia granted a concession to build a canal across Panama; the Interoceanic Canal Company of Ferdinand de Lesseps was the recipient. The French firm committed itself to neutrality and to open access for all, but President Hayes was sufficiently aroused to declare that "the policy of this country is a canal under American control." Garfield's inaugural address, echoing Hayes, called for United States "supervision and authority," and in 1881, Congress passed a joint resolution affirming that the United States would have to consent before an inland waterway could be constructed.[14]

In some ways, the United States was still being cautious. In January 1881, Congress appropriated $200,000 for coaling stations at Golfo Dulce in Costa Rica and Chiriquí Lagoon on the Isthmus of Panama. Yet neither Garfield's nor Arthur's secretary of the navy followed through, as claims to the land were decidedly uncertain.

Blaine, however, was quick to assert his nation's prerogatives. When his minister to Colombia supposedly boasted that intransigence on its part would force the United States to negotiate independently with Panama, the secretary felt compelled to recall him. On other matters, though, he soon made America's anger known. When Blaine learned, for example, that Colombia had permitted the kings of Belgium and Spain (as well as the president of Argentina) to arbitrate a boundary dispute between Panama and Costa Rica, he immediately protested. The United States, he warned, would be most unfriendly towards any European power that interfered in Colombian affairs. Moreover, the American government, so he claimed, would not consider itself bound by any such collective judgment, a move that forced the king of Belgium to decline Colombia's invitation and forced the Spanish government to assure the United States that the latter's interests would not suffer. The secretary had another chance to make his views known. In May 1881, Blaine learned that Colombia had invited Britain, France, Germany, Spain, and Italy to join in a multilateral treaty that would guarantee Colombia's sovereignty over a neutralized isthmus. On June 24, he accused the Europeans of engaging in "an uncalled-for intrusion." He denied that he was seeking privileges in peacetime or opposing European investment. At the same time, he claimed that the security of the Pacific states—states "imperial in extent and of extraordinary growth"—needed United States control of the area. To Blaine, as to Hayes, any projected canal in Panama must be considered as an integral part of the United States coastline; indeed it was "as truly a channel of communication between the Eastern and far Western States as our own transcontinental railways."[15] In his communique he distorted the terms of the 1846 agreement; for, contrary to Blaine's claims, the treaty with Colombia had not given to the United States sovereign rights over an isthmian canal. President Arthur, in his first annual message, backed the State Department. A joint European guarantee, he said, would violate "our obligation as the sole guarantor of the integrity of Colombian territory."[16]

Given Blaine's sentiments, it would not take him long to assail the Clayton-Bulwer Treaty itself. This agreement, notes one expert, "had floated for decades across the sea lanes of Anglo-American relations like a great iceberg, largely submerged and often hidden by fog."[17] Though its terms were unclear and its language vague, it had often prevented conflicts. Yet, as time passed, the growing United States commerce on the Pacific, fears of isthmian upheavals and subsequent European intervention, and the completion of the Suez Canal (a waterway lying totally under British control) made many Americans increasingly uneasy with the 1850 agreement.

As part of his new departures in diplomacy, departures that included the Pan-American conference and the Trescot mission, Blaine sought to amend the treaty. Particularly alarming was an arbitration ruling, made by Emperor Franz Joseph of Austria, practically giving Britain control over the Mosquito Coast off the Caribbean. With England thereby dominating the eastern outlet of any canal, her entire interest in the area would be much greater. In a much publicized note to James Russell Lowell, United States minister to Britain, dated November 19, 1881, Blaine called obsolete the 1850 provisions concerning joint participation. England, he said, had fortified Gibraltar, Malta, Cyprus, and Aden and also possessed total jurisdiction over the Suez Canal and Red Sea. Hence it was not unreasonable, he claimed, for the United States alone to fortify and control any canal in Nicaragua and to avoid joint control over other isthmian routes. Neutrality of such a canal, asserted the secretary in a memo that began to sound more and more like a stump speech, could never be submitted to Europe; it was "strictly and solely . . . an American question, to be dealt with and decided by the American governments."[18]

Ten days later, Blaine again wrote to Lowell, this time declaring, by making use of selective evidence, that both powers had long considered changing the treaty. He implied that joint participation referred only to a canal in Nicaragua (but did not include Panama and Tehuantepec) and claimed that the agreement by no means limited the rights that the United States had gained in the 1846 accord with Colombia. Arthur concurred, vaguely declaring in his first annual message of December 6 that the Clayton-Bulwer Treaty needed modification.

Such logic was unusually loose, even for a diplomat as slippery as

Blaine, and Britain's foreign secretary, Lord Granville, had little difficulty in making a devastating reply. In January 1882, the British statesman denied that Britain had fortified Cyprus, asserted that his nation had made no effort to limit use of the Suez Canal, and met Blaine's frequent historical examples with ones of his own. He quoted former President James Buchanan, for example, as having claimed that the treaty had "resulted *in a final settlement entirely satisfactory to this government.*" Any canal that linked Europe and eastern Asia, Granville said, was "a work which concerns not merely the United States or the American Continent, but the whole civilized world."[19]

Blaine was extremely vulnerable. His claim that changed conditions had abrogated the 1850 treaty was not only dangerous; it had no standing in international law. The eighth clause of the Clayton-Bulwer Treaty explicitly transcended Nicaragua, covering other routes as well. It would take more than crude arguments or sophistic logic to force Britain to recognize that the United States had exclusive control over the isthmus.

Blaine faced more immediate problems in Europe, and here the issue was nothing less than the continued prosperity of the United States. The nation had been slow in emerging from the depression of 1873. For example, as late as July 1878, over half of America's iron and steel furnaces were idle. Only disaster in the Old World rescued much of the New. In 1879, at the very time that Europe was confronting the worst harvest in a century, American farmers were reaping bonanza crops. At the same time, American railroads had just finished establishing a network that permitted the United States husbandman to enter the world market. The new prosperity helped to pull the entire nation out of the depression, and in his inaugural address, Garfield noted that agricultural staples furnished "much the largest part of all our exports."[20]

Soon, Americans were exporting over 60 percent of their pork and lard; in fact, the United States was becoming the world's greatest exporter of pork. The *London Economist* hardly exaggerated when it reported: "It is the American supply . . . alone which has saved Europe from a great famine."[21] Britain in particular, because of its free trade, huge increase in population, and concern over pleuropneumonia in European cattle, turned to the United States and, during the second half of the century, received 97 percent of all cattle exported from America.

Once the emergency was over, however, the European powers grew increasingly fearful of the American influx. As they found traditional sources of farm products again opening up, they started to exclude American beef. Conservative landowners, who were alert to the burgeoning of the United

States economy, began to demand firm barriers. Cheap American pork, they believed, might fill many stomachs in European cities, but it might also destroy their own markets. Hence, even in the critical year of 1879, Italy, Portugal, and Greece prohibited the importation of American meat, and in 1881, Spain banned American pork. Austria-Hungary, Turkey, and Rumania followed. Their reasons varied: Hungary found the United States was cutting into its own pork markets; the Moslems of Turkey were forbidden by religious law to eat pork; and Rumania sought to safeguard its pork trade with Austria-Hungary.

Rumors that American pork was diseased, in particular with trichinosis, aided the militant protectionists; and they were not slow in making the most of it. The whispering campaign had first begun in 1878, when a Viennese doctor warned that one-fifth of America's hams were carrying infection. Europe's experts genuinely differed as to what was causing the disease; they could not prove that American pork was the most infected. Undoubtedly, some American cattle had been stricken with another disease, pleuropneumonia; equally undoubtedly, some European officials put the public's health foremost. Nevertheless, it surely was questionable whether meat from the United States produced more disease than its European counterpart. The European practice of eating unboiled pork, for example, probably created far more illness and deaths.

᠊Britain was one of the first nations to level accusations. The acting British consul in Philadelphia, George Crump, first warned his countrymen of seven hundred thousand cholera-ridden cattle in Illinois; then he took the liberty of describing one human victim, who found worms "in his flesh by the millions, being scraped and squeezed from the pores of the skin." Secretary Blaine disputed the cause of the disease, writing Minister Lowell in anger: "Had it been Mr. Crump's specific purpose to cause a panic among the British consumers, by misrepresenting and associating isolated statements, he could hardly have framed his report more appropriately."[22] Although the British cited official Illinois statistics to support Crump's allegation, Blaine denied that any meat from the diseased cattle had ever been packed. True, the secretary had characteristically weakened his argument by overstatement, but the British government soon realized how much its wage earners depended upon cheap beef. It briefly checked imports of live hogs and pork but declined to exclude American meat totally.

The United States fared less well with France, a nation that succeeded in excluding all American pork products. The French action, which took place in February 1881, came most unexpectedly. There had been no scare stories concerning trichinosis and no prior warnings of governmental action; furthermore, the French government lacked a consistent protectionist tradition. But as cheap American bacon and lard had consistently undersold their own domestic pork products, the pork-producing regions in the interior welcomed their government's action. The American consul at Nantes noted that the French minister of agriculture and commerce, Pierre Tirard, had realized that the French Parliament was not of a mind to vote protection. Therefore, Tirard resorted to executive decree. True, the French government itself could not ascribe one single case of trichinosis to American pork. Equally true, the French Academy of Medicine approved American pork by an overwhelming vote. Tirard, however, obstinately refused to appoint a scientific commission. American minister Levi P. Morton could not resist commenting to Blaine's successor, "It is admitted openly that public health has little bearing upon the subject in its present stage; it is simply now a question of protection."[23]

America's greatest battle over pork lay with Imperial Germany, for in 1880, Bismarck's Reich terminated its huge commerce in American pork sausage and chopped pork. Though the new German Empire had inherited a tradition of free trade, it found itself responding to growing protectionist sentiment in its farming and manufacturing regions. The Iron Chancellor, Otto von Bismarck, genuinely believed that free trade might ruin his nation. Restrictions on commerce could never have passed the Reichstag, for there the voices of consumers and labor were powerful. The Bundesrat, however, had been entrusted with administering sanitary regulations, and it was the body that could exclude the United States products. German customs officials, knowing full well that American pork was both relatively cheap and relatively safe, devised ways of skirting the new law, even going so far as to classify canned goods as "iron wares" and sugar-coated hams, covered with linen cloth, as "fine linen." Only in 1882 was the prohibition fully felt, and by then it was no longer Blaine's problem.

This is not to say that Blaine was indifferent, any more than his predecessor Evarts had been. Particularly as recession grew, the secretary vigorously objected to having European countries exclude American products. He considered a quid pro quo: American tariffs would be reduced once the European governments dropped the ban on meat. He also offered to have all American pork products inspected and certified before they were exported. In March 1881, the State Department ordered the chief of its Bureau of Statistics to investigate the alleged perniciousness of American pork. The search proved that, contrary to accusations from overseas, the American product showed a much lower incidence of trichinosis than did that from Europe.

Other problems involving Europe, and Britain in particular, were less serious. The Treaty of Washington in 1871 had settled most of the outstanding issues, and the bitterness engendered by the Civil War became more of a memory with each passing year. Some friction had been created in 1878 at Fortune Bay, Newfoundland, when native fishermen had destroyed the nets of their American rivals and forced them from the coast. In late October 1880, Granville offered £15,000 to cover damages. At the very last minute, however, the British tacked on an additional demand, one that specified that the £15,000 be accepted for all claims against Newfoundland fisheries up to January 1, 1881. Although Granville's reasons for unexpectedly interposing the additional condition were unclear, Blaine—who was usually feisty where the British were concerned—acceded to the foreign secretary's terms.

Britain's real quarrel with America involved, not meat or fish, but Irish nationalists. True, it lacked the intensity of the United States' dispute with Germany, but the rancor—had it been left unchecked—could have poisoned relations with Great Britain.

In 1881, to squelch the latest manifestations of a rebellion that had lasted for centuries, the British Parliament passed the Coercion Act. Similar to the preventive-detention acts used by many countries today, the law enabled British agents in Ireland to imprison anyone suspected of committing or, more important, of being likely to commit illegal acts. Such suspects could be held without trial, and held indefinitely. This legislation was passed in order to weaken the Irish Land League, an organization seeking to boycott and intimidate British landlords. Under its provisions, the league's famous leader, Charles Stewart Parnell, and his followers were soon jailed. And among those imprisoned were naturalized Americans of Irish birth, individuals who had returned to their original homeland to support Parnell's case.

Blaine, ever ready to twist the lion's tail, first demanded immediate trial or release of the prisoners. But he was soon burned; for after taking part in one controversy, he learned that the defendant had falsified information on his passport. ("A pestiferous fellow," said Blaine, who "deserved what he got.") At one point, he privately told the British minister that he considered the Irish-American agitators "the scum of Europe."[24]

The British stood their ground, producing no information beyond the actual warrants for those arrested. For Britain to try Americans, while keeping its own citizens in jail without trial, would have involved discrimination against British nationals. If the American suspects were freed, this might lead to further subversion, as the Irish-Americans would always see themselves as being immune from prosecution.

Most of the time, James Russell Lowell was in charge of negotiating any releases. Faced with over a dozen internment cases, he was fully aware that some Irishmen were relying upon their American citizenship simply for protection. He therefore promised only to intervene on behalf of a bona-fide American citizen who was "attending exclusively to his business." A confidant of Granville's, Lowell believed that the British were genuinely trying to solve the Irish problem. Yet far from being the Anglophile that he was considered by his opponents, Lowell was highly sensitive to issues of American honor, found the Coercion Act self-defeating, and wanted to see the Irish given the opportunity to own their own land. At one point he thought that England would be wise to make either Parnell or nationalist Michael Davitt chief secretary for Ireland. Despite Lowell's personal sentiments, the issue stood deadlocked as Blaine's secretaryship came to an end.

In addition to Latin America and Europe, Asia demanded the attention of the Garfield administration, with Korea in particular becoming a focus of American interest. Pletcher has described the Far East in the eighties as "a disorganized solar system in which several planets—China, Japan, Britain, France, and Russia—wandered to and fro, drawing satellites out of each other's control."[25] The Hermit Kingdom was one such satellite: it had been a vassal state of China since the Manchu conquest of 1637, although it had traditionally controlled its own domestic affairs. Not until 1876 did Japan break through Korea's isolation, negotiating a commercial treaty that opened three ports to Japanese trade and recognized Korea's independence of China. China's powerful foreign minister, Li Hung-chang, was fully aware that China was too weak to stop Japan's penetration; but he sought some means of curbing Japanese influence. Li proposed that Korea build up its military strength and conclude treaties with Western powers, a strategy that, so he hoped, would give foreign nations a vested interest in Korean independence. In his effort to use "barbarians" to check "barbarians," Li singled out the United States, one Western power that possessed no territorial designs.

Li's strategy dovetailed nicely with newly formed American ambitions. In 1878, the Navy Department sent Commodore Robert W. Shufeldt on a trip around the world. When he arrived at Korea, so he was ordered, he was supposed to give "special consideration" to initiating trade. Shufeldt, a blue-eyed, brown-haired sailor of possessing mien, was an appropriate choice, for he had long believed that economic depression and its consequent domestic unrest could be alleviated by exporting American surpluses.

Upon reaching Korea in April 1880, Shufeldt found himself blocked by the Japanese, who were hopeful of preserving their own commercial monopoly. He was permitted to go only as far as Pusan. Only when Li promised aid in securing a Korean treaty did the commodore take hope. Li extended a bit of personal bait, offering Shufeldt the post of adviser to the

Chinese navy and, with it, the power to organize China's naval forces. Li's motive by no means centered on fostering American commerce. Rather, the Chinese diplomat was beginning to fear Russian penetration of Chinese Turkestan as well as Japan, and therefore he welcomed any United States involvement on the Asian mainland.

Shufeldt was sufficiently encouraged to return home with a highly optimistic report. Arriving in San Francisco in November 1880, he suggested that the United States follow up his visit by sending a squadron of ships. "The Pacific Ocean," he said, "is to become at no distant day the commercial domain of America."[26] Ironically, the commercially minded commodore believed that trade with Korea itself was unimportant; the country, he claimed, was rugged but unproductive.

Shufeldt urged the government to send him back to China, there to make a treaty with Korea and to aid Li in organizing the Chinese navy. Blaine concurred heartily if vaguely, simply telling the commodore to report on trade opportunities. When Shufeldt arrived in Tientsin late in June 1881, he discovered that Li's enthusiasm for American assistance had cooled. Li had recently concluded a treaty with Russia, thereby eliminating any threat to the north, and he faced Japanese opposition to possible American influence. Only in the middle of July, when Li grew intolerant of Japanese pressures, did he again envision an American counterweight in Korea. Even then, although he paid careful heed to Shufeldt's suggestions concerning naval affairs, he did not repeat his offer of a naval post. Finally, the frustrated commodore, realizing that he was appearing more and more foolish, refused to advise the Chinese any further. Lacking specific instructions from Blaine (who by now was occupied with the assassination crisis), Shufeldt was unaware that on November 14 the secretary had sent him instructions to seek a treaty regarding shipwrecks. If possible, the commodore should also negotiate a commercial agreement, one that would secure most-favored-nation privileges and give American consuls the same extraterritorial privileges that they already possessed in Japan and China.

Finally, at the end of the year 1881, Li told Shufeldt that the king of Korea was ready to negotiate. The commodore, who had long been fuming about Li's deliberately protracted delays, remained suspicious, and on New Year's Day of 1882, he wrote to his personal friend Aaron A. Sargent (Rep., Calif.), chairman of the Senate Foreign Relations Committee. In his letter he accused the Chinese of "deceit and untruthfulness" and labeled the empress, in particular, "an arrogant, capricious and immoral woman." China, he said, would "exclude every article of foreign manufacture from her shores." Hence American policy must be determined by self-interest alone: "The only appeal or argument appreciated is *force*."[27] Sargent, acting without Shufeldt's permission, released the letter to the press; therefore, Blaine's successor felt forced to recall the commodore. Shufeldt's request to be allowed to head the Asiatic Squadron was refused, and he believed that his government career was over. Then, with Blaine's departure from the State Department, negotiations over Korea appeared to have been suspended.

Africa too demanded Blaine's attention. Here the focus was on Madagascar, the world's third largest island and a nation dominated commercially by the United States. America, in fact, supplied half of the island's imports, which amounted to an annual trade of a million dollars. As consul William W. Robinson stated in 1881, "American brown cotton is king here, and even the foreign merchants, including the English, bow in allegiance." "But," he could not help but query, "how long is the reign going to last?"[28]

The question was indeed moot. The United States, although lacking a single steamship line, found itself increasingly embroiled in Madagascar's internal intrigue, particularly when Robinson became adviser to the court of Queen Ranavalona. Ranavalona headed the Hova tribe, the largest and most Europeanized group on the island.

French imperialist ambitions complicated Robinson's role. France had proclaimed a protectorate over the nation as far back as the eighteenth century but had only recently exercised sovereignty. In order to forestall any conquest, the Hova government attempted a full-scale campaign against the virtually autonomous Sakalava tribe of the west coast. Robinson sought to have an American warship ferry troops of the Hova government to western Madagascar, but Blaine refused the request. (The British, long protective of the Hovas, agreed to supply a warship.) The secretary did support a treaty of friendship and commerce, one that included acknowledgment of Hova sovereignty over all of Madagascar. In return, the United States was promised special commercial and shipping privileges on the island's west coast. On May 13, 1881, the Hova government, attracted by possible trade benefits, signed the agreement. American merchants were pleased with the new trade concessions, but the Hovas believed that the United States was now committed to their sovereignty over the entire island. It would soon be disillusioned, but the worry would no longer be that of Mr. Blaine.

Even today, scholarly appraisals differ over the statecraft of the Maine politico. Some historians assert that, like William H. Seward before him, Blaine contributed much to the shaping of his nation's foreign policy. Blaine, so they claim, attempted to make the United States respected by the European powers, expand the country's commercial interests, bring peace to the hemisphere, assert American dominance of the Isthmus of Panama, and foster a sphere of influence in the Pacific. Milton Plesur finds him to have been a man "far ahead of his generation with his definitive plans for commercial expansion." According to Edward P. Crapol, Blaine advanced "a comprehensive domestic and foreign program designed to transform the United States into the world's greatest power."[29]

Some evidence supports such eulogies. According to Edwin Hurd Conger, a farm businessman from Illinois and a prominent Republican, both Blaine and Garfield had the wisdom to recognize in 1881 that reciprocal trade could supply needed markets for American cereals, beef, pork, and farm machinery. "We shall," said Garfield, "develop a policy during my administration which will make the Republican party more popular with the people of this country than it has been since the day of its birth."[30] In the same year, Secretary Blaine commented: "Throughout the continent, North and South, wherever a foothold is found for American enterprise, it is quickly occupied, and this spirit of adventure, which seeks its outlet in the mines of South America and the railroads of Mexico, would not be slow to avail itself of openings for assured and profitable enterprise, even in mid-ocean."[31] The secretary obviously believed, as we shall see in chapter 10, that the nation's economic scope could reach as far as Hawaii.

Blaine's critics stress the opportunistic streak in his diplomacy. Irrespective of his ultimate vision, they claim, his performance was marked by amateurism, opportunism, and sheer bluster. Some historians doubt whether the secretary's policies centered on Open Door imperialism. David M. Pletcher, for example, finds Blaine primarily concerned with prestige, not markets; his intervention into such areas as Latin America and Hawaii, Pletcher says, sought to make the United States the arbiter of hemispheric conflict. Other historians see irresponsibility as being characteristic of his leadership. John A. Garraty notes that Blaine opposed "even the most harmless kind of European intervention," such as Belgian arbitration in a Central American dispute. Charles S. Campbell concurs. Blaine's restless, impulsive nature, Campbell claims, could only have produced tension.[32]

As far as the Garfield and Arthur presidencies are concerned, Blaine's critics have the best of the argument. During the early 1880s, American diplomacy was singularly ill equipped to cope with the crises that invariably accompanied industrialization. If, during that time, James G. Blaine ever did possess a grand strategy for commercial expansion—a proposition surely open to question—he was the wrong man to execute it. Indeed, it is difficult to conceive of more clumsy statecraft. His tenure in office was marked by showmanship and demagoguery, evincing little of the maturity needed for any "large policy."

5

★ ★ ★ ★ ★

NO LONGER CHET

In addition to inheriting such a volatile secretary of state, the new president faced other obstacles. Arthur's lack of national experience did little to establish public confidence; the circumstances of his vice-presidential nomination, the Delmonico's speech, the deliberate undercutting of President Garfield, and the continual closeness to New York Stalwarts offered even less. In addition, he had inherited a divided and factionalized party, with Blaine, Sherman, and other leading Republicans all hoping to receive the presidential nomination in 1884.

Arthur did have some advantages: he was bright, he was a good administrator, and his conduct during the assassination crisis had won him public sympathy. As president he attempted to capitalize on all three assets, temporarily keeping the Garfield cabinet as a symbol of unity.

And when he changed his cabinet, he usually did so responsibly, almost as if to prove that the Stalwarts were not bereft of talent. The new secretary of state, former New Jersey senator Frederick T. Frelinghuysen, was an obvious improvement over Blaine. For secretary of the treasury, Arthur chose Charles J. Folger, chief justice of the New York State Supreme Court, whom Garfield had once slated to head the Justice Department. The president asked Wayne MacVeagh, who had pushed the star-route prosecutions, to stay, but Garfield's attorney general could not envision himself in a Stalwart administration. To replace MacVeagh, Arthur selected Benjamin Harris Brewster, once attorney general of Pennsylvania and long one of Arthur's comrades. Since Brewster had already been employed by MacVeagh as government counsel in the star-route cases, civil-service reformers considered him to be one of their own. Senator Henry M. Teller (Rep., Colo.) took over the Interior Department from the elderly and ineffective Kirkwood, a man who had voted for Arthur's removal from the customhouse. Although Teller was a member of the "306" and a strong opponent of civil service, he won Godkin's praise as being a "man of ability." The colorless Robert Todd Lincoln retained the War Department post.

Some of Arthur's appointments to the Supreme Court were strong: Senator Edmunds declined an associate justiceship, but Horace Gray was a distinguished scholar who had sat on the Massachusetts Supreme Judicial Court, and Samuel Blatchford of New York had served for fifteen years on the federal bench. Arthur did choose Conkling, who was an able attorney, to serve on the Supreme Court, but the Utica politician, who had wanted to replace Blaine as secretary of state, turned the offer down. Entering corporation law, Conkling soon became what one Senate colleague called "a gorgeous reminiscence."[1]

Other appointments were more suspect. Arthur pleaded with James to remain, but the postmaster general found a New York banking position far more lucrative. Not heeding Frelinghuysen's advice to balance his cabinet between Stalwarts and Half-Breeds, he replaced James with sixty-five-year-old Timothy O. Howe, a former Wisconsin senator. Howe had never held an administrative office; he possessed no commitment to reform, and his son-in-law had served as attorney for the star-route defendants. Reformers were even more strongly suspicious of the new secretary of the navy, William E. Chandler, an ardent Half-Breed who had managed Blaine's convention efforts in 1880.

Once he became president, Arthur ceased to act like a "Gentleman Boss." While he still welcomed Stalwart cronies to sumptuous feasts, he refrained from doing favors to such a degree that one Conkling follower complained, "He has done less for us than Garfield, or even Hayes." Thousands of jobs were available for patronage in the Treasury Department alone, but by the summer of 1882, only sixteen removals had been made. Arthur resisted appeals to fire Robertson, and soon Conkling was finding the Hayes administration "respectable, if not heroic" in comparison. As one of the president's old customhouse associates said, "He isn't 'Chet' Arthur any more; he's the President."[2] In fact, when Folger ran for the governorship of New York, Arthur refused to assist him. True, the president did not strongly dissociate himself from the campaign activities of others, but he did not want his office tarnished by partisan warfare. Critics suspected covert political activity, but they were wrong.

Arthur saw little reason for challenging congressional initiative; at any rate, he lacked the political strength to do so, because Republican majorities in both houses were slim. The president's annual messages, however, contained a host of suggestions, ranging from a government for Alaska to a building for the Library of Congress. Reporting a large surplus in the treasury, Arthur wanted to repeal all internal taxation save excise duties on tobacco and liquor. He sought an item veto whereby a president could block certain portions of a bill while keeping others; he even went so far as to suggest a constitutional amendment on the subject. He asked Congress to consider the entire matter of presidential succession, so as to avoid the kind of political limbo that existed just before Garfield's death. He also wanted Congress to decide who was to count the electoral votes, making his request in order to prevent the confusion that existed during the Hayes-Tilden election. Accusing the railroads of price collusion and rate discrimination, Arthur endorsed the regulation of interstate commerce. "No individual and no corporation," he said, "ought to be invested with absolute power over the interest of any citizen or class of citizens."[3] Yet, with its focus on favor and patronage, Congress felt little compunction about ignoring such suggestions and others as well.

It was probably just as well that Arthur did not fight the Congress, as there was little in his background to prepare him for executive leadership. The new president had been born in 1829 in the farming community of Fairfield, Vermont, the son of a Baptist minister. After growing up in various parishes in Vermont and New York State, he attended Union College, where he was elected to Phi Beta Kappa. He taught school in North Pownal, Vermont, where he had been principal of an academy for three years before James A. Garfield arrived to teach penmanship. In 1851, he became a principal in Cohoes, New York. He then became an attorney in New York City, where in 1858 he took an active part in the famous *Lemmon* case, which involved two Virginia slaves who were seeking freedom.

A Whig as far back as 1844, he joined the Republican party at its inception and became a protégé of the New York State boss Thurlow Weed. In 1861, the six-foot, sturdily built man, with his silken wavy hair, black eyes, and grey sideburns, became engineer-in-chief to the military staff of the Empire State's powerful governor, Edwin D. Morgan. At the outset of the Civil War, the states assumed many responsibilities for the recruiting and equipping of troops, and Arthur became so expert in providing supplies that he was appointed quartermaster general of New York State. Here he proved invaluable to the state's war effort, showing both honesty and ability. When Morgan lost the governorship in 1862, Arthur reentered civilian life. Perhaps he was influenced by his wife, Ellen Lewis Herndon, a southerner who had close relatives fighting for the Confederacy. Perhaps, unlike Garfield, Arthur did not want to see the war turn into an antislavery crusade.

Perhaps he simply sought more money and was holding out for a more significant position.

After the conflict, Arthur rose steadily in state Republican ranks, eventually becoming the leading lieutenant of Roscoe Conkling. The portly, dignified Arthur possessed orthodox Republican views on such issues as the tariff and the currency, and he believed in limited government. Even more important as far as his political future was concerned, he was ever loyal to his chiefs. In 1871, Grant appointed him collector of the New York Customhouse, where he presided over a large patronage empire. Arthur tolerated, indeed at times encouraged, the illegal conduct that made the office a national scandal and that, in 1878, caused President Hayes to suspend him.

Personally, although he grew increasingly corpulent, he was always a man of refined tastes, as much at home with Prince Alberts and imported high hats as he was with the most sumptuous of dishes. In office or out, his world—as Thomas C. Reeves notes—was "the world of expensive Havana cigars, Tiffany silver, fine carriages, and grand balls; the 'real' world where men manipulated, plotted, and stole for power and prestige and the riches that bought both."[4]

Despite the glitter and gold, however, Arthur's life was marred by tragedy. When he was thirty-four, one of his sons died; when he was fifty-one, his wife, nine years his junior, passed away. The latter event in particular caused him grief, for he realized how often he had neglected her in order to devote late hours to machine politics. The marriage, in fact, was on the verge of dissolution when, in 1880, she succumbed to pneumonia.

Because of the recent death of his spouse and because of the assassination of Garfield, Arthur would enter the White House without any sense of triumph. He would enter, although few people would see this side of him, as a deeply emotional person, one loyal to friends, sensitive to suffering and death, and sobered by the august office that he was now assuming.

If the man was haunted by hidden tragedies as he entered the presidency, he still possessed a magnificent sense of style. Few presidents have been as concerned with the ceremonial and the symbolic. Arthur renovated the White House on a grand scale, supervising the project himself. Twenty-four wagonloads of furniture and clothing were auctioned off, including Nellie Grant's birdcage and a pair of Abraham Lincoln's trousers. From paneling of Japanese leather to pieces of Limoges china, the refurbished executive mansion betrayed Arthur's love of the elaborate and the sumptuous.

The widowed president had two living children, but neither one received much publicity. His daughter, Ellen, called Nell, was not quite ten when Arthur assumed the presidency. She remained in New York with a governess and servants until late in 1882, when she moved into the White House. Although she sometimes appeared at an afternoon reception or was seen with her father in the presidential carriage, her life was indeed a private one; her time was occupied by piano lessons and French grammar. Arthur's son, Alan, attended the College of New Jersey (later Princeton University), where his activities centered on girls, parties, and splendid clothes. The young man was not an intellectual.

Arthur entertained in a warm yet refined manner, having his youngest sister, Mary Arthur McElroy, serve as surrogate first lady. Almost seeming to act in a conscious effort to forget the death of his wife, he threw himself into state dinners and private suppers. Former president Hayes might rail about "liquor, snobbery, and worse," but most guests found his fourteen courses and eight varieties of wines a refreshing contrast to the reign of "Lemonade Lucy." Few citizens could match Arthur's penchant for fastidious dress; it was even rumored that he would try on twenty pairs of trousers before finding the one he desired. Wearing tweeds for business hours, frock coats for the afternoon, and tuxedos for dinner, Arthur was correctly described by Thomas C. Platt as "a veritable Chesterfield."[5]

A man of impeccable manners and charming conversation, Arthur would bow profusely to everyone he met. His carriage, drawn by two matching bay horses, was elaborately trimmed and had dress blankets and lap robes bearing the monogram "C.A.A." Such a conscious attempt at style, not to be matched until the Kennedys came to the White House, helped to make Arthur most welcome in Washington. When he died, a city newspaper declared that "no president since the war has been so universally popular here."[6]

Yet in many ways Arthur was a loner. Although his son claimed that Arthur was a nonbeliever, he occasionally worshipped—out of respect for his wife—at St. John's Episcopal Church. As a widower, his name was frequently linked with eligible women; however, he displayed no affection or commitment. Once, when he felt that he was being subjected to prying, he snapped, "Madam, I may be President of the United States, but my private life is nobody's damned business."[7]

Arthur's apathy toward administrative tasks was almost in inverse ratio to his love of high living. As a White House clerk later commented, "President Arthur never did today what he could put off until tomorrow."[8] He arrived in his office about ten in the morning, received congressmen until noon, ate lunch, and saw callers by appointment until four or five. From five to seven thirty, the president's time was his own—to read, rest, or ride horseback. In addition, he reserved two days to himself—Sunday and Monday. Twice a week, at noon, he met with his cabinet; three times a week, for an hour, he greeted the public. Arthur's staff often had to force him to pay attention to matters of state, and even then they were not entirely successful. For example, it once took him a month to copy a letter of condolence, which had already been drafted by the State Department and was destined for a European court! Even his annual messages, it was said, were written by an aide. A sensitive, moody, shy man, he appeared deeply troubled to those who knew him best. General callers and office seekers irritated him the most, and only retreats to the presidential cottage at Washington's Soldiers' Home or late evening walks gave him respite.

If the president had an Achilles heel, it was his relations with the press. He granted few interviews and consistently refused to discuss political issues. He had been burned by press coverage of his Delmonico's speech and of his trips to Albany while vice-president. He not only cherished privacy; he possessed an aristocratic disdain for the masses. Most of all, he wanted to keep news of his ill health from the public, and in this he was usually successful.

His deteriorating condition was probably the best-kept secret of his administration. Only after eighty years have Americans learned all the facts of the case. Part of Arthur's lethargy was due to Bright's disease, a fatal kidney ailment that leads to spasmodic nausea, mental depression, and inertness. Arthur learned that he had this illness in 1882, a year in which he was often fatigued, irritable, and physically ill. On August 1, Brode Herndon, his physician and cousin by marriage, wrote in his private diary, "The President sick in body and soul."[9]

By March 1883, Arthur's condition was deteriorating rapidly, and during the summer he started to delay official business until noon. A vacation trip to Florida had only served to weaken him further, because the president contracted malaria and could well have been close to death. He was indeed a courageous man, for he refused to court the sympathy of the public. In fact, he found it undignified to burden others with his pain. He took few into his confidence, talking optimistically about future plans.

There was always some activity. For example, in May 1883, he attended ceremonies for the opening of the Brooklyn Bridge. Principally in an effort to recoup some strength, he traveled through Yellowstone Park during the summer. He avoided making political visits and speeches. Although still failing, he refused to go into seclusion. His public receptions continued to be popular. At one such event, the White House was so crowded that General Philip H. Sheridan had to enter through a window, and the president had to face some three thousand admiring women in order to reach the Blue Room. Arthur realized that the performance of presidential tasks was hastening his end, but he did not, as Reeves notes, want to "be remembered merely as a sickly caretaker of the White House, a pitiable misfortune to his party and country."[10]

If the president had any positive role to play in government, it centered on the veto. On July 1, 1882, he vetoed a steamboat safety bill, claiming that its wording contained several serious technical errors. Congress yielded, passing the measure after making the changes that he had suggested.

Then, on August 1, he blocked a pork-barrel rivers-and-harbors bill that would have reduced the surplus by nineteen million dollars. Many newspapers had opposed the legislation, as had Conkling, New York business leaders, and the cabinet. The legislation included some $5.4 million for a Mississippi River commission, with the South obtaining 50 percent of the total appropriation. A coalition of southerners and westerners supplied 90 of the 120 supporting votes in the House, 25 of the 38 votes in the Senate.

Arthur was not opposed to internal improvements in general or to southern improvements in particular. In April, he had endorsed a report of the Mississippi River Commission that called for improvements on the whole length of the river. But in his veto message to Congress, he claimed that the rivers-and-harbors grants would only benefit "particular localities." Such parochial appropriations, he continued, did not advance the common defense, interstate commerce, or the general welfare and hence went "beyond the powers given by the Constitution to Congress and the President." In addition, they set a bad precedent: further demands could only lead to "extravagant expenditure of public money," thereby demoralizing the nation.[11]

Congress, acting almost immediately, again passed the bill. There was the expected public outrage, and Senator Hoar later recalled that many of its supporters in the House soon lost their seats. In the Senate, the same coalition of southern Democrats and Republicans of the upper Mississippi Valley states supplied twenty-eight of the needed forty-one votes. Although Whitelaw Reid called it "the worst River and Harbor bill that was ever invented," the editor of the *New Orleans Times-Democrat* rejoiced because the government had recognized that "the people of the Northwest as well as those of the South may share the advantages of deep water to the sea."[12]

Ironically, the South did not benefit as much as it had hoped. The Mississippi River Commission now received between two and four million dollars annually, but the development of railroad trunk lines cut heavily into its traffic. Water freight on the lower Mississippi rose only slightly from 1880 to 1889, then fell precipitously.

Arthur's most significant veto came slightly earlier, on April 4. It concerned a major wave of settlement to the United States, that of the Chinese. During the gold rush, California had welcomed large masses of Chinese laborers. Indeed, West Coast communities had found Chinese labor so desirable that, as one expert notes, it was "looked upon as a veritable god-send."[13] The Chinese in turn welcomed the chance to leave their homeland. Overcrowded living conditions (particularly in the southeastern provinces), droughts, floods, devastating wars with Britain and France, the Taiping Rebellion—all had made them highly receptive to opportunities in America. By 1882, some 288,000 Chinese had entered the United States, doing so as free laborers not coolies, although a good many of these eventually returned home.

Within three decades the attitudes of many Americans had changed drastically, and Chinese settlers were met with waves of hostility. Aggressive Chinese merchants in California had become highly successful in such industries as boots, shoes, broom-manufacturing, and cigar-making; therefore, native Californians feared that the Chinese would monopolize these fields. Several prominent Americans, such as U. S. Grant and James G. Blaine, had other fears, centering on a contract-labor system they considered smacking of slavery. In addition, Chinese found their customs attacked as "anti-Christian," their living quarters branded as hotbeds of filth and prostitution, their very bodies perceived as carriers of venereal disease, smallpox, and leprosy. Until the 1870s, Chinese immigration was disproportionately male, a circumstance that led to accusations that they had little interest in family life.

Defenders of the Chinese attempted to reply to these charges. They noted that the Chinese drank little, that they did not exhibit any more "immorality" than Europeans, and that in San Francisco, where many of them lived, they were no more subject to arrest than were other elements of the city's population. Yet, even if those who were friendly to the Chinese often had the better of the argument, they lacked political power.

During the depression of the seventies, voices seeking for total Chinese exclusion became particularly loud. Early in 1879, Congress passed a bill that virtually restricted Chinese immigration. Although Hayes vetoed the measure, he negotiated a treaty in 1880 that recognized America's right to "regulate, limit, or suspend" the immigration of Chinese laborers whenever it found its own "interests" or "good order" were affected. Agitation, however, still continued, and in 1880 all of the major national parties, including the Greenback, condemned unrestricted Chinese immigration. The role of the Morey letter in Garfield's campaign shows how inflammatory the issue was. Two years later the Knights of Labor endorsed the Chinese exclusion movement, and thereafter its members formed a major part of every anti-Chinese mob.

In 1882, Senator John F. Miller (Rep., Calif.) introduced a bill that would have excluded Chinese laborers for twenty years and would have denied citizenship to Chinese residents. Because the Senate was so evenly divided between Republicans and Democrats, the Pacific Coast bloc held the balance of power. Southern senators added their own arguments regarding racial supremacy, with James Z. George (Dem., Miss.) insisting that this was "a white man's government." By the end of March, Miller's bill had passed the Senate 29 to 15 and the House 167 to 66. Opposition came mainly from Republicans in the Northeast; Hoar, Edmunds, Platt, and Sherman had combined memories of the abolition crusade, a tradition of free immigration, and protests against such a blatant violation of the 1880 treaty.

Almost immediately, the president vetoed the measure. Though Arthur claimed that American institutions, and some American livelihoods as well, might be threatened by unrestricted Chinese labor, he believed that twenty years—"nearly a generation"—would be an unreasonable suspension. Moreover, by violating the 1880 treaty, it would be "a breach of our national faith." In addition, Arthur found the bill's registration requirements particularly "undemocratic and hostile to the spirit of our institutions." The Chinese, the president continued, had made a major contribution to the American economy, and he pointed specifically to their labor on the transcontinental railroad. In his veto message he also stressed Asia's commercial potential, commenting that "experience has shown that the trade of the East is the key to national wealth and influence." Such exclusionist policies, if not designed with care and sensitivity, might "have a direct tendency to repel Oriental nations from us and to drive their trade and commerce into more friendly hands."[14]

Brahmin journals welcomed Arthur's veto, but labor groups—in both the East and the West—denounced the president. Californians found Arthur to be more responsible to the commercial interests of the eastern states than to the desires of the Pacific Coast. In San Francisco, flags hung at half-mast, and merchants draped their stores as if in mourning.

Congress, however, heeding the president, revised the bill. The new measure reduced the term of exclusion from twenty years to ten, but it still retained features to which Arthur had objected, such as the exclusion of all Chinese from American citizenship. The bill's preamble went out of its way to be insulting, declaring that "in the opinion of the Government of the United States the coming of Chinese laborers to this country endangers the good order of certain localities within the territory thereof."[15] As in the case of the first bill, both the Democrats and the western Republicans backed the measure, and it passed the Senate 32 to 15, the House 201 to 31.

This time, although the New Englanders were still dissatisfied, the president signed the legislation. Secretary of State Frelinghuysen confided to China's representative in Washington that he personally opposed such a discriminatory law. Promising to do all he could to curb California's racists, Frelinghuysen offered to return the unused portions of the Chinese Indemnity Fund, established in 1868, and he endorsed legislation the intent of which was to ban the American shipment of opium to China. The Chinese minister in turn assured the secretary that the immigration law would not unduly disturb China's relations with the United States.

The issue was temporarily over; only in retrospect does it appear as a harbinger of much greater exclusion policies. As far as its immediate consequences were concerned, Congress's action led, for many years, to a negative picture of Chinese settlers. Even those eastern businessmen and Protestant clergymen who had long defended the Chinese joined in the attack.

Chinese were not the only unpopular minority. Few groups in America were as suspect as members of the Church of Jesus Christ of Latter-day Saints, whose practice of polygamy had long kept Utah a territory, not a state. In 1882, Mormons outnumbered non-Mormons there eight to one. In 1862, Congress had ruled plural marriage illegal, as did the United States Supreme Court in 1879; but local Mormon courts would not prosecute a coreligionist.

Garfield was adamant in his opposition, claiming in his inaugural that Mormon polygamy was a "criminal practice," one that offended "the moral sense of mankind," destroyed "family relations," and endangered "social order." Arthur's first annual message referred to polygamy as "this odious crime, so revolting to the moral and religious sense of Christendom."[16] Because such marriages were secret and obtaining convictions was difficult, Arthur suggested that wives of bigamists should be permitted to testify against their husbands. In addition, so he requested, all marriages should be certified by the Utah Supreme Court.

In the winter of 1882, Congress passed and then Arthur signed the Edmunds Act, drafted by the Vermont senator. This legislation, a reenactment of existing statutes, made plural marriage a crime, disfranchised all polygamists, disqualified polygamists from jury duty, and prohibited polygamists from holding office. It also established a five-man "Utah commission" to supervise voting in Utah. The commission barred from the voting everyone who professed a belief in polygamy—in short, all faithful Mormons—even if they were not personally guilty of the practice. Government was now taken out of Mormon hands.

Mormons resisted. By October, John Taylor, president of the church, told members that "any man or set of men who curtail or deprive us of our constitutional rights are tyrants and oppressors. We intend to lawfully contend for our rights inch by inch."[17] In the first local and territorial election under the Edmunds Act, held in August 1883, Mormons were resoundingly returned to office. The new legislature did not outlaw polygamy, thus causing Arthur to call for direct congressional control of Utah. And despite the Edmunds Act, the practice of polygamy was growing. Late in 1884, the federal commissioners for Utah reported that at least 196 men and 263 women had entered into polygamous marriages since the law had been passed, but only two people had been convicted in the federal courts.

Congress kept up the pressure. Edmunds advanced a new bill, one that permitted the compelling of the husband or wife of a polygamist to testify, abolished woman suffrage, declared that all existing offices were vacant, and provided for the compulsory filing of every marriage. Senator Shelby M. Cullom (Rep., Ill.) introduced a law calling upon the president to name a governor and council of nine to run Utah Territory. Hoar sponsored legislation that would turn over the Mormon church's corporation to fourteen trustees, who would be appointed by the president with the consent of the Senate. In June 1884, the Senate passed what was called the Utah bill, which would have abolished all laws incorporating the LDS church; but the House failed to act. In time, however, polygamists began to be arrested, and a Mormon underground was organized to help the offenders escape from federal officials.

The "threat" of Mormonism might evoke consensus, but the fate of the Native American did not. Instead, opinions were far more diverse. Beginning with the Grant administration, the government sought to concentrate all western tribes on a few reservations in Indian Territory (later Oklahoma) or in similar areas in the Northwest. Such removals created much opposition. As time passed, white settlers found it contrary to "the principles of Christian society," much less to "common sense," to allow millions of acres to rest idle; railroad promoters wanted no interference with projected lines; humanitarians sought a maximum of interracial contact and assimilation; and the Indians themselves disliked being told where to live. It was only, so it appeared, economy-minded government officials who endorsed the removal policy.

Indians still occupied the anomalous position of being aliens and wards. Administrators sought to apply federal criminal laws to them, and the Board of Indian Commissioners claimed in 1881 that "no good reason can be given for not placing them under the same government as other people."[18] Many westerners, however, opposed legal equality, arguing that the Indians could not understand, much less obey, criminal codes.

In practice, certain penalties would be applied to Indians that would not apply to whites, and an Indian who committed a crime against another Indian would be given lighter treatment. For example, when the well-known Sioux chief Spotted Tail was murdered late in 1883, the Supreme Court ruled that his murderer, another Sioux chief named Crow Dog, was not subject to United States statutes. In fact, Justice Stanley Matthews declared, Indians were a people "separated by race, by tradition, by the instincts of a free though savage life, from the authority and power which seeks to impose upon them the restraints of an external and unknown code."[19] As a consequence, Congress ruled—by passing the Indian Appropriation Act of 1885—that Indians who lived on reservations were subject to federal laws regarding such crimes as murder, manslaughter, rape, arson, and burglary. Hence, for the first time, the United States asserted its jurisdiction over crimes of Indian against Indian, thereby striking a major blow against the autonomy of Native Americans.

Strictly speaking, in fact, Indians were not citizens. The Supreme Court, ruling in the case of *Elk* v. *Wilkins* (1884), declared that Indians were no more subject to the Fourteenth Amendment than "the children of subjects of any foreign government." In Omaha, John Elk, an Indian who lived outside of a reservation, was prohibited from voting in a local election. In deciding Elk's case, the Court ruled that the mere surrender of tribal allegiance did not, in itself, constitute grounds for formal admission to the privileges of American citizenship; indeed, it would not do so unless Congress specifically so provided. Senator Dawes, a man close to Indian reformers, compared the decision to the fugitive-slave cases. He introduced a bill granting citizenship for all Indians who lived apart from the tribe.

The issue was more complex than one would at first think, because many reformers emphasized that premature citizenship held dangers of its own. Indians possessing civil rights, they declared, would lack the special federal patronage they needed in order to defend themselves. The reformers pointed to the example of the Pueblos, a group that had been treated as citizens since 1848. Local courts, noting their citizenship, held Pueblos responsible for acts that could not have been charged against wards, thereby permitting them to be robbed of their property.

Problems were compounded by the lack of any clear policy. Loring Benson Priest writes that "instead of setting a goal, administrators drifted aimlessly, meeting difficulties as they arose without thought of the future." Governmental officials changed so frequently and policies so rapidly that it was impossible to have any permanent method of dealing with the tribes. Congress paid little attention to these matters, always hoping to expedite business as quickly as possible. No longer were large funds voted; in fact, they were being cut at the very time that extermination of the buffalo made such appropriations more needed than ever. Even the most heartless system, Priest notes, would have been less disastrous if it had been steadily pursued.[20] Indians needed to know what was expected of them; administrators, what they were supposed to achieve.

Indian affairs were primarily located in the Department of the Interior, or, as Leonard D. White called it, "The Department of the Great Miscellany."[21] Organized in 1849 to relieve existing departments of unwanted burdens, it gained Lands from the Treasury Department, Patents from State, Pensions and Indian Affairs from War. The Office of Indian Affairs supervised some sixty or more Indian agents, appointed to four-year terms by the president with Senate approval. Responsibilities included the management of Indian relations, distribution of annuities and goods, removal of trespassers and fugitives, and seizure of alcoholic beverages.

Because duties were often ill defined and agents riveted to party organization, it is little wonder that the Indian service became ridden with corruption. At times, agents were totally ignorant of Indian culture. One might see the strange situation of instructors in agriculture who could not farm, clerks who could not write. True, top pay was only about $1,500 a year, but the Indian service always had an abundance of applications, for contracting could be as lucrative as it was corrupt. Various religious denominations had nominated Indian agents, a practice disapproved of by President-elect Garfield, and by 1880 most churches preferred to surrender the right of nomination rather than to battle the Indian Bureau.

The Department of the Interior had primary responsibility, but the army also played an important role. Soldiers protected Indians against intrusion; they occasionally administered relief and served as Indian agents. Much work centered on policing the traffic in liquor and arms, although more time was taken up in suppressing Indian uprisings on the frontier, where many skirmishes took place. For example, in 1883, General George Crook chased Apache bands, which had raided mining settlements and ranches in Arizona, sometimes pursuing them to the Sierra Madre in Mexico. Of course, jurisdictional conflicts between the departments of War and the Interior were inevitable; their bickering covered such issues as the debasing of Indian women and the army's use of timber from the reservations.

The military took a particularly prominent role in reservations inhabited by nomadic and hunting tribes. It used Indian auxiliaries in its Division of the Pacific, and somewhat begrudgingly in 1882, it assisted Indian education by converting vacant posts and barracks into schools. When Congress cut appropriations and when the price of staples fluctuated, military commanders protested vigorously. In April 1882, Major General John Pope, commander of the Department of the Missouri, saw starvation ahead for the Cheyennes and the Arapahoes; therefore he acted upon his own authority to borrow beef from neighboring lands. Such generals as George Crook, John Pope, William T. Sherman, Philip H. Sheridan, Nelson A. Miles, and John M. Schofield were often consulted by civilian authorities and served on special commissions. Many army spokesmen supported the same changes that were advocated by civilian reformers: Crook, for instance, stressed the need for federal criminal laws and praised the behavior of Indian juries.

By 1879, a budding reform movement was calling for education and citizenship for Indians, abolition of the reservation system, and private ownership of land. A host of organizations were being established, including the Women's National Indian Association (1879), the Boston Indian Citizenship Committee (1879), the Connecticut Indian Association (1881), the Indian Rights Association (1882), the Lake Mohonk Conference of the Friends of the Indian (1883), and the National Indian Defense Association (1885). In 1882, a joint conference of missionary boards declared: "For Indians, we want American education! We want American homes! We want American rights!"[22] Humanitarianism, of course, grew increasingly more pronounced the farther one got from the frontier; it was at its fullest strength in New England. Westerners were still inclined to condemn Indians, and in 1881, a bill was introduced in the Colorado Legislature calling for the "destruction of Indians and Skunks."

The Nez Percé War of 1877 and a conflict the next year with the Ute tribe in northwest Colorado generated much public sympathy for the Indian. The year 1878 also saw the unsuccessful flight of Dull Knife's Cheyennes from the Indian Territory to their old homes in Dakota, an incident that resulted in the Fort Robinson Massacre of the captive band. It was, however, the forced march of the Poncas from Dakota Territory to Indian Territory in 1877 that focused the most public attention on tribal expulsion. Helen Hunt Jackson's *Century of Dishonor* (1881) was an impassioned, if polemical, tract indicting white betrayal, and in March 1881, Congress voted to compensate the Poncas for their land.

Far wider problems, however, remained. Some reformers sought the immediate abolition of Indian political systems; others wanted gradual change. Those in charge of Indian policy differed among themselves. Interior Secretary Kirkwood called tribal arrangements a hindrance to Indian improvement. His successor, Teller, agreed, as did most army officers and such humanitarians as Episcopal Bishop Henry B. Whipple. Other sympathizers, as well as most administrators, argued that persuasion, not forcible conversion, was necessary. But whether they favored coercion or voluntarism, reformers believed that only by destroying tribal identity could racial antagonism be overcome. Most champions of assimilation saw few features of Indian life worth preserving. Priest paraphrases this attitude: "To save the individual Indian the race must be destroyed."[23]

For some Americans, Indians had long been on the path to oblivion. Among these was Congressman James A. Garfield. Contemptuous of the Native American, Garfield claimed in 1868 that "the race of red men" would "be remembered only as a strange, weird, dream-like specter, which had once passed before the eyes of men, but had departed forever." They should, he suggested, be allowed to slip down the road to extinction "as quietly and humanely as possible."[24] Even as president, he never indicated a change of mind.

Arthur was different. Like those reformers who sought to change nomadic tribesmen into individual husbandmen, he spoke of introducing "the customs and pursuits of civilized life." Indeed, he looked forward to their gradual absorption "into the mass of our citizens." In his first annual message, he noted an important need for a severalty law, one that would include from twenty to twenty-five years protection and the extension of federal law to cover Indian reservations. "Their hunting days are over," he said, but give them "the assurance of permanent title to the soil," and they would gladly till it.[25] Apportioning tribal lands to individual members was a policy that had long been used on a minor scale, and by 1885, over eleven thousand land patents had been issued. Yet Indians were easily cheated, often ending up as landless paupers.

Hence it was hardly surprising that severalty was hotly debated. Senator Teller, appointed secretary of the interior in the spring of 1882, had claimed that "the Indian mind" possessed an "inherent objection" to severalty; it still clung to the belief that territory belonged to the tribe in common. Congressman Charles E. Hooker (Dem., Miss.) predicted that Indians would continue to lose private holdings "by fraud, force, or violence."[26]

Such sentiments caused the defeat of allotment bills in 1880 and 1881. In 1882 and again in 1884, severalty bills introduced by Senators Richard Coke (Dem., Texas), chairman of the Committee on Indian Affairs, and Henry L. Dawes passed the Senate but found insufficient support in the House. The fact that Coke's bill provided the tribes with an inalienable title for twenty-five years, thereby nullifying the immediate opening of surplus lands to speculators and settlers, undoubtedly helped to cause its defeat.

Leasing was one way in which whites could legally penetrate Indian settlements. The Indian Bureau believed that leasing would give Native Americans additional income as well as the opportunity to learn the cattle-raising skills. Such tribes as the Cheyennes and the Arapahoes rented out land for as little as a cent and a half an acre. But it was whites who primarily benefited from this opportunity. By 1883, about one hundred thousand untaxed cattle were grazing in the Cherokee Strip, and many cattlemen were building ranches there.

Arthur's administration usually attempted to restrict white settlement of the Indian Territory. Both the president and Teller proposed that penalties for intruders be increased. Each year, thousands of squatters invaded Indian lands, and in 1884, some six thousand to ten thousand claims were reported to have been made in Cherokee territory alone. An executive order kept relatives of Senator Logan from acquiring Zuni land, but just a week before his administration ended, Arthur opened Crow Creek Reservation in Dakota Territory to settlers. Teller had convinced him that the tribes did not hold title to the land, but a subsequent investigation proved otherwise, and in 1885, President Cleveland revoked the order.

Like his predecessor Kirkwood, Teller sought to preserve the reservation system while curbing its size. If the Indians found their territory restricted, so Teller maintained, they would no longer hunt but rather would raise livestock and cultivate land. The secretary's eyes, however, were always on opening more territory to whites. "Very many of these reservations," he said in 1881, "contain large areas of valuable land that cannot be cultivated by the Indians." Industrious whites, acting as "neighbors," could "become valuable auxiliaries in the work of civilizing the Indians residing on the remainder of the reservation."[27]

Surprisingly enough, in some ways Teller was an Indian reformer. Corporation lawyer, mine owner, and president of a small railroad, he had only displayed liberalism with regard to the cause of woman suffrage. While senator from Colorado, he had called for the removal of Utes from his state. "We ought not to forget that we are dealing with savages—brutal, bloody savages," he had once declared, "and we never should deal with savages as we deal with civilized people."[28] However, Teller created a system of courts to deal with Indian offenses, by which three Native American judges punished such "heathenish" tribal customs as polygamy, "immoral" dances, and the sale of wives. In 1882, he had reformer Helen Hunt Jackson investigate conditions in southern California, where white settlers were encroaching on the lands of the Mission Indians. She wrote the romantic novel *Ramona* (1884) on the basis of her experiences; but when she made her specific recommendations, they were blocked by the House.

In his first annual message, Arthur stressed Indian education. He found boarding schools particularly important, for they separated Native American youth "from the surroundings of savage life."[29] He also wanted to provide livestock and farm equipment to graduates of manual-labor schools and to establish a permanent school fund, which would be financed by the sale of public lands.

Congress was not willing to go that far, but it did boost appropriations considerably. In 1881, funds were allocated for the Carlisle Indian Industrial School in Pennsylvania, and a year later the federal government started to finance programs at Hampton, Virginia, and Forest Grove, Oregon. In May 1882, Congress created the office of Indian-school superintendent and appointed a veteran Indian agent to the post. In 1881, only 14 percent of Indian appropriations went to education; by 1885, it was over 25 percent. Secretary Teller strongly supported vocational instruction and agriculture, finding it to be the greatest agency available for the civilization of the Indian, and he increased the number of national schools from two to six. By the time he made his last report, he was demanding education for Indian youths of both sexes. Sometimes, education was perceived as a panacea, with Senator Hoar declaring in 1882 that a few more years of spending would make the Indians completely self-supporting.

Unfortunately, such heralded schools as Carlisle were counterproductive, for the skills that were taught to the Indian boarders had little application to reservation life. Girls would learn laundering and the mass production of food; boys, the handling of farm machinery. Yet both groups either had to forget such skills on the reservation or remain discontented. In a sense, Indian education was Booker T. Washington's Tuskegee experience writ large.

By 1886, as Robert Winston Mardock has noted, "The old frontier, with its lack of law and order, its boisterous expansionism, and its belligerent Indian-white relations, was rapidly disappearing."[30] Indeed, President Cleveland announced the closing of the Indian frontier in December of that year, soon after the Apaches under Geronimo had surrendered. The Dawes Severalty Act of 1887, introduced by the Massachusetts senator while he was chairman of the Committee on Indian Affairs, empowered the president, if he so wished, to allot land to individual Indians. The head of each family that was living on a reservation could receive 160 acres. Furthermore, the Dawes Act bestowed citizenship upon all Indians who received such acreage. The act fulfilled the dreams of Arthur and the reformers, and in so doing, it turned into general national policy what had long taken place piecemeal. Such legislation led to further degradation, because many Indians soon lost their personal holdings. The administrations of Garfield and Arthur, despite good intentions, remained unaware of many problems related to Indian life. Much less did they know how to tackle them.

In looking at the above politics, we see Arthur as a typical president of the Gilded Age genre. He made many recommendations but offered little follow through. He seldom initiated legislation, yet he did use the veto in an attempt to block bills he found offensive. In short, he saw his role fundamentally as that of an administrator, and as his Indian policy indicates, he tried to be a good one.

6

★ ★ ★ ★ ★

SCANDAL AND REFORM

Despite concerns with Chinese, Mormons, and Indians, Arthur had more immediate problems on his hands, and in particular the star-route scandal that Garfield had discovered so soon after his inauguration. Arthur undoubtedly knew of the frauds before he became president, for—as Reeves notes—"he worked closely with Dorsey and Brady in the struggles of 1880, and surely had a solid understanding of the sources of Republican financial income."[1] Arthur, Dorsey in fact declared, was not only aware of the postal profits that Dorsey had made in 1880; the future president had personally tapped Dorsey for a $40,000 contribution to the party. Nine days after becoming president, however, Arthur ordered a series of removals. He told his new attorney general, Benjamin Brewster, that he wanted the proceedings executed "earnestly and thoroughly."[2] And in his first annual message, he promised to prosecute offenders "with the utmost vigor of the law."[3] If as a man, Arthur was saddened to see his cronies indicted, as president he wholeheartedly supported the prosecuting attorneys.

By the spring of 1882, the government was ready with its case. An old friend of Postmaster General James's, attorney George Bliss, headed the prosecution. On March 4, 1882, a grand jury indicted nine men, including Thomas J. Brady, Stephen W. Dorsey, and Montfort C. Rerdell, claiming that they had tampered with nineteen mail routes. Bliss led off with the Dorsey-Brady case, first because of the notoriety of the accused and second because there seemed to be abundant evidence of conspiracy to defraud the government.

Only on June 1, however, did the trial begin. Errors in the indictment,

93

disagreement among counsel, an unfortunate choice of a special assistant attorney general (who had received $2,500 from a prominent star-route contractor), the stalling tactics of Dorsey's lawyer, Robert G. Ingersoll, the temporary disappearance of Stephen's brother John—all had caused delay. During the trial, the jury heard some 150 witnesses and examined some 3,600 exhibits. The government relied upon the postal workers who were well acquainted with the particular routes; the defense drew upon congressmen and other government officials who claimed that population growth and the needs of the army had made irregularities inevitable. The prosecution's case was a complex one, and undoubtedly the jury was often confused. During the trial, Dorsey released several letters showing his closeness to Conkling and Arthur. The jury found only Rerdell and another minor defendant guilty, a decision that sat well with few Americans. When the foreman of the jury charged a government agent with attempting to bribe him, the judge—who believed that the jury's findings were generally unreasonable—granted a retrial.

The second trial, which began on December 7, 1882, and lasted until June 14, 1983, was even longer than the first; it involved some 4,481 pages of testimony. Before the proceedings started, the president removed five federal officeholders for revealing sympathy with the defendants. And Brewster, in a letter to the president that he made public, called the defendants "public enemies," individuals who had engaged in "infamous conspiracy."[4] Again, defense attorneys attempted to confuse the jury, with Ingersoll alternating between sarcasm and maudlin pleas that reduced spectators to tears.

Although the evidence was more complete and the judge's charge to the jury more severe, the defendants were all found innocent. The country, which had become apathetic during the interminable proceedings, was suddenly jolted. The defense had probably tampered with the jury, a poorly educated group to begin with. The government issued eight warrants for attempting to influence the jury improperly, yet it brought only one case to trial. Scores of local cases came before various courts, but only two minor convictions were secured. The Cleveland administration later dropped all charges.

Arthur, obviously embarrassed, was reported to be extremely irritated. At best, he appeared ineffectual; at worst, slightly corrupt. Democrats claimed that the decision revealed that the administration's protestations of reform were hypocritical: the first verdict gave their party a campaign issue in the congressional elections of 1882; the second helped it in Grover Cleveland's presidential bid of 1884. Republicans in general were unhappy; Independents believed the Arthur government insincere; Half-Breeds saw Blaine's cause strengthened; Stalwarts condemned the president for approving of the proceedings. Dorsey called Arthur "the stalled ox feeding at the rich trough of accident."[5] The president undoubtedly realized that the trials had halted the postal frauds, thereby saving the government some $2 million a year, but in every way he found the price a high one.

The case of Charles J. Guiteau had possibilities of being even more embarrassing. Upon being arrested, Garfield's assassin had blurted out words to the effect that he was a Stalwart and that Arthur would now be president. Born in Freeport, Illinois, Guiteau had long been a drifter, with a record of charlatanry and petty fraud. He had spent the Civil War years in John Humphrey Noyes's Oneida Community (where he dreamed of becoming ruler of the world), then had served a brief stint as an attorney and bill collector. He had written a companion to the Bible and had given public lectures on the coming millennium. In 1880, he had first supported Grant for president, then had endorsed the Garfield-Arthur ticket. Although usually ignored by party leaders, Guiteau had lingered around the New York GOP headquarters, writing some petty party propaganda and addressing minor rallies. After the election, he had briefly met Garfield and Blaine and had sought a diplomatic post in Paris or Vienna. Nevertheless, all he had received was the coldest of shoulders.

One scholar calls him "a victim of mental illness"; another finds that he had manifested "a common garden variety of paranoid schizophrenia."[6] At the time, people saw in Guiteau's deed the revenge of a disappointed office seeker, one whose supposed indolence and deceit contrasted markedly with Garfield's honesty and industry. To many, the spoils system itself was responsible for Guiteau's act, a judgment that Guiteau had fostered when he called Garfield's death "a political necessity." He was brazen enough to make recommendations for a new cabinet, one in which Conkling would be secretary of state; Morton, of the treasury; and Logan, of war.

The trial, which lasted from mid November 1881 until the third week in January 1882, was the most celebrated insanity case of the nineteenth century, fully matching the Leopold-Loeb affair of the 1920s. Stalwarts, of course, were the first to desire Guiteau's execution, and Arthur personally pressed for conviction. In the words of Attorney General MacVeagh, the president wanted "no slip." Although a negative verdict was extremely unlikely, the prosecution—composed of some of the nation's most gifted lawyers—made extensive efforts to construct an ironclad case. Guiteau acted as a most peculiar defendant, interrogating prospective jurors on biblical doctrines, shouting at hostile witnesses, and in general implying that he spoke for the Deity. He told the court that during the 1880 campaign, he "used to go to General Arthur and talk just as freely with him as I

95

would with anybody"; he did admit, however, that no Republican leader had ever acknowledged his desire to aid the party.[7]

It took the jury little more than an hour to find Guiteau guilty. The defense's efforts to prove him insane went unheeded. MacVeagh's successor, Brewster, claimed that any stay of execution would "shake the public confidence in the certainty and justice of the courts."[8] Arthur heard one plea on the matter, but he accepted the attorney general's judgment. Guiteau, upon hearing of the president's decision, declared that Arthur and his cabinet were possessed of the devil. The assassin was publicly executed on June 30, 1882, crying out from the scaffold, "I saved my party and my land, Glory hallelujah!"[9]

Guiteau's trial could only remind civil-service reformers of the president's shady past. Henry Adams commented, "Luckily, it will be hard for Arthur to begin worse than Garfield did, although he can but try." Educator and diplomat Andrew Dickson White later reported: "It was a common saying of that time among those who knew him best, '"Chet" Arthur President of the United States. Good God.'" A debonair manner only added to this concern, for the new president, as Morgan notes, "looked at the world through slightly closed eyes, as if most things were comfortably out of focus."[10]

Critics would nevertheless soon be in for a most pleasant surprise. In his first annual message, Arthur repeated his earlier pledge, given when he had accepted the vice-presidential nomination, that civil service should conform to the "conduct of successful private business," and by this he meant "fitness" for the position, stable tenure of office, and prompt investigation of abuses. He suggested that a central examining board make certain nominations, but he objected to competitive examinations on the grounds that immature college youths might monopolize appointments. He promised, however, to support any bill that Congress might pass, even one containing such examinations. If Congress failed to act, he would seek an appropriation of $25,000 to reactivate the Civil Service Commission.[11]

The Democrats already had a bill in mind. They realized that the cause of civil-service reform could attract Independents, while it would curtail the Republicans' exploitation of government personnel, and they were, of course, actively aware that assessments of federal employees put them, the Democrats, at a decided disadvantage. On December 15, 1880, Senator George Hunt Pendleton introduced legislation to create a five-member civil-service examination board, which would have authority to supervise many government activities, including the removal of officeholders.

The Ohio Democrat was the last person one would have expected to advance such a cause. Few individuals, on the surface, could have been more of an anathema to reformers. Pendleton possessed an elegant beard and a genial personality. He was, as Morgan notes, known more "for cravats and manners than ideas"; and his colleagues called him "Gentleman George."[12] He had been McClellan's running mate during the Civil War, he had promoted the "Ohio idea" of paying the national debt with inflated greenbacks, and he had successfully negotiated a shady railroad claim against the government while serving as the company's president.

Pendleton's proposal appeared most sincere, however; and even the usually skeptical *Nation* praised it. After consulting with New York reformer Dorman B. Eaton, who had been chairman of Grant's Civil Service Commission, Pendleton scrapped his own proposal and substituted a bill written by the executive committee of the New York Civil Service Reform Association. This new bill, substantially Eaton's own creation, also provided for a supervisory commission and competitive examinations, but it retained for the executive the right to remove officeholders. Outside of the federal offices located in Washington, the bill would only apply to post offices and customhouses employing over fifty people. During the spring of 1881, Congress ignored Pendleton's proposal as well as an association bill, introduced by Congressman Albert S. Willis (Dem., Ky.), that would have banned political assessments.

On the very day that Arthur's message was delivered to Congress, December 6, 1881, Pendleton again introduced his bill. If it were implemented, the president would appoint a five-member commission to devise civil-service rules, suggest action, and report annually to the chief executive. Other provisions included competitive examinations for positions on a classified list (which could be expanded by the president at will); entrance to civil service at such low grades as government clerks; a probationary period; the abolition of compulsory assessments; and promotion solely on the basis of merit and competition. Removal and tenure were not mentioned. In his supporting speech, Pendleton stressed that the examinations would be designed to test professional fitness and would not touch on unrelated subjects; he incorrectly remarked that about one hundred thousand federal employees would be protected by its terms. A more accurate estimate would have been in the neighborhood of ten thousand.

Congress stalled on Pendleton's proposals, suggesting, as Hoogenboom notes, "almost as many reform plans as it had members."[13] Senator Benjamin H. Hill (Dem., Ga.) advocated frequent changes in the civil service, claiming that a party that had possessed federal power for twenty years was bound to be corrupt. Various westerners sought direct election for offices located outside Washington; but Pendleton himself, who introduced such a proposal, apparently was oblivious to the potential for corruption. Congressman William McKinley (Rep., Ohio) opposed any discrimination against Union veterans.

Such prominent figures as Harvard's president Charles W. Eliot, poet Henry Wadsworth Longfellow, psychologist William James, and author Brooks Adams signed the usual number of petitions, but Congress remained apathetic. At first, in fact, it turned down Arthur's plea for a $25,000 appropriation to reactivate the Civil Service Commission; only after several votes and widespread reaction did it appropriate $15,000. The House Select Committee on Civil Service Reform flaunted its disdain. One of its members was Jay Hubbell of Michigan, the notorious collector of "voluntary contributions"; another was an Ohio congressman elected in part through the efforts of a convict. The committee paraded its indifference by simply proposing a bill to enlarge the duties of the Department of Agriculture.

While Congress remained unconcerned, assessments continued. Most federal assessments involved 2 percent of an officeholder's salary, but state obligations could raise the total levy up to 7 percent. Despite alarming reports from reformers, the power of the Republican machinery was growing thin. In 1881, only about one-third of the employees at the New York Customhouse contributed to the state party's executive committee. The assessment of navy-yard laborers, which was evidently done for the first time in 1882, reveals how desperate the GOP had become.

Arthur received additional criticism when General Newton M. Curtis, a special agent of the Treasury Department, demanded that assessments be made. As an employee of the national government, Curtis had been forbidden, by a federal statute passed in 1876, to seek political funds. In December 1881, the New York civil-service organization protested. Secretary Folger permitted Curtis to resign, but the United States district attorney prosecuted the case. The first indictment was quashed on a technicality (the defendant's name was given as Nehemiah, not Newton); a second indictment resulted in conviction. Despite the advice of New York's former Governor Edwin D. Morgan, who told Arthur that Curtis only did what "most of us have ourselves done," the president refused to issue any pardon.[14]

Despite Arthur's personal backing of the Curtis conviction, Republican politicos remained active. Hubbell, acting in his role as chairman of the Republican Congressional Campaign Committee, tapped officeholders for assessments, although this time he stressed the "voluntary" nature of the contributions. When the counsel of the New York Civil Service Reform Association complained to Arthur's attorney general that Hubbell was violating the statute of 1876, Brewster responded that the 1876 statute did not apply to congressmen. In addition, Folger assured an employee in his department that assessments were quite legal.

Arthur himself was not above using the patronage, filling almost all vacancies with Stalwarts; but only twice did Independents and Half-Breeds become alarmed. In one case he ignored senatorial courtesy by appointing the editor of a Stalwart newspaper as collector for Boston. In another, he selected two friends of John F. Smyth, a corrupt New York boss, to occupy federal posts in Albany. Smyth himself was chosen chairman of the Republican State Committee of New York. Because Smyth had narrowly escaped conviction when he was state superintendent of insurance, young Theodore Roosevelt, then running for the state assembly, found the decision an insult to honest men.

Such blatant practices led to popular reaction. George Frisbie Hoar claimed that Hubbell was acting improperly. Dorman B. Eaton did not know whether to compare Hubbell to Luther's enemy John Tetzel or to "Arab robbers." George William Curtis warned that continued abuses would result in the formation of a new political party. Almost all the state party conventions in 1882, including those of the Greenbackers, the Prohibitionists, and the Anti-Monopolists, favored some kind of civil-service legislation. Even such unlikely partisans as James G. Blaine and former Massachusetts Congressman Benjamin F. Butler proposed specific reforms, with Butler going so far as to advocate a competitive examination for the governorship of Massachusetts, the very office he was seeking.

Such sentiments were soon reflected at the polls. Hubbell, who had his eye on Michigan's Senate seat, could not even gain renomination to Congress. The GOP lost Ohio in October, an event that was blamed on the temperance issue, the defection of German-Americans, and what Hayes saw as dissatisfaction with the boss system. Arthur's efforts to give some patronage to Ohio Stalwarts only perpetuated the mutual party suspicions.

In the November elections, the Republicans suffered far heavier defeats. The Democrats were unusually united, with Senator Arthur P. Gorman of Maryland and Congressman Samuel J. Randall of Pennsylvania serving as skillful if inconspicuous managers. The new House had 200 Democrats to 119 Republicans, and the GOP possessed a margin of only four in the Senate. Newspapers called the results "A Democratic Cyclone," pointing to the victories in New York, Pennsylvania, Indiana, Connecticut, New Jersey, and Massachusetts to prove it. The mayor of Buffalo, Grover Cleveland, defeated Secretary of the Treasury Folger for the New York governorship by what was, until then, the greatest margin in the Empire State's history. Cleveland received the backing of Republicans who were angry over Stalwart appointments and Smyth's new position. The defection of one hundred thousand Republican Independents in Pennsylvania toppled the Cameron organization, and stay-at-home Republicans caused the election of the demagogic Ben Butler as governor of Massachusetts.

It was the election of 1882, more than any other event, that prompted Congress to consider the Pendleton bill. If, as Mrs. Henry Adams claimed, the lame-duck Congress was acting like "a pack of whipped boys," it moved rapidly to end assessments.[15] Even John A. Logan, who had helped to kill Grant's civil-service system, was converted to the reform cause. By acting quickly, the Republicans could pose as reformers to their constitutents, while protecting the tenure of their officeholders and protecting it even if the Democrats won the coming presidential election.

The 1882 election also had its impact on Arthur. In his second annual message, he called for the passage of the Pendleton bill. By this endorsement he not only reiterated his approval of tenure but came out for competitive examinations and the banning of assessments. The president admitted that officeholders often made political contributions because they were afraid of being dismissed. And with more than a bit of disingenuousness, Arthur declared that he had always opposed forced contributions. Supervising the larger part of some one hundred thousand federal employees, he said, was keeping him from more important duties.

Senate Democrats were particularly partisan; they even turned votes on adjournments into party issues. Mississippi's James Z. George proposed a constitutional amendment that would have provided for local elections of all federal officials. Alabama's James L. Pugh sought to have all appointed officials apportioned according to population, a provision that would have given the Democrats an equal share of offices and his own state of Alabama a more equitable share of the patronage. Pendleton strongly backed Pugh's amendment, as did all Democrats but the reformist Thomas F. Bayard. When Joseph B. Hawley (Rep., Conn.), chairman of the Senate's Committee on Civil Service and Retrenchment, sought a provision to permit voluntary contributions, Democrats—voting strictly by party—immediately moved to dam up a rival's source of revenue. Zebulon B. Vance of North Carolina (who, after the Democratic victory of 1884, sought the total repeal of the Pendleton Act) wanted the proposed bill to apply to all internal-revenue offices that employed over fifty people. All Democrats knew that their strength lay in branch offices, not in Washington departments. Hence they supported Vance's amendment, while all but one Republican opposed it.

The Democrats were only able to alter Pendleton's bill in one particular: they unanimously supported a proposal, advanced by Georgia's Senator Joseph E. Brown, to extend civil service to all ranks, not just the lower ones. Such a move, which he justified on the grounds that certain higher positions demanded special skills, would equalize the party distribution of offices far more quickly. Obviously the nature of the Pendleton bill was not always determined by principles of clean government but by the political potential of the posts that would be affected.

Brown did fail in two proposals. First, he could not delay action until after the 1884 election, because Pendleton was arguing that procrastination would only foster a Republican victory. Second, he was unable to achieve the equal division of offices among all parties.

Some Republicans also wanted the Pendleton bill modified. John A. Kasson pushed a compromise measure that would have eliminated competitive examinations while providing for fixed terms. John Sherman wanted to limit terms of tenure. Henry L. Dawes revived a proposal to permit each department to supervise its own examinations. Kansas Senator John J. Ingalls simply claimed that the bill would permit either party to defraud the other. As Hoogenboom notes, "The undertone was one of expediency rather than of sympathy."[16]

Differences were sectional as well as political. The West and the South, two areas markedly underrepresented in the civil service, feared that educational qualifications would result in further discrimination against them. Therefore, Pendleton sponsored an amendment that would help to distribute offices according to a state's population. Western Republicans and southern Democrats pushed the measure through, little worrying as to whether such a proposal would violate reformist principles.

In the final Senate vote, taken on December 27, 1882, thirty-eight senators from both parties supported the Pendleton Act. Although fifteen Democrats approved of the proposal, twelve either spoke or voted against it. Pendleton was the only Democrat outside of the South who favored his own bill. All thirty Republicans backed it, including Cameron and Louisiana's corrupt carpetbagger William Pitt Kellogg. After the final tally, Senator Brown labeled the measure "a bill to perpetuate in office the Republicans who now control the patronage of the Government."[17]

Thanks to the skillful legislative maneuvering of Abram S. Hewitt (Dem., N.Y.), on January 4, 1883, the House debated the entire issue within thirty minutes. William E. Robinson (Dem., N.Y.) wanted the bill to go into effect on July 1, 1885, a move that might give a victorious Democratic party a few months to fill vacancies. "Little Phil" Thompson (Dem., Ky.) unsuccessfully moved to recommit the legislation; he then sought to add amendments that would have forbidden all political contributions by officeholders. The final vote on the bill itself was 155 to 47, although the declared views of abstainers would have made the total 162 to 48. Republicans, except for six from the Old Northwest and the South, had supported the proposal. So had many Democrats, even if forty from the South and the Old Northwest had opposed it. Arthur then signed the measure, thereby launching civil service in the United States. The entire effort had been made most reluctantly.

The Pendleton Act had a limited application, as it was restricted to officials in Washington and to employees in major customhouses and post offices. The vast majority of federal employees, as well as all municipal and state ones, were still not protected. Some 47,000 postmasters were still not affected, nor were "old soldiers" or "mere workmen" appointed by the president. In fact, when the bill was passed, it covered only 11 percent of the federal government's employees—some 14,000 of a total of 131,000. If one combined Arthur's political appointments with those of Garfield, some 72 percent of the fourth-class postmasterships changed hands within four years. Furthermore, although the vast majority of postmasters earned less than $100 annually, they still were required to honor political obligations.

Reformers remained suspicious of Arthur's motives, protesting strongly in December 1882 when a Stalwart was nominated for commissioner of the District of Columbia. Although the president withdrew the nomination, they suspected that Arthur was still unrepentant. Similarly, he appointed one of Grant's partisans, Randolph De B. Keim of Pennsylvania, as chief examiner of the Civil Service Commission. Protests from the press led Keim to withdraw, at which point Arthur chose a less controversial figure.

Such suspicions were increased by the controversy over Silas Burt. Once a friend of the president, with whom he had attended Union College, Burt had long been an outspoken reformer. Early in 1883, he held the commission as naval officer to the New York Customhouse, where his performance was praised by such civil-service spokesmen as the *New York Evening Post* and *Harper's Weekly*. Even Edwin D. Morgan, by no means a reformer, told Arthur that Burt was "an exceptionally good Officer, giving satisfaction to our merchants and importers."[18] In March, however, Arthur nominated surveyor Charles K. Graham to replace Burt, whom he then nominated for chief examiner of the Civil Service Commission. Graham's military record was distinguished, and he was not a political figure, much less a Stalwart. Burt, in turn, could have contributed much in his new post, although his salary would have been reduced from $8,000 to $3,000. Arthur unquestionably knew in advance that Burt would decline the appointment. Burt had recently withheld a list of naval-office employees from the New York Republican State Committee, and now the president was retaliating. It was, writes Reeves, a petty act of spite against a man whom Arthur had known for thirty-five years, and reformers were not amused.[19]

Yet, on the whole, Arthur administered the Pendleton Act conscientiously. He appointed Eaton, who had been one of the few reformers who had praised him in 1880, as chairman of the Civil Service Commission. Other selections for the new body were equally lauded by reformers: John M. Gregory, president of what later became the University of Illinois, and Leroy D. Thoman, a young Democratic judge from Ohio. When, in May 1883 and in November, Arthur adopted major recommendations made by the commission, George William Curtis, president of the newly formed National Civil Service Reform League, told his organization that the president desired "to give the reform system fair play." Even though such politicos as Mahone complained about Arthur's indifference to their own party machines, within two years, postmasters were sharing their enthusiasm regarding the Civil Service Commission. In 1885, the commission paid direct tribute to "the constant, firm, and friendly support" of the outgoing president.[20]

Arthur's later cabinet appointments could only serve to allay remaining fears. When Postmaster General Howe died in March 1883, the president replaced him with Walter Q. Gresham, a respected federal judge from Indianapolis. Then, in September 1884, the death of Folger caused Gresham to be moved to the Treasury Department; soon, however, Arthur appointed him to a circuit judgeship. The president's last secretary of the treasury, Hugh McCulloch of Maryland, had been a London partner of Jay Cooke's and had headed the Treasury Department under Abraham Lincoln, then Andrew Johnson. And the president's last postmaster general, thirty-eight-year-old Frank Hatton of Iowa, had helped to direct the national postal bureaucracy since 1881.

Hence, in the short run, the odyssey of civil-service reform was quite stormy. Arthur's successor, Grover Cleveland, did not advance the cause, for he awarded jobs primarily on the basis of party service and, in fact, effected almost a clean sweep of fourth-class postmasters. Pendleton's association with reform displeased Ohio Democrats and ultimately cost him his position in the Senate.

The bureaucracy still housed much inefficiency, with the General Land Office being a particularly miserable institution. Long suspected of corruption, lacking forceful leadership, and always behind schedule, the office lacked support in Congress as well as in the Great Plains, where so much of its work took place. Laws were not adequate for protecting small settlers; administrators were lax and at times corrupt; official policy was uncertain. In 1883, Commissioner Noah C. McFarland reported widespread fraud, and in the early 1880s, a special agent of the General Land Office uncovered a large timber scandal involving some of the choicest California redwoods.

The Pension Office, if anything, offered even greater opportunities for corruption. That agency suffered from an excessive volume of work, lack of coordination, incessant congressional pressure, and GAR lobbying. Given such chaos, it was hardly surprising to find thousands of soldiers and their attorneys who, according to Leonard D. White, "seemed to have been engaged in a gigantic conspiracy to defraud their own government."[21]

Under Arthur the Pension Office was headed by a former Union general, William W. Dudley, who had lost a leg at Gettysburg. Dudley's administration became synonymous with dishonesty. In his first annual message, Arthur sought an appropriation for the prevention of fraud, but Congress failed to act. In 1882, the Senate, in order to combat misrepresentation, printed the names of all pensioners. However, pension attorneys, in order to continue various swindles, soon obtained the volumes that were not being used by officials.

In the long run, the reformers got much of their way. Not only was the number of people entering government service increasing sharply, but individuals of higher social status were being attracted. Bryce soon commented that the rank and file of the federal civil service had reached a level as high as in England or Germany, and Dorman B. Eaton found that the overwhelming majority of political hacks had been eliminated from government employment. Remote sections of the Union had received greater representation in the bureaucracy. Since many civil servants were no longer under obligation to a political boss, the proceeds from assessments dropped by as much as one-half.

Business benefited in several ways: there was a marked improvement in postal and customs efficiency; it was able to replace the coercive assessments with contributions of its own, thereby exerting greater control over party activities; and by the 1890s, it could deal with the quiet, steady, sympathetic party manager, not the independent and capricious spoilsman.

Even more important, civil-service reform was necessary in order to rationalize the bureaucracy, a development that in turn helped to pave the way for the emergence of a modern United States. Indeed, it would be difficult to envision the sweeping economic and social legislation of the twentieth century without a nonpartisan civil service. Writes Paul P. Van Riper, one historian of the movement, "The civil service reformers diagnosed better than they knew or than others have usually given them credit. They did put first things first."[22]

Although Arthur had endorsed civil service, he still hoped to strengthen his party, especially its Stalwart wing. Many of his wishes centered on the South, and it is first to the general condition of the South, and then to the role played by the Republican party there, that we now turn.

7

★ ★ ★ ★ ★

"ARTHUR IS FOR US":
THE PRESIDENT AND THE SOUTH

During the 1880s, what has long been known as the New South was emerging. When the depression ended in 1879, both northern and British capital found an outlet for surplus investment there. The area was so attractive for several reasons. First, for several years, the South had been systematically opening rich timber, coal, and iron lands to outside entrepreneurs, who thereby controlled the pine, cypress, and much else as well. Second, the labor turmoil so prevalent elsewhere had bypassed the area. Third, in 1879, there was a great boom in railroad construction, and within a decade, track mileage had doubled.

Because of these circumstances, the South was becoming an economic unit in a way undreamed of during the Confederacy. By 1883, the Southern Pacific Railroad had tied New Orleans to San Francisco, and other lines were about to join St. Louis to southern cities. Steel rails began to replace iron ones, rolling stock was modernized, and track was relaid to conform to a national guage. The banking syndicates of New York and Philadelphia invested heavily in southern roads, controlling most southern railroads by 1882.

Railroad investment led to more general economic development, with the most important spurt lying in the iron industry. The mill areas followed a belt that extended along the Piedmont into Georgia and Alabama. Such industrial towns as Chattanooga, Atlanta, and Knoxville first took on a reddish tinge, then a uniform grayness.

In contrast to the railroad industry, the capital and enterprise used in the development of iron were largely southern. The Louisville and Nashville

Railroad, whose general counsel was a hero of Appomattox and former governor of Alabama, played a crucial role, for it tied the central works at Birmingham to other coal and iron towns. So successful was iron production that during the depression of 1884, southern iron successfully invaded the northeastern market, and by the end of the decade, the South was producing more pig iron than was the entire United States before the Civil War.

Other southern industries showed similar growth rates. Timber production doubled between 1880 and 1890, making the region the nation's leading source of lumber and turning such places as High Point, North Carolina, into furniture-manufacturing centers. During the same ten years, the production of coal increased from six million tons to twenty-two million. Recovery in the tobacco industry did not wait until the eighties, although the processing of the crop was still done by ante-bellum methods and was restricted to such cities as Richmond, Durham, and Louisville.

Cotton remained king, and by 1879, the South once again dominated world production. In that year, cotton production exceeded prewar figures by over a million bales. The British bought over 75 percent of the total yield. By 1880, the South, together with the Northeast, was using more cotton products; therefore, the southerners began to invest much of their own surplus capital in new mills. Despite predictions of failure by such prominent northern textile merchants as Edward Atkinson, appeals to regional patriotism were effective, and the number of spindles rose from something over 500,000 in 1880 to 1.6 million in 1890. In 1881, Atlanta held an international cotton exposition, which displayed far more than cotton exhibits, and in 1883, Louisville sponsored a southern exposition. These served both to advertise the region's resources and to demonstrate a revived sense of belonging to a wider United States.

Accompanying such development was an entire ideology, one called the New South mystique. Prominent editors in the urban South preached the work ethic, sought an end to the bloody shirt, and welcomed northern investment. They advanced a new model of southern life, and in 1883, Mark Twain described them as "brisk men, energetic of movement and speech; the dollar their god, how to get it their religion." Romanticism might sometimes baptize, sometimes obscure this process, for in the post-Reconstruction South, there was more knifing, manslaughter, and murder than there had been before the Civil War. Twain again spoke to the issue, writing of "practical common-sense, progressive ideas, and progressive works, mixed up with the duel, the inflated speech, and the jejune romanticism of an absurd past that is dead."[1]

The essential message of the New South's creed was clear: as Henry W. Grady, editor of the *Atlanta Constitution*, told a group of northern bankers in 1883, "We need the money. You can make a profit off the development."[2]

There was, however, a real gap between New South ideology and New South reality, a hiatus so great that Paul M. Gaston frequently uses the term "myth" in discussing the region during the Gilded Age. By any indices of accomplishment, be it per capita wealth or percentage of urban population, the area remained well behind the North's development. Its rate of industrialization was no faster than that of the nation as a whole; in fact, it was quite modest in comparison to its own development during the 1850s and early 1860s. Never had the South been so far behind the North in wealth and social well-being.

Despite increasing outside investment, the South was often forced back upon its own meager supply of capital. Credit, even Grady admitted, was ruinously expensive; in his own Georgia, he found that it cost 54 percent on everything a farmer could purchase. And though a number of factories were erected, they were largely limited to cotton manufacture. Furthermore, most southerners still preferred to grow cotton, not produce textiles. Many southerners welcomed railroads, immigration, and capital, not in order to transform the region, but out of the belief that efficient cotton-growing would enrich the area without its needing further industrialization.

It is hardly surprising that industrialism was neither extensive enough nor revolutionary enough to change living standards for the great mass of southerners; therefore, the area remained the most rural and impoverished part of the nation. Such propagandists as Grady might well have served the South poorly, because they sought industrialization on the most disadvantaged of terms. Only in a few areas, such as the Yazoo Mississippi delta, were New South objectives realized.

To understand the weakness of the New South and the sketchiness of its industrial development, one should note that the southern economy took on an essentially colonial pattern. The region remained overwhelmingly an area of staple-crop agriculture, to which were added such extractive industries as forestry, fishing, and mining. Since most manufactured goods and much food were imported into the region and since railroads and natural resources were increasingly controlled by outside capital, decisions that could affect the life of almost every southerner were made in northern boardrooms. As a result, the North drained off profits that could otherwise have been reinvested in regional enterprises. The industries that did emerge, such as textiles, paid low wages; they frequently depended upon child and convict labor. The new mills quickly fell into the colonial pattern, for final processing often took place above the Mason-Dixon line. The relative lateness of southern industrialization, an inferior educational system, and lack of skilled workers only reinforced the dependency of the South.

The comparatively slow growth of industry made little impact on the hold agriculture had upon the area. Indeed, the South was more agricultural than it had been before the Civil War, and by any standards, it was an agriculture that entrapped the people in a grinding poverty. As early as 1880, one-third of all farmers in the lower South were tenants, and the plantation system, under a different name, persisted in the black belt.

What C. Vann Woodward has called the New Order in agriculture was marked by the lien system, whereby the farmer pledged his future for such supplies as plow points and hay. Because merchants charged exorbitant prices and interest, farmers were often unable to meet their obligations at the end of the season. Hence, they would be forced to renew the lien on their next crop or, at times, to sell their farms outright. Yet, merchants were as much victims as victimizers, for they in turn had to pay outrageous interest rates to factors, individuals who were themselves dependent upon distant lords of credit. "The merchant," writes Woodward, "was only a bucket on an endless chain by which the agricultural well of a tributary region was drained of its flow."[3] A relatively good year for cotton crops, such as 1880, could bring a sharecropper some fifty dollars for his year's work. Probably neither he nor his landlord, however, would have touched any cash, for both were deeply enmeshed in an oppressive and impersonal system.

This system, together with sharecropping, created much outrage. So also did the brutal leasing of convicts, fixed elections, high taxes and interest rates, huge land grants for corporations, and the lack of public schools. The South experienced a major cleavage between poor and rich, country and town, with the Bourbon, or "Redeemer," governments often aligned against much of their own populace. As southern farmers no longer feared "black Reconstruction," they became increasingly alert to personal exploitation, and soon after the restraints of occupation were cast off, they formed independent movements, renouncing allegiance to the dominant Democrats. In 1881, the new Greenback party, "readjuster" crusades, and various other insurgent movements became quite visible.

In order for any protest movement to break the hold of Bourbon Democracy, new groups would have to be recruited. One such group could be southern blacks.

As late as the 1880s, many leading whites accepted some black voting, even if intimidation was by no means absent. In some areas, Negroes worked with whites on political committees and conventions. They voted in large numbers, although patterns varied widely from state to state, and within a state as well. In the presidential election of 1880, a majority of adult black males voted in almost every southern state, and they voted Republican. Only in Mississippi, which had an extraordinary amount of violence, and in Georgia, which had adopted a cumulative poll tax, was

black voting severely restricted. Patrician Redeemers of the black belt frequently defeated their opponents by courting or coercing Negroes, who—
with dependable regularity—gave them support. Even in Alabama, few
whites before the 1890s recommended that the black vote be eliminated,
because as long as black belt Democrats could control Negro suffrage, they
found it an asset. The Redeemers deliberately sought to keep blacks in control of the Republican units; such leadership would make whites reluctant to
join, while putting the Jim Crow label on the GOP. Bourbons would also
give offices to blacks, either as Republicans or Democrats, in return for tacit
support for state positions. Hence, it is not really surprising in 1880 to see
eleven blacks in the lower house of Louisiana, four in the upper. National
politics was a slightly different story. Here most blacks, or at least their
leaders, adhered to the adage of Frederick Douglass, who, in 1872, had
claimed that the GOP was the deck; all else, the sea.

This is not to say that blacks felt no squeeze, and by the 1880s, some
states made this squeeze quite tangible. South Carolina, for example, in
1882, required a confusing series of special voting boxes and ballots for each
office. The stick and the carrot were both used: blacks were punished for
voting Republican but rewarded for voting Democratic. By that year, 1882,
Negro Republicans of the state had also stopped offering congressional candidates except in their own gerrymandered black district. Although Democratic Senator Wade Hampton might boast, in 1884, that every pledge made
to the state's blacks had been kept, his party made sure that no Republicans
were represented on election boards.

Some black politicians called for blind loyalty from their constituency,
while they amassed much personal wealth. Blanche K. Bruce of Mississippi
owned a thousand-acre plantation; Congressman John R. Lynch of Mississippi reportedly possessed vast tracts of land. If such black politicos
benefited, rank-and-file Negroes were often exploited.

White-sponsored dances, parties, barbecues, and whiskey were subtle
pressures; the herding of black laborers to the polls was a bit less so. At
times, whites would nominate black candidates in order to divide the Negro
vote. At other times, but far less frequently, insurgent whites courted black
voters. For example, when Tom Watson ran for the Georgia Legislature in
1882, he called for Negro schools and condemned the convict-lease system.

If the Bourbons thought that blacks were inferior, they saw no need to
humiliate them publicly. The times, as Woodward notes, were ones of "ex-
periment, testing, and uncertainty," with alternatives still open and real
choices being made.[4] Much legal segregation in public accommodations was
still to come; in the 1880s, blacks could attend plays with whites, drink at
bars, eat at ice-cream parlors, and make purchases in general stores. They
could ride a train—and even ride it first class in Virginia and Sou~

Carolina—or a streetcar, live in mixed neighborhoods in older cities and towns, and appeal to courts with the knowledge that they might well get redress. Discrimination was common only in hotels, and this practice lacked the force of law.

Of course, legal rights were one thing; custom, another; and beyond a certain point, blacks and whites seldom mixed. Slavery had created lingering stigmas in bearing, stress, and manner; and both black and white realized this. Even if blacks were permitted access to restaurants and theaters, they seldom had the cash to make use of them. Separation continued in churches, schools, military life, and public institutions. New public services—such as hospitals and asylums—applied existing practices of segregation, sometimes legally, sometimes not. The number of lynchings started peaking in the 1880s, with the number averaging one hundred fifty a year. Blacks were proportionately more in debt as a result of the crop-lien system; they were more frequently jailed for petty offenses; they had even fewer educational opportunities than whites; and when they were hired by industry, they were relegated to the lowest-paying jobs. Obviously, segregation, disenfranchisement, and black subordination were increasing, although this growth was as yet sporadic.

And given the increasingly worsening conditions, many blacks migrated. Within the South, such movements involved journeying from country to town, from older states in the Lower South to newer ones in the Southwest. A second pattern of migration, which was strong enough by 1879 to be labeled the Exodus, involved traveling from the South to the Midwest. Led by Henry Adams of Louisiana and Moses ("Pap") Singleton of Tennessee, some forty thousand southern Negroes, writes Rayford W. Logan, "virtually stampeded" to Kansas, Iowa, and Nebraska.[5]

Conditions were not always better in the North, where segregation was also prevalent. By the 1880s, Negroes had won the right to an education, but black teachers were often expelled from mixed educational systems. Antidiscrimination laws were generally ignored in such states as those in the Ohio Valley and in other areas of the North as well.

Migration was only one way of coping with declining economic and political strength. The twin ideologies of self-help and racial solidarity constituted another. Blacks were abandoning the integrationist ethos of Reconstruction in order to create segregated institutions. By separation, white hostility and competition might be averted, opportunities for leadership might be expanded, and vested interests might be retained. The Gospel of Wealth was supported by Frederick Douglass, who declared in 1880, "If the time shall ever come when we shall possess in the colored people of the United States, a class of men noted for enterprise, industry, economy and success, we shall no longer have any trouble in the matter of civil and political rights."[6] Such a philosophy was obviously manifested in a number of ways, ranging from the development of small businesses to informal taboos on intermarriage. In 1884, Douglass himself was strongly criticized by black leaders for marrying a white woman.

During the eighties, Negro education had already gravitated towards the philosophy of industrial education as represented by Virginia's Hampton Institute. The Hampton philosophy stressed "uplift" through moral values and the acquisition of a specific trade, and it stressed these at the expense of broader learning, political action, and demands for civil rights. Conservative northern and southern whites welcomed this development, sincerely believing that blacks could best benefit from a curriculum limited to home economics, farming, manual training, and other skills useful in rural areas. (Congressman Garfield once served as a Hampton trustee, but lost interest as his reservations about vocational education grew.) In 1882, for example, the Connecticut textile merchant John F. Slater gave a million dollars to create industrial and agricultural departments in black schools. Former president Hayes was chosen to head the Slater Fund's board of trustees.

Hence the famous Atlanta Compromise of Booker T. Washington went into effect almost a decade before the black educator had become nationally prominent. Indeed, as August Meier notes, Washington became powerful not because he initiated a trend but because he articulated it so well. Believing that blacks had few alternatives, Washington commented that industrial education "secures the cooperation of the whites, and does the best possible thing for the black man."[7] When, in 1881, he was called to lead Tuskegee Institute, he genuinely thought that it was through thrift, industry, and "Christian character" that blacks would have their constitutional rights recognized. And in an address given in Madison, Wisconsin, in 1884, he called for an alliance with the more powerful southern whites. Negroes, he assumed, would not remain in subordinate positions; rather, by their own efforts, they would create a propertied class of landowners and businessmen. Gaston goes so far as to find Washington's entire life and doctrine "wonderful examples of New South precepts put into action."[8] The Tuskegee educator had risen out of slavery, achieved eminence by his own industry, minimized the importance of politics, stressed economic skills, and was generally conservative on political and economic questions.

Of course, even on its own terms, the Washington approach had obvious limitations, although few people were aware of them at the time. Industrial education was equipping blacks with the type of skills that the technological revolution was making obsolete. For instance, such millionaires as Andrew Carnegie and John D. Rockefeller—both of whom contributed to Tuskegee—might have had all their clothing made by a tailor, but most Americans were now buying manufactured garments. Small individualistic entrepreneurs in general were having a more difficult time, and yeoman farmers, both white and black, would find themselves increasingly reduced to farm tenancy. Given political and economic relations in the South, the blacks had a dim future.

If blacks found little support in the political system, they found even less in the judicial one. True, some northern states, such as New Jersey and Illinois, opposed segregation in local schools. In 1880, the Supreme Court outlawed a Delaware law restricting jury service to whites, and in 1883, it did the same for a Kentucky law concerning grand juries. However, a circuit court sustained railroad segregation in one northern state, Ohio, on the basis of the separate-but-equal doctrine. In fact, the major thrust of court decisions, both state and national, was to bolster segregation, with intermarriage being the first item given attention and education the second. In 1882, by sustaining an Alabama statute, the Supreme Court lent its authority to laws prohibiting miscegenation.

One Supreme Court case involved mob violence. In *U.S.* v. *Harris* (1882), the Court ruled that the beating of several Negroes and the murder of one did not constitute a federal offense. The mob action was a private one, and while the failure of the state of Tennessee to prevent it was regrettable, no federal crime was involved. By declaring that the first section of the Fourteenth Amendment applied only to states, not to individuals, it suddenly made the Enforcement, or Ku Klux Klan, Act of 1871 meaningless indeed.

The Harris decision was a harbinger of things to come. The greatest impediment to black advancement, however, came in 1883 with the Civil Rights Cases. Eight years earlier, in 1875, Congress had passed the Supplementary Civil Rights Act. It was, in a sense, the abolitionist Senator Charles Sumner's last legacy to his countrymen. In an effort to counteract southern black codes, the law provided that all persons, regardless of race, were entitled to "the full and equal enjoyment of the accommodations, advantages, facilities and privileges of inns, public conveyances on land or water, theaters, and other places of public amusement."[9] The aggrieved individual, if successful in a suit, could recover $500; federal courts were given exclusive jurisdiction. It was section 5 of the Fourteenth Amendment in particular, or so proponents of the law believed, that offered ample authority for this legislation.

In the Civil Rights Cases, the Supreme Court upheld private segregation in public accommodations. Several incidents were combined for argument and decision: they concerned seating in a restaurant, access to a railroad car, lodging in a hotel, and attendance at New York's Grand Opera and at a theater. Because southerners did not have as much integrated contact with blacks as did northerners, only two of the five cases had originated in the South. All but the railroad incident involved federal prosecutions.

"There was," writes Morton Keller, "a weary, empty quality to these cases, as indeed there was to the cause of civil rights itself."[10] The defendants submitted no briefs, and the arguments of the solicitor general were not convincing. It was far from an auspicious beginning.

The Court ruled that the Fourteenth Amendment applied only to state law, not to persons or activities private in nature, and the category "private" was given a wide interpretation. As Justice Joseph P. Bradley put the issue, "Individual invasion of individual rights is not the subject-matter of the amendment."[11] White supremacy was thereby placed beyond federal control, for southern society rested on just such "individual" arrangements. The desire for national reconciliation merged with the prevailing laissez-faire ideology, one that sought to limit all regulatory powers of the federal government.

In his dissent, Justice John Marshall Harlan found the Thirteenth Amendment, which ended slavery, clearly authorizing the Civil Rights Act. Racial discrimination by businesses of a public character, he said, was a form of unconstitutional servitude. As for the Fourteenth Amendment, certain enterprises—such as railroads, hotels, restaurants, and theaters—served important public functions and therefore came under its jurisdiction.

An important segment of the Republican press applauded the decision, including the *New York Journal of Commerce*, the *New York Evening Post*, and *Harper's Weekly*. Most party leaders, however, disapproved. Robert G. Ingersoll found the decision "as cruel as slavery's lash." John Sherman, again in the Senate, accused the judges of undermining "the foundation stone of Republican principles."[12] Senator Benjamin Harrison of Indiana promised that the Republicans, if necessary, would amend the Constitution in order to safeguard Negro rights. Within the decade, a dozen northern states passed civil-rights laws, although most segregation above the Mason-Dixon line remained undisturbed.

Booker T. Washington took the news complacently, but northern blacks were incensed. They held protest meetings at Chicago, Pittsburgh, and San Francisco, and they formed a group to lobby for the reenactment of the law. Frederick Douglass thought that the United States would appear "before the world as a nation utterly destitute of power to protect the rights of its own citizens."[13] T. Thomas Fortune, editor of the *New York Age*, urged fellow Negroes in first-class railroad coaches to defend themselves; indeed, one could not die in a better cause.

Despite the decision in the Civil Rights Cases and despite the worsening situation of American blacks, the vast majority of Negroes opposed emigration. Commenting on the Supreme Court ruling, Bishop Henry M. Turner of the African Methodist Episcopal Church claimed that "a conclave of human donkeys" had "made the ballot of the black man a parody, his citizenship a nullity and his freedom a burlesque."[14] Turner, a vice-president of the American Colonization Society, called for emigration to Africa. He had few followers. When blacks responded to their predicament, they sought the traditional avenues of self-help, racial solidarity, and protest.

It would take another seventy-five years before the principles embodied in the 1875 Civil Rights Act were again put into force. In 1964, Congress ruled, on the basis of the power to regulate interstate commerce, that discrimination in public accommodations was illegal. During the early 1880s, the condition of the American Negro was at what Rayford W. Logan has called its nadir.

At first, southern Republicans thought that Arthur would support the traditional party organizations. This belief was particularly strong because he had turned over strategy regarding the South to Navy Secretary William E. Chandler, a man who had cultivated many of that region's leaders during the Hayes-Tilden election. Chandler, who had protested emphatically against Hayes's "new departure," called for strict enforcement of the Fourteenth and Fifteenth amendments.

Once in power, Chandler changed his sentiments, finding that the salvation of the party lay in such Democratic defectors as Mahone. With reform movements in Ohio, New York, and Pennsylvania threatening to weaken the Republican party in the North, he thought that a new approach was necessary in the South. Victory in the 1882 congressional elections lay in serious doubt; the 1884 presidential race, even more so.

"You are rightly regarded as the Carnot of our American politics," a GOP politico from New Orleans wrote Chandler, "doing politically, for the Republican party, what the great Frenchman did for France as War Minister,—organizing victory out of the incongruous elements of a disrupted party and forging them into thunderbolts against the enemy."[15] Chandler lost little time in devising new plans, ones that transcended support to traditional Republican machines and that made bids to disaffected Democrats. In the fall of 1882, he wrote to a suspicious James G. Blaine: "Our straight-out Republican, carpetbag Negro governments, whether fairly or unfairly, have been destroyed and cannot be revived. Without these coalitions in support of independents we cannot carry southern votes enough to save the House from Bourbon democratic control and carry the next presidential fight. Beyond that, the safety of the colored race, while exercising the suffrage, depends upon this new departure."[16] In short, to Chandler, occasional blurring of Republican identity was preferable to defeat. Hoping for a new lease on political life, the Arthur administration had no qualms about backing people who favored greenbacks, endorsed unlimited silver coinage, attacked national banks, and championed the cause of the black. Chandler's paper declared, "The cry should be 'anything to beat the Bourbons,'" an attitude that Woodward finds "a test for the social conscience of a Machiavelli."[17]

Throughout the South, various voices called for the rethinking of old alignments. A Chandler correspondent from Jackson, Mississippi, reported that clinging to the name "Republican" solidified the Bourbons; a man from New Orleans wrote, "We must have a political transfusion of blood."[18] In the North, Carl Schurz predicted that the Independent movements might split the Democratic South and even eliminate the race issue in the process. The *Nation* reported, "We are told that the breaking-up of the 'solid South' on the Mahone plan will result in making the Republican party independent of a united North."[19]

The phrase "Mahone plan" was the crucial one, because Virginia was the site of the administration's most visible success. Although the Senate Democrats were able to block the appointments of Riddleberger and Gorman, Old Dominion Readjusters had done well in the 1882 elections. Indeed, they were at the zenith of their power, giving a strong rebuff to the Democratic party. William E. Cameron was elected governor; Harrison H. Riddleberger, Mahone's close friend, was chosen senator; and six Mahone men were elected to Congress. Readjusters controlled the legislature and the courts; in fact, they were powerful enough to remove the Bourbons from every significant office. The Virginia Legislature passed the Riddleberger Law, which foisted one-third of the state's debt onto West Virginia and issued fresh bonds paying a lower rate of interest. It also engaged in a host of other reforms, including reduction of the general property tax, care for the insane, and abolition of the poll tax. Blacks as a group benefited from several laws: an appropriation of $100,000 for black higher education; the doubling of the number of Negro elementary schools; enfranchisement of some twenty thousand Afro-Americans; jury service for blacks; and the elimination of the whipping post, a device that had been used to humiliate Negroes.

Chandler gave Mahone much patronage power, and the Virginia politician soon controlled some two hundred treasury offices, seventeen hundred post office ones, seventy court appointments, and the Norfolk Navy Yard. All such employees were assessed by the administration, a move endorsed by Grant, Ingalls, and Sherman, who—as Hayes's secretary of the treasury —had bitterly denounced all repudiators. Federal officials who failed to cooperate with Mahone were removed, even if they claimed to be faithful to the national party.

Blaine, however, was bitterly opposed. First of all, he detested repudiation. In addition, he was well aware that the Readjusters would support Arthur's renomination in 1884. When Blaine refused to relent on the issue, Arthur and Chandler suspected him of secretly backing Virginia's Bourbons.

Mahone served as a catalyst for general southern dissent, and many disaffected Democrats told him that they had finally found their leader. In Mississippi, in particular, Republican chances of cracking Bourbon control looked promising, because, in the 1881 governor's race, the Greenback party had pulled approximately 52,000 votes to the Democrats 77,700.

The GOP there, however, was split into white and black wings, each of which was antagonistic towards the other. The blacks had control of the party machinery and federal patronage, and they were strong in such cities as Jackson. In 1880, eight Negroes served in the Mississippi House; in 1882, the number was ten. Black leaders included James Hill, state collector of internal revenue; Blanche K. Bruce, former United States senator and registrar for the Treasury Department; and John R. Lynch, chairman of the Republican State Committee.

White Republicans, led by George C. McKee, resented black control. McKee, postmaster of Jackson and formerly a Union general and a congressman, suspected Negro leaders of selling out to the Democrats, in particular to Senators L. Q. C. Lamar and James Z. George. The black triumvirate, so McKee and other white Republicans believed, would persuade rank-and-file Negroes to support Democrats in state and local elections in return for receiving petty patronage. The whites pointed to Lamar's endorsement of Bruce's registry post as evidence of hidden collusion. McKee complained to Chandler that "Bruce & Lamar humbug the different administrations, and keep up negro role in the Rep party in order that fear of negro rule in the State may keep white men in the Dem. party." As a member of the Republican Congressional Committee in Washington commented, "Miss. is the hot-bed of faction. . . . the feuds are deep and deadly."[20] In fact, had black and white Republicans been united and had they been able to combine with Greenbackers and Independents (who controlled some counties), they could have taken Mississippi from the Democrats. Yet they were not able to do so.

It took an aggrieved Democratic politician, James R. Chalmers, to take advantage of this enmity. Chalmers, once a Confederate general and a slaveholder, had been one of the primary officers involved in the "Fort Pillow Massacre" in western Tennessee, an incident that took place in 1864 when southern troops wiped out a Negro regiment attempting to surrender. He had been elected to Congress for three successive terms as a regular

Democrat, when, in 1880, Lynch successfully contested his House seat. When the "Lamar legislature" changed Chalmers's district—a move designed to "punish" him for an insubordinate attitude—Chalmers accused Lamar of betrayal, left the Mississippi Democracy, and announced his candidacy as an Independent. His platform included the coinage of silver dollars, a free ballot, tariff protection for southern manufacturers, and an elective judiciary. Although one-fifth of Mississippi's small farms were located in his second district, Chalmers's platform made no mention of corporations, monopolies, and the agricultural lien law. He was by no means an agrarian spokesman.

By the fall of 1882, Chalmers had made overtures to the Republican party. Although the Arthur administration realized that it needed Hill's support at the next national convention, Washington party leaders found Chalmers's prospects so fair that they did not think they could ignore him. Envisioning him as the Mahone of Mississippi, they placed jobs and money at his disposal.

At this point, the black leaders Hill and Lynch, fearful of losing their patronage power, openly urged fusion with the Democrats. The Arthur administration, via Bruce, asked Mississippi Negroes to "give Chalmers a chance at the Bourbons," but the blacks still nominated their own candidate. As the components of the regular Republican party, they were still allowed some federal patronage, which they used to fight the Chalmers group.

In November 1882, Chalmers defeated his Democratic opponent for the House, but a fraudulent maneuver prevented him from taking his seat. Because of a clerical error in one county, 1,472 votes had been awarded to one "J. R. Chambless." This error enabled Mississippi's secretary of state to declare that Vannoy H. Manning, the Democratic incumbent, was the winner. Only in June 1884 did the House recognize Chalmers's title to a seat. All in all, however, Chalmers was quite pleased with the general results of the elections, for Mississippi had experienced its closest race since Reconstruction. One district had gone Independent, another had gone Republican, and certain counties in other districts had shown anti-Democratic majorities.

In South Carolina, the Arthur forces attempted to merge the Greenback party with dissident Democrats. Blacks here were not a political factor, having been already reduced to silence. When the Greenback party was first organized in South Carolina in 1880, it could only poll 3.5 percent of the vote. In 1882, over the protests of Republican blacks, the GOP state convention endorsed Greenbacker J. Hendrix McLane for governor. To McLane, the Democrats were "fossilized"; he urged "the Progressive element" of the state to back him.

Arthur quickly followed suit, although McLane's platform was hardly calculated to elicit more than token support from the GOP. It endorsed greenbacks as legal tender, condemned all government bonds, and denounced the lien law, "rings," "monopolies," and high railroad rates. A sop was thrown to the Republicans and blacks by denouncing South Carolina's rigid election rules, but in general the platform made no specific appeal to the state's Negroes. McLane, suspected of being in the pay of northern interests, was no Mahone, and his running mates were totally unknown to the public. South Carolina Democrats were not only suspicious of the Greenback platform but also of what they saw the Republicans standing for, and Conservatives defined any Independent as a Radical. Senator Wade Hampton declared that anyone "not with us, with the Democratic party, is a traitor to his State," while the *Charleston News and Courier* called the Greenbackers the Negro party.[21] In the 1882 elections, the Greenbackers won no contests, although they drew some Republican votes.

Then there was Georgia, where a budding Independent movement was attracting Republican attention. Its base lay among the poor farmers of the Piedmont, white yeomen who felt little kinship with the more prosperous lowland planters and who opposed the Bourbons' alliance with industry. As the mountain counties contained comparatively few blacks, it was hard to frighten white voters there. Moreover, the area had possessed Unionist sentiments before the Civil War.

A country doctor, William H. Felton, served as the Independent leader; his platform included cheap money, an honest ballot, and an end to the convict-lease system. Having experienced fraud in 1880, when he ran for a third term in the House, he sought cooperation with the Republicans. His wife, Rebecca, also politically prominent, was not afraid to denounce the Democrats for their "crusade against the colored race."[22] Felton was encouraged by General James Longstreet, who, in July 1881, came to Atlanta as federal marshal. Although one of Lee's chief lieutenants, Longstreet was a personal friend of Grant's and had cooperated with the Radicals after the war. During Reconstruction he had held several federal and state appointments in New Orleans, where he had become involved with some thoroughly corrupt politicians.

True, the Republican-Independent alliance was an extremely tenuous ut Arthur endorsed cooperation as a means of building up the ia GOP. The Republicans did not nominate a candidate for Congress; d, they backed Felton. Both Longstreet and the Feltons sought to have ressman Alexander H. Stephens, a former Whig and once the Con- acy's vice-president, as the coalition candidate for governor. A con- d old neurotic, Stephens was considered a dissenter, though he had er broken formally with the Democratic organization. In fact, in 1882, he accepted the nomination of the Bourbons, thereby striking a death blow to Independency.

In addition to Stephens's maneuver, the Republicans faced another problem: factionalism. Longstreet controlled only one wing of the party; William Pledger, a black editor, and A. E. Buck, a white carpetbagger, led another. Both groups vied for federal patronage. On August 2, 1882, the night before the state convention assembled, the black caucus tried to break into the white one. It met with violence, and Pledger was arrested. The factions held separate conventions, and only in September were their forces united enough to adopt a coalition slate.

The Bourbons swept the 1882 elections, and in November, they won complete control of the Georgia congressional delegation. Republican support for an Independent was the kiss of death, because the Democratic apostates were not able to shake off charges of party desertion, economic radicalism, and Negro domination. The victorious Stephens, an ailing man, died several months after the election.

As far as Alabama was concerned, Republicans had cooperated with Greenbackers and other anti-Bourbon groups that, in 1880, nominated the Reverend James M. Pickens for governor. His platform too was a reformist one: it denounced the leasing of convicts and advocated equitable taxation, less restrictive election laws, and a better school system. Yet, as black-belt Negroes had no incentive to vote for Pickens, party strength was limited to the Republican and Unionist northern part of the state, and the Bourbons won easily. Aid from the GOP continued during 1882, but the party disintegrated within two years. If there was any class struggle in the South, the voting behavior of Alabama's dirt farmers did not yet reflect it.

Other states offered variations on the same theme. In North Carolina, the Republican party remained formidable in the 1880s, drawing upon large numbers of both whites and blacks. An Independent movement emerged from Greenbackers and opponents of prohibition, although its platform covered a wide variety of proposals: equal rights for both races, local self-government, federal aid to education, and measures against monopolies. In the spring of 1882, Republicans endorsed the Independent ticket, urging every GOP supporter in the state to vote for it. In Texas, Congressman "Wash" Jones, an ardent Greenbacker, revolted against the regular Democratic organization. His platform called for free schools, honest elections, and encouragement of northern investment. Although Jones was obviously an economic radical, Arthur called upon the Republicans to merge their party with his. And in Arkansas, Arthur urged the GOP to fuse its forces with those of Rufus K. Garland, a Greenback leader in that state.

Some patterns varied, and not all administration efforts lay in recruiting inflationists and Independents. In Tennessee, for example, Arthur and Chandler favored those Democrats who were opposed to repudiation. They endorsed the "State-Credit" or "Whig" industrialist group, which had gained control of the legislature in 1880 but had lost it two years later. In Louisiana, the administration rejected an alliance with E. John Ellis, Democratic congressman and would-be Mahone. Chandler became convinced that the state's blacks were solidly behind the carpetbagger Senator William Pitt Kellogg and therefore backed him. As Kellogg's reputation was nothing if not unsavory, Arthur's move decreased Republican chances of winning the state. In Florida, Arthur did not back the Independents; instead, he supported a regular Republican for Congress.

In each of these states—North Carolina, Texas, Arkansas, Tennessee, Louisiana, and Florida—the cause of the president did poorly. And elsewhere, as we have seen, Chandler's strategy was not working. In the spring of 1882, the secretary of the navy had told Blaine that the GOP needed some twenty congressmen from the South in order to hold the House and that it could only obtain these by fostering coalitions with white Independents. And in April, at an informal meeting, the Republican National Committee had endorsed the strategy of a GOP-Independent alliance. But aside from Mahone's spectacular success in Virginia, the election of a single independent in North Carolina, and the pyrrhic victory of Chalmers in Mississippi, all was defeat.

Hopes remained, however, that Chandler's strategy might work in 1884. A Florida editor, in pleading with Chandler to stay at the helm, wrote: "I need not tell you that unless we can carry two or three Southern States in 1884, the Republicans will lose the next Presidency." The chairman of the Republican Executive Committee in North Carolina said, "The hope of our party is the division of the democracy in the Southern states."[23] In the summer of 1883, some Independents, including Mahone, Longstreet, and Chalmers, met in Washington, there to prepare for the coming state elections and to work towards Arthur's renomination the following year.

Yet the beginning of the end was already in sight, and it came, appropriately enough, in Virginia, where it had all begun. By 1883, Old Dominion Funders had launched a counteroffensive. True, they had acquiesced in the Riddleberger debt settlement, but they had protested against "Mahoneism," had played upon popular fears about blacks, and had formally used the label "Democrat." Some conservative Readjusters had joined them, believing that their program had been accomplished.

Real trouble came for the Republicans early in November, just a few days before the state elections, when a riot took place in Danville in which a white mob murdered several blacks. The governor called out the state militia, and order was soon restored. The incident might have been deliberately planned in order to permit the Democrats to clinch the election. As blacks held a good number of state offices in the town, Democrats raised the cry of "Africanization," even though Mahone had never placed Negroes in important state positions. Voters turned out for the election in large numbers, and the Democrats resorted to fraud in such areas as Danville, Charles City County, and Charlotte County.

When the results had been tallied, the Democrats had won nearly two-thirds of both houses. Virginia's new General Assembly accepted the Riddleberger debt settlement as well as increased appropriations for schools and charities, lower taxes, and more liberal suffrage. At the same time, it broke Mahone's hold on the patronage, reorganized congressional districts, and started filling positions by appointing Democrats. Blacks no longer played a significant role in Virginia politics.

As a result of the 1883 elections, Arthur knew that Virginia was lost. Hence he sought to rally the North by keeping the Danville incident, as well as crass intimidation in Mississippi, before the public. The president blamed Blaine and Whitelaw Reid's *New York Tribune* for the collapse of the Independents, claiming that opposition to the Readjusters had paved the way for the Bourbons. But he was enough of a realist that he no longer expected Mahone to carry the state. With Mahone's aid, Senator Sherman introduced a resolution to investigate "alleged election outrages in Virginia and Mississippi." Congress adopted it by a party vote, and the ensuing reports followed expected political lines: the Republican majority charged fraud; the Democratic minority claimed that reports of the incidents had been greatly exaggerated.

By 1884, the Readjusters were calling themselves "the Republican party of Virginia." In their platform, they denounced Bourbonism, sought a protective tariff, and endorsed the Arthur administration. Mahone headed its delegation to the national convention, and despite protests from the "straight-out" Republicans, his group was recognized as the official delegation of the state GOP. Mahone delegates held to the slogan "We are for Arthur because Arthur is for us," although they acquiesced in Blaine's nomination. In August, Blaine's advisers told the Readjusters that they would no longer be needed, and they received no aid from the Republican National Committee. Cleveland won the state by a vote of 145,497 to 139,356, and the Democrats gained eight out of ten congressional seats.

Mississippi was scarcely more promising, for from 1882 to 1884, Chalmers's group had accomplished little. Chandler saw to it that Chalmers received an appointment as a federal attorney, and he kept the patronage flowing, but the prolonged delay in Chalmers's seating hurt the nominee's prospects. In June 1883, Lynch attacked Chalmers at a meeting of the state

Republican Executive Committee, accusing him of working solely for "selfish ambitions." A year later, when the Republican state convention met, the white wing was given more voice in party matters; nevertheless, it still was forced to acknowledge black control. The convention confirmed this black domination, electing Lynch as permanent chairman, choosing Bruce to address the body, and selecting Lynch, Hill, and Bruce as delegates to the national convention.

In the 1884 elections, the Democrats won every district; Chalmers, who again ran for the House, carried only one county. Because his platform was vague and because he failed to court the vote of the small farmer, his revolt, as Albert D. Kirwan notes, was simply that of a rebellious personality fighting against a party dictatorship. Unlike Mahone, Chalmers lacked any critical issue—such as debt readjustment—that might have split the opposition. Although he was supported by an influential newspaper, he never attained the power of a senator or of a chairman of a state committee. He had no ally in the governor's chair, and he controlled relatively little of the patronage that would have been needed in order to build a political machine.[24]

Undoubtedly a fusion between blacks and Democrats had increased Chalmers's margin of defeat, and in some counties that had Negro majorities, the coalition was openly recognized. Democrats gave blacks a few low-paying jobs as well as representation on county boards of supervisors, but the fusion principle was limited to, at most, eight counties where whites constituted a small minority. Bourbons saw the system as gaining valuable objectives at low cost; Lynch found fusion the best bargain that Negroes could make.

Circumstances were little better in South Carolina, where, in 1884, conservative Democrats again trounced a Greenback-Republican coalition. The South Carolina Republican party remained torn by internal dissension and handicapped by poverty. Composed of little more than a corrupt political faction and a motley group of federal officeholders, it stood no chance of delivering electoral votes to the GOP.

In Georgia, wounds were slow in healing. Early in 1883, one Georgia politico wrote to tell Arthur that Longstreet's reluctance to work with blacks had damaged the party's chances in the recent state elections, and by 1884, Longstreet himself had given up hope of controlling the regular party organization. Arthur had seemed genuinely interested in cooperating with the Georgia Independents but realized that the regulars, not the Longstreet faction, offered the safest support at the coming national convention. In fact, after the convention was over, Arthur called for Longstreet's resignation, basing his demand on the findings of his attorney general. Although Longstreet personally was honest, ill health and general unfitness had made him an easy mark for corrupt and incompetent assistants. Within three years, the administration's hopes to capture the state of Georgia had been reduced to a petty victory at the national party assemblage.

Several points can be made concerning Arthur's strategy. First, while he energetically aided the southern Independent movements, he also sought to preserve regular Republican organizations. Knowing that the state GOPs controlled the delegates to the national convention, Chandler and Arthur sought to maximize their strength within the party. Second, in the early 1880s, Independents and Republicans made a surprisingly good showing, in Virginia in 1881 reaching over half the vote. In at least seven states, blacks gave the bulk of their votes to foes of the Democrats; in three other states, the returns were probably tampered with. In addition, except for South Carolina, a sixth to a third of the white voters had bolted the Democracy. One can argue, with justice, that the Arthur administration paid more attention to southern affairs than did that of any other president from Grant to Wilson. Though its assaults on the Democratic party had garnered few offices for the GOP, Republican efforts were more successful than has usually been realized.

Of course, the Republican cause had its drawbacks. One should note that the GOP's reputation for corruption and crass office-seeking was hard to live down. A leading black Republican and former acting governor of Louisiana, P. B. S. Pinchback, said of his own state party: "For corruption and venality, for dishonesty, it has not its equal anywhere on the face of God's earth. . . . from head to foot, from centre to circumference, there is not an honest drop of blood in it."[25] Louisiana's Senator William Pitt Kellogg, for example, had been indicted in the star-route frauds. And if one looks at the Louisiana delegation to the 1884 convention, what does one see?—a surveyor, a deputy surveyor, a naval officer, a customhouse clerk, two customs inspectors, a postmaster, two revenue collectors, a deputy collector, a subtreasurer, a district attorney, a member of Congress (Kellogg), and a state senator. Only one delegate was not on the public payroll, which caused the *Nation* to muse that when the group got to Chicago, "there will be few white Republicans left in Louisiana."[26]

Then there is the general role that racial turmoil has so often played in southern politics. The Danville case was not an isolated one. In South Carolina alone, Chandler learned about the shooting of four blacks in cold blood, the firing upon of a secret service man, and the hanging of a black just before the 1882 election. The United States attorney for South Carolina sent Chandler a forty-eight-page report on election violations, sorry spectacles that included beatings, knifings, and shootings.

And even within Republican ranks, the administration's southern policy faced continual attacks. Fiscal conservatives opposed any alliance that included debt repudiators and inflationists; civil-service reformers deplored Mahone's use of the patronage; Union veterans could not envision former Confederates in the Grand Old Party; and Blaine's partisans feared that a large body of southern officeholders might swing the 1884 convention to Arthur. The GOP was too divided to put up a united front, much less to co-opt Greenbackers and Independents.

Some blacks found Arthur neglecting them. Two militant editors, T. Thomas Fortune of the *New York Age* and W. Calvin Chase of the *Washington Bee*, castigated the administration for courting dissident Democrats. A national convention of Negroes, held in Louisville in September 1883, hotly debated a resolution endorsing the GOP, but the measure was never voted upon. Frederick Douglass called himself "an uneasy Republican," declaring that "if the Republican party cannot stand a demand for justice and fair play, it ought to go down." (Douglass later commented, in referring to Arthur, that "there is nothing in his career as President of the U. S. that proves him to have had any sympathy with the oppressed colored people of the South.")[27] In 1884, a similar convention, meeting at Pittsburgh, refused to back any presidential candidate.

Some historians, such as Rayford W. Logan, claim that Arthur was reticent concerning blacks. The president, Logan writes, made no reference to blacks in his inaugural address, spoke only in terms of education in his annual messages, and was silent concerning such discrimination as the Eight-Box Ballot Law of South Carolina.[28] Arthur himself told a delegation of white Republicans from Georgia that he found white officeholders more helpful to the party; Southern blacks, he said, excelled only in "office begging." Another historian, Stanley Hirshson, believes that Arthur revealed his indifference when the Supreme Court abrogated the Civil Rights Act of 1875. Republicans in Congress introduced five new bills to replace the one that had been declared unconstitutional, but the president offered little support for any of them, and hence the proposals were defeated.[29]

The critics made another point—namely, that blacks received far less than their share of civil-service jobs. Though prominent Negroes held certain patronage posts—P. B. S. Pinchback became surveyor of the port of New Orleans, for example—most blacks still remained in the most menial of positions. In the Department of the Interior, for instance, only a handful of blacks held posts that paid over one thousand dollars a year; the bulk of them—charwomen, messengers, and laborers—received fifteen dollars per month.

Now, however, several historians challenge the indictment against Arthur. Thomas C. Reeves notes that the president—an abolitionist before the Civil War—made significant gestures of sympathy, such as contributing funds to a Negro church and personally awarding diplomas at a black high school in Washington. More important, when the Supreme Court knocked down the 1875 Civil Rights Act, Arthur did assure Congress that he would unhesitatingly support any "right, privilege and immunity of citizenship" that it might pass.[30] In addition, he called for federal aid to education, with particular stress upon the need to combat Negro illiteracy.

Another historian, J. Morgan Kousser, finds administration opportunism exaggerated, claiming that every significant Independent candidate supported Negro suffrage. In addition, general public education, a cardinal plank in the Independent platform, would have been bound to aid poor blacks as well as poor whites. Indeed, Republican policy, Kousser writes, "promised additional congressional and electoral votes for the national GOP, political equality and education for the blacks, office for any white Southern Democrat disgruntled by a factional dispute, and a two-party system for the South as a whole."[31]

Blacks in turn gave Arthur real support. Almost every Negro newspaper in the country endorsed the administration's southern policy. Out of 120 black journals, only 2—the *New York Age* and the *Washington Bee*—believed that blacks should form their own party, and both Fortune and Chase, their respective editors, backed Blaine in 1884. Douglass and Fortune also endorsed the Mahone movement, the latter claiming that the Readjusters had put an end to a long-time "hell for blacks." At no time did Douglass encourage Negroes to leave Republican ranks; in fact, in 1884, he accused Mugwump defectors of betraying "the cause of liberty itself."[32]

Yet, despite black efforts and despite the sympathy of a failing president, real progress would have to wait for half a century. Power in the South was destined to remain in the hands of the whites and of the Democratic party. If Arthur wanted to leave his office with any sense of accomplishment, he would have to move in quite different directions.

8

★ ★ ★ ★ ★

MR. FRELINGHUYSEN'S
INHERITANCE

The direction that might hold the most promise for Arthur was foreign policy. At the time of the assassination crisis and immediately thereafter, the State Department faced several problems. William Henry Trescot was attempting to mediate between Chile and Peru, thereby seeking to remedy the blundering statescraft of Hurlbut and Kilpatrick. Blaine sought to promote a Pan-American conference that, so he hoped, might reduce tension between the two warring nations and between Guatemala and Mexico as well. The secretary also tried to terminate the Clayton-Bulwer Treaty, which gave Britain joint control with the United States over any isthmian canal. Putting an end to French and German discrimination against American pork was another item on Blaine's agenda, as were efforts to free Irish-American prisoners. As far as other parts of the world were concerned, Commodore Shufeldt was trying to arrange a commercial treaty with the king of Korea, and Consul Robinson had completed a trade agreement with the Hovas of Madagascar.

Arthur was well aware that Blaine's diplomacy was under fire but at first kept him in office. The secretary, because of his White House aspirations, sought to free himself for future campaigning, but Arthur persuaded him to remain until Congress convened. During this time, the president gave him virtually a free hand. Arthur was—quite understandably—concerned with party unity. In addition, the two men were more friendly than were many a Half-Breed and Stalwart, for Blaine, while a senator, had defended Arthur's administration of the New York Customhouse.

Other Republicans, particularly among the Stalwarts, wanted Blaine removed immediately. In late October, acting upon the suggestion of Grant, Arthur asked Frederick Theodore Frelinghuysen to become secretary of state, and the sixty-four-year-old attorney was confirmed by the Senate a month later. Blaine's successor was a man of quite different temperament and background. The Maine politician had, to some degree, been a parvenu, the first in his family to achieve national political prominence; Frelinghuysen was merely the latest of a long line of public servants. Blaine was flamboyant, a man who—in the words of Russell H. Bastert—"loved to flex his muscles in public"; Frelinghuysen was quiet and conservative in temperament and had unquestioned integrity.[1] Even the focus of their policies diverged: Blaine stressed national prestige; Frelinghuysen emphasized markets.

The new secretary came from Dutch background. One ancestor played a major part in the Great Awakening; another served as Clay's running mate in 1844. Frelinghuysen was born in Millstone, New Jersey, in 1817, graduated from Rutgers, and became a leading attorney whose clients included the New Jersey Central Railroad. He first became nationally prominent in 1866, when New Jersey's governor appointed him United States senator, a position he held until 1877. Always a Stalwart partisan, Frelinghuysen backed the impeachment of Johnson, promoted Grant's scheme to annex Santo Domingo, and was part of the commission that in 1876 declared Hayes legally elected. Like many other Stalwarts, he never believed the charges of corruption that were levied against the Grant administration. Indeed, he had hoped that Grant would again be president in 1881, and he was in turn a Grant protégé.

Frelinghuysen, however, was never a party hack. A devout and prominent layman in the Dutch Reformed denomination, he saw both domestic and foreign policy in terms of religious stewardship. He said in 1866, "My life must run the mission that God intended it, and until God recalls it," and his sentiments were entirely sincere.[2] His most recent biographer stresses Frelinghuysen's persistent efforts to win equality for the freedman, which culminated in his fostering the passage of Charles Sumner's Civil Rights Bill of 1875.[3]

Because he was an ill man, Frelinghuysen at first hesitated to accept the appointment. Arthur assured him (incorrectly, it turned out) that he would primarily be dealing with patronage matters and that career diplomat John Chandler Bancroft Davis, the new first assistant secretary of state, would bear the burdens of policy-making.

Davis's influence was felt immediately. He had long been close to Hamilton Fish, Grant's able secretary of state, who continually warned him against Blaine's policies. Upon reading the State Department's dispatches from Peru and Chile, Davis suspected "guano diplomacy" and found that America was "on the highway to war for the benefit of about as nasty a set of people as ever gathered about a Washington Dept."[4] Frelinghuysen too saw only scandal ahead. The threats to Chile embodied in Blaine's instructions to Trescot, so Frelinghuysen believed, would further embroil the United States. Similarly, Blaine's overtures to Brazil and Argentina might justifiably leave the nation open to charges of partiality. The new secretary consulted with Arthur, then ordered what Davis called "an instant halt and about face."[5]

The final phase of United States involvement in the War of the Pacific commenced early in January 1882, when Frelinghuysen began cabling Trescot. The United States, said the secretary, could extend its good offices immediately; nevertheless, it had no intention of dictating terms, much less of severing relations with Chile. He also told Trescot not to visit Buenos Aires on his way home and informed him that Arthur was reconsidering the whole matter of a peace conference. True, Frelinghuysen considered Chile's demands exorbitant, particularly its demands for a high indemnity, the cession of Tarapacá, and the ten-year's occupation of Tacna, Arica, and the Lobos Islands. But by refusing to apply Blaine's solution of creating general pressure on Latin America, he blunted what might have been the only real diplomatic weapon the United States possessed. Both Frelinghuysen and Davis were acting in the firm, if mistaken, belief that "guano interests" were behind Blaine's moves; therefore, they attempted to remove the new Arthur administration from any taint. Even had Trescot's trip and an inter-American conference been able to bring peace, the two men did not see them as worth the political risk.

Unaware of the sudden shift in policy, Trescot and Walker Blaine, the son of Frelinghuysen's predecessor, had blithely continued on their journey. After being feted in Callao and Lima by Peruvians who mistakenly saw the United States as their deliverer, the two diplomats arrived at Santiago on January 7. Chile's foreign minister, José M. Balmaceda, attempted to assure the envoys that the arrest of Calderón had by no means been intended as an insult to the United States.

For the most part, however, the new envoys found nothing but embarrassment. Minister Hurlbut, working with characteristic incompetency, had prematurely issued the conference invitation to Peru, thereby forcing Trescot to deliver one immediately to Chile. Yet when Trescot saw Balmaceda on January 31, the foreign minister told him that the United States had withdrawn the invitation three weeks earlier. In addition,

Balmaceda informed Trescot that Frelinghuysen had published the instructions that Blaine had sent to him. Trescot experienced even more surprises, for he learned that new orders, which the envoy himself had not yet received, now called for strict United States neutrality. It was rare to see a diplomat so crudely undercut by his superiors.

In March 1882, Trescot, aware that he was appearing both ineffective and foolish, wrote Davis, "Get me home at the earliest practicable moment. I can't stand this much longer."[6] The publication of confidential communications, complained the special envoy, had made Chile intransigent. However, he stoically accepted Frelinghuysen's orders to remain in Latin America, and he continued to work for negotiation. Finally, in the middle of May, Trescot and the young Blaine started back to the United States, and three weeks later, Trescot told Frelinghuysen that Peru would have to give up Tarapacá. He then came down slightly on the side of the Peruvians, declaring that total indifference on the part of the United States would only encourage European intervention.

While Trescot was continuing his abortive peace mission, Blaine was attempting to fight back. In a *Washington Post* interview dated January 30, 1882, and in a public letter to President Arthur published within the week, Blaine accused Frelinghuysen not only of using Trescot for a "fool's errand" but of truckling to European monarchies and acquiescing in the destruction of Peru. He also claimed, probably incorrectly, that the martyred Garfield had warmly approved the peace conference and asserted, probably correctly, that Arthur had originally endorsed the project. Soon Blaine was stressing commercial advantages, thus making it appear that export imperatives had always been a primary consideration. (The text of his original invitations had made no references to trade.) He attacked "the English bondholders and speculators" who supposedly had furnished "the money and the guns and the iron-clads that destroyed Peru"; at one point he called the conflict "an English war on Peru, with Chili (*sic*) as the instrument."[7]

In his comments on Britain, Blaine had once again revealed his genius for oversimplification. He had long feared that England would capture the markets of Latin America, thereby preventing United States penetration. The *Nation*, however, pointed out that the United States only exported $109,696 worth of goods to Peru in 1881; the loss of this sum, it claimed, would resemble the "failure of a dry-goods store in Bangor, Me."[8] As far as Chile was concerned, British steamship lines were doing a thriving business in Valparaiso, British merchants were faring well in Santiago, and British shipyards were building new warships for the Chilean navy. Chile in turn attempted to play off Britain against the United States by taking such actions as exploiting Hurlbut's efforts to gain the Chimbote lease. Yet the British Foreign Office never did consider actively intervening, and England sold arms freely to whatever side could pay for them. Although British capital was closely tied to Chilean finance and although the war strengthened British influence, the conflict—contrary to the claims made by Mr. Blaine—was by no means "an English war."

After the immediate furor over Blaine's policies and the Trescot mission had died down, the rest was anticlimatic. On April 18, Arthur asked Congress to advise him as to whether the proposed Pan-American conference should be held. When Congress responded with characteristic apathy, Frelinghuysen withdrew the invitations, even though nine countries had already accepted. The secretary also sent a new set of diplomats to the warring nations. Cornelius A. Logan, then minister to Guatemala, was moved to Chile, and James R. Partridge, a Maryland lawyer, was sent to Peru. Logan, once a practicing physician and a cousin of the Stalwart senator from Illinois, had represented the United States in Chile during Grant's regime. Partridge had served as minister to a host of Latin American nations, including Venezuela and Brazil.

Washington's continual efforts to make Chile moderate its demands proved futile. The peace efforts of both men dragged on for a good many months but eventually proved unsuccessful. As had happened with Kilpatrick and Hurlbut, the diplomats fell out, and early in 1883, Partridge's unauthorized maneuvering among European diplomats stationed at Lima forced Frelinghuysen to recall him. President Arthur, in his annual message dated December 12, 1882, attacked Chilean intransigency; he maintained, however, that any dictated peace would have to "be supplemented by the armies and navies of the United States. Such interference would almost inevitably lead to the establishment of a protectorate—a result utterly at odds with our past policy, injurious to our present interests, and full of embarrassments for the future."[9] Peru finally knew, and knew unmistakably, that the United States would not come to her aid.

Finally, it was a Peruvian general, Miguel Iglesias, who assumed control of his nation and then made peace with Chile. In the Treaty of Ancón, made in October 1883, Tarapacá was ceded outright, and Chile was given permission to occupy the provinces of Tacna and Arica for ten years. At the end of that time, there would be a plebiscite to determine the fate of the occupied territory; the country that retained permanent possession would have to pay the other nation $10 million. Chile had achieved all her war aims, including domination of the most valuable part of Peru—some 250 miles of valuable coastline. And there was nothing the United States could do about it. Only in 1929 was Tacna, and Tacna alone, returned to Peru.

American diplomacy, in short, had been a total failure. Arthur uncritically permitted Blaine to initiate both the Trescot mission and the peace conference, thereby finding himself in the embarrassing position of having to reverse his policies within two weeks. Frelinghuysen also bears much responsibility. Had he not so drastically and irresponsibly undercut the Trescot mission, he could have speeded up the peacemaking process. True, Arthur's eventual firmness did stifle Peru's last hope for American intervention and indirectly forced it to the conference table. Nonetheless, aside from a belated policy of neutrality, the United States had not contributed much towards ending the conflict. There was little in the nation's response to the War of the Pacific to which it could point with pride.

Another change was soon in order, this one centering on the Mexican-Guatemalan dispute. As soon as the State Department changed hands, Frelinghuysen and Davis turned down a treaty that had been jointly proposed by Guatemala, Honduras, and El Salvador. Under its terms, the United States would have offered the three countries protection from outside attack. In return, it would have had the right to station troops and occupy ports in those countries.

In addition, Frelinghuysen soon made it clear that Blaine's Pan-American conference would not be held, and in March 1882, he told Mexico's minister that he did not intend to force mediation. Informally, President Arthur made it clear to Grant, a man close to the Mexican government, that United States policy had shifted radically. In May, the Guatemalan foreign minister, Lorenzo Montúfar, offered low tariffs and rights to build a canal, in return for United States protection. Frelinghuysen refused, as he did when Montúfar asked the United States to assume all of Guatemala's negotiations with Mexico. Even a trip to Washington by Barrios himself could not sway the Arthur administration. Blaine's erstwhile protégé, Guatemala, was clearly on its own.

Once Guatemala realized that it could not draw upon United States support, the dispute was quickly settled. In September, the two nations signed a treaty calling for direct negotiation over the disputed boundary, and until 1895, the question was dropped. Blaine and Logan, by not making the limits of United States commitment clear at the outset, had created a highly explosive situation. Frelinghuysen's cautious policy turned out to be the wise one.

A continuity of Blaine's policies, however, was shown in the new administration's policy concerning an isthmian canal. The United States was still trying to alter the Clayton-Bulwer Treaty, but with little success. Frelinghuysen, in fact, went even further than Blaine had gone, suggesting total abrogation. In a letter sent to Minister Lowell on May 8, 1882, the secretary claimed that the 1850 agreement never had applied to Panama. Joint rights, he continued, were calculated to "breed dissension." Therefore, he endorsed a United States protectorate over any canal built across the isthmus. In brief, so Frelinghuysen maintained, the thirty-two-year-old treaty was no longer binding.

Lord Granville, as usual, replied patiently, quoting documents over twenty-five years old in order to establish that the agreement applied to all isthmian routes. He saw no reason to surrender significant treaty rights on demand, and similar notes that Frelinghuysen sent to him in May and November of 1883 could not persuade him. Only nineteen years later would the United States, through the diplomacy of John Hay, fulfill the goals of Frelinghuysen and Blaine by securing recognition for American control of any canal across the isthmus.

Frelinghuysen's concern over the Clayton-Bulwer Treaty was just the beginning. Because of the efforts of the Frenchman de Lesseps to establish a Panama route and because of the fear of possible penetration by Chile or Britain, the Arthur administration focused increasingly upon a route in Nicaragua. In 1880, the Maritime Canal Company, organized by Rear Admiral Daniel Ammen and navy Captain Seth L. Phelps, had obtained a concession from the Nicaraguan government. Supported by such luminaries as Generals Grant and McClellan, as well as by financier Levi P. Morton, the company intended first to follow the San Juan River, then cross Lake Nicaragua, and finally pierce the steep mountains along the Pacific Coast. The cost, so the promoters promised, would only come to $93,000.

In December 1881, Senator John F. Miller introduced a bill providing for the incorporation of this enterprise as well as for a government guarantee of its profits. Miller's bill was reported favorably by the Senate Foreign Relations Committee and, thanks to the efforts of Representative Kasson, by the House Foreign Affairs Committee as well. Congress adjourned, however, before it could vote, and the bill remained dormant in subsequent sessions.

Other projects had even less backing, such as the proposal made by engineer James B. Eads, who advocated a ship-railway across the Mexican territory of Tehuantepec. Some Americans were more cautious, hoping first to clarify the status of the Clayton-Bulwer Treaty. Others sought to allocate such sums for pork-barrel projects. Northern Democrats feared that the precedent of granting a canal "bounty" might be used to foster ship subsidies, which in turn would deplete the treasury and lead to high tariffs.

Frelinghuysen himself was at first suspicious of the Nicaraguan project. It would bestow too much power upon private individuals, he believed, while failing both to exclude European investment and to guarantee neutrality in wartime. Yet, suspecting that such a concession might temporarily keep Europe out of the isthmus, the secretary did not object when, in May 1882, Nicaragua extended the Maritime Canal Company's concession for two and a half years. Phelps's company continued to make little progress, and by 1884, it became all too clear that it would not be able to honor Nicaragua's conditions. Now the Arthur administration, fearing that the Maritime Canal Company was about to seek capital in Europe, attempted to purchase the firm itself. In April 1884, Frelinghuysen offered Phelps a flat price of $12,000 plus 1.2 percent of the construction cost of the canal.

The secretary had been making other preparations as well. Less than two months earlier, Frelinghuysen had instructed Henry C. Hall, United States minister to Central America, to negotiate for canal rights as well as for ownership of the waters and islands of Lake Nicaragua. In return, the United States promised Nicaragua a defensive alliance, one-fourth of the toll profits, and civil jurisdiction over the canal strip.

Nicaragua's president, Adán Cárdenas, presented a counteroffer, one that retained the defensive alliance with the United States while including a 3 percent guarantee for the private Maritime Canal Company and permission, if war threatened, for the United States to occupy the canal strip temporarily. (Nicaragua's junta of notables rejected the last point.) Frelinghuysen then offered $5 million for the needed shoreline; but his offer was refused, and in May, discouraged American diplomats suspended the negotiations.

After much subsequent bargaining and after congressmen and journalists had accused the hapless Frelinghuysen of bribing Nicaraguan leaders, Nicaragua finally came to terms. The final treaty, signed on December 1, 1884, gave the United States co-ownership over a two-and-one-half-mile strip for a canal; Nicaragua would retain civil jurisdiction. According to this agreement, the defensive alliance would be continued, but the wartime rights of the United States would not be defined. Nicaragua would gain equal representation on a six-man board of directors, as well as one-third of the net profits. In addition, the United States promised to give Nicaragua a $4 million loan for public works, the money to be paid out of canal receipts. As Alice Felt Tyler has noted, the treaty established a protectorate over Nicaragua, "a step far in advance of any which Mr. Blaine had given any evidence of willingness or desire to take."[10] It was indeed an unprecedented act.

Some of the negotiations involved overt corruption. On the insistence of Nicaragua's former President Lorenzo Zavala, the United States agreed to purchase the steamboat rights owned by Zavala's private secretary. Hence, the official terms of the treaty permitted Nicaragua's leaders to sell land and second-hand concessions. "If she had sold her virtue," writes Pletcher, "she had obtained a good price for it."[11]

Soon the United States became involved in heated debate, particularly after December 18, when the *New York Tribune* published a pirated text of the treaty. If some supporters, such as Frelinghuysen himself, must have had to hold their noses, they found the commercial advantages particularly welcome during a time of economic recession. Frelinghuysen went so far as to tell the Senate Foreign Relations Committee that the Clayton-Bulwer Treaty had "lapsed by neglect." And in asserting that the funds allocated to Nicaragua had involved no bribes, he cited Zavala as his authority! In the endorsement that Arthur submitted to the Senate on December 10, he stressed that the treaty would result in closer ties between California and the East as well as giving the United States access to Latin America's west coast ("a natural market") and to the Far East. "Our vessels and productions," he said, "will enter upon the world's competitive field with a decided advantage, of which they will avail themselves."[12]

Opponents of the treaty offered a variety of objections: Britain and France would get the most benefit, perhaps being able to dominate Pacific commerce and put an end to America's monopoly of transcontinental railroad traffic; the canal would never make substantial profits; the cost, estimated as high as $150 million, would far outweigh any advantage; it would result in a confrontation with Great Britain. Holding land in a foreign country, so critics claimed, was unconstitutional; so were efforts to turn Nicaragua into a United States "colony." Senator Bayard, who led the Democratic opposition, thought that all parts of the Clayton-Bulwer Treaty were still valid. Blaine's unsigned editorials for the *New York Tribune* branded the proposed loan as a "corruption fund."

When the Senate decided on January 29, the bill was nine votes short of the two-thirds needed for ratification. With the exception of Democratic members on the Foreign Relations Committee, only one Democrat voted for the agreement. Its Republican sponsorship, at a time when the Democrats controlled both the incoming presidency and the House, harmed its passage. So did the sudden and sweeping responsibilities for the construction, operation, and defense of such a project. Foreign policy was still determined by partisan considerations and an insular ideology.

Soon after he entered the White House, Cleveland withdrew the treaty. Any "offensive and defensive alliance for its protection," he commented, would go "beyond the scope of our national polity or present means."[13] For the time being, the government and people of the United States would remain relatively complacent about the isthmus.

True, one could say that the groping policy makers were paving the way for more active and systematic intervention and that by 1900, the nation would have a much clearer grasp both of its interests in Latin America and of the means that it could use in order to secure them. During the presidencies of Garfield and Arthur, however, Americans as a whole perceived few major interests in the area, and neither the stormy and blustering diplomacy of Blaine nor the more purposeful statesmanship of Frelinghuysen could make them change their mind. For the time being, a consistent and potent Latin American diplomacy would remain stillborn.

In Europe, the Arthur administration occasionally met with more success, but not concerning the battle over pork. In November 1883, President Jules Grévy of France withdrew the bans that had been imposed two years before. Nevertheless, members of the Chamber of Deputies, voting by a decided majority, set aside his action until they could devise their own inspection system, a policy totally unacceptable to the United States. One of the French arguments was ingenious: a deputy noted that trichinosis could be communicated to French hogs if they ate rats that had become infected by American pork!

The news from Germany was little better. On March 6, 1882, it had extended its ban to include virtually all United States meat products. Germany's free-trade liberals wanted to provide lower meat prices for the German poor, and its merchants feared that their thriving export trade was doomed. Yet protests had no effect, and American meat shipments were cut many fold. Rudolf Virchow, an eminent German pathologist, called the government's prohibition "unjustifiable"; he could attribute few cases of trichinosis to American pork. In fact, it was common knowledge that most deaths caused by trichinosis came from meat freshly slaughtered in Russia, Hungary, or Germany itself. Bismarck confessed his real motive: to protect Germany's Junker—the so-called pillar of the monarchy—from ruin.

Many Americans were furious. Meat packer Philip D. Armour claimed that the German ban would unquestionably cause "disaster to the farming interests of Illinois and the Northwest." Midwestern farmers, packing companies, and swine producers sought retaliation; they even wanted to go so far as to ban the importation of French and German wines. The *New York Herald* spoke in terms of "avenging the American hog."[14]

One economic group, the National Livestock Association, called, in 1883, for "a rigid system of inspection of all meat products for foreign export . . . the expense . . . to be borne by the exporter."[15] Hence, American ministers and consuls, who backed the inspection idea almost to a man, had found some surprising allies within the business community.

President Arthur wanted to make his own investigation, and on February 15, 1883, he informed Germany that he would soon appoint an impartial commission to examine American packing plants. He also invited the Germans to send over their own inspection group, but responding in July, the German government sent its refusal. The United States could not, said Germany with obvious casuistry, obligate it to accept the judgment of a foreign country.

Arthur's commission, which consisted of representatives of the meat industry and the federal government, came up with ambivalent findings. It declared that existing inspection methods were inadequate; in fact, the United States might still be exporting diseased meat. The report, claimed Frelinghuysen, proved conclusively that United States meat was not transmitting cholera; a judgment regarding the possibility that trichinosis was being transmitted would have to await further study. In May 1884, Congress created the Bureau of Animal Husbandry. Although the new agency ultimately effected an improvement in the quality of American meat, it did not reduce the demands for retaliation.

Despite Germany's continued affronts, both Arthur and Frelinghuysen remained extremely cautious about additional pressure. In December 1883, Arthur endorsed "equitable retaliation," but he did so without specifically alluding to the German ban. Frelinghuysen realized that the United States lacked effective weapons; Europe, on the other hand, had the power to exclude all American manufactured goods. The secretary regarded the mere consideration of retaliatory legislation a sufficient threat. France's temporary retreat of November 1883, he believed, could well serve as precedent for ending such bans everywhere. When the French reaffirmed their prohibition, the *Chicago Tribune* commented: "Having been kicked, it is time to kick back."[16] American farmers continued to be dissatisfied with the administration's policy, and Arthur's apparent lethargy in regard to it undoubtedly contributed to Cleveland's victory.

The activities of the United States minister to Germany, Aaron A. Sargent, only increased friction between the two nations. A peppery machine politician from California, Sargent showed little deference to Bismarck, freely consulted with the Liberal opposition on the pork issue, and threatened that the United States would retaliate. Early in 1884, he presented to the German Foreign Office a provocative House resolution, one that mourned the death of the German Liberal leader Eduard Lasker. Bismarck not only refused to accept it; he even went so far as to claim that Sargent's continued service was inconsistent with the Reich's national dignity. When Sargent resigned in April, Frelinghuysen replaced him with the far more tactful John A. Kasson, former congressman from Iowa and minister to Austria. The new emissary had only been in Germany a few weeks when he was able to report that he had the situation well in hand.

Germany continued to ban United States pork until the Harrison administration, when, in 1891, Congress passed an act making meat inspection compulsory. American pork again entered Germany. On one level, United States policy had been a failure; Frelinghuysen was not able to get either the French or the Germans to rescind their bans. On another, however, it was an able holding action. Although Great Britain began to fear the entry of other American exports, such as wheat, it did not retaliate by excluding pork or manufactured goods. In a time of recession, diplomatic caution had helped to keep some markets open.

Frelinghuysen inherited another source of friction, the matter of Irish-American prisoners. The issue was put graphically by one Brooklyn congressman who, noting the current pork dispute with Europe, said, "Oh, that we only had as much . . . protection given to a live American citizen as there (is) given to a dead Cincinnati hog!"[17] By this time the ministry of William E. Gladstone had come to realize that only some sort of accommodation with Parnell could prevent the continued growth of Irish extremism. On April 2, 1882, the Gladstone government, acting more from the prime minister's own concerns than from any United States pressure, quietly released the prisoners, and by the following day, all but three of those who had been interned had been freed.

Yet it was the secretary of state himself who would not let the matter die. On April 25, Frelinghuysen admitted that naturalized Americans who were living in the British Isles had to expect to obey British laws. He denied, however, that Britain had given "sufficient reason why an American citizen should remain incarcerated without accusation, without chance of trial, without opportunity for release."[18] By unfavorably contrasting British liberties to those of the United States, he implicitly criticized the Coercion Act itself.

Though the last Irish-American prisoner had gained his liberty some days before October 1882, the time that the Coercion Act expired, rapprochement with Britain was still not secure. On May 6, 1882, in Dublin's Phoenix Park, a band of Irish terrorists knifed and killed two high British officials. As a result of the murders, the British passed the Prevention of Crime Act. This law replaced jury trials with judicial tribunals and gave broad search powers to the authorities. Frelinghuysen accused the British of violating traditional civil liberties: "It is hardly to be expected," he wrote to Lowell, "that an Irish-American citizen, however innocent he might be in act and intention, should consider his person or his property safe in that country."[19]

There was a related issue, one that did not deal with the status of Irish-Americans but with the smuggling of explosives. Irish-American publicists had been advertising their intentions to buy dynamite and subsidize terrorism in England. Such Irish-American newspapers as the *United Irishman* and the *Irish World* advocated widespread use of arson, encouraged the assassination of the Prince of Wales and Gladstone, and claimed responsibility for various explosions that had already occurred. One editor, O'Donovan Rossa, boasted that he would strike Britain "in five or six different places in one night."[20]

The United States, so it appeared, was actually aiding some rebels. In 1881, three weeks after two Fenians had tried to blow up the town hall of Liverpool, British police searched a steamship arriving from Boston and found six detonating machines. In addition, the British chargé in Washington called Secretary Blaine's attention to a torpedo ship that the Fenians were building in New York. Soon even the most pro-Irish partisans became embarrassed. Members of the New York Legislature unanimously censured the terrorists; United States marshals in New York aided British consular officials in searching ships as they arrived from Ireland.

The controversy was still far from over. After a bombing of the House of Commons on the evening of March 15, 1883, the British immediately renewed their protests. Lionel S. Sackville-West, England's minister to the United States, demanded the suppression of the Irish-American press. Frelinghuysen replied, claiming that the American government had no legal power to prohibit the expression of unfriendly sentiment.

The administration was more responsive in February 1884, when it learned that terrorists had used American-made bombs in their effort to dynamite English railroad stations. Reacting to British protests, Arthur ordered federal marshals to concentrate upon preventing such traffic in munitions. His commands probably could not accomplish much, for an individual could easily sail to Britain with a can of nitroglycerine in his pocket; but they did reveal American sympathies.

Even after the election of 1884, the Irish issue was not over. On January 24, 1885, two dynamite bombs partially wrecked the House of Commons. Senator Edmunds introduced a bill calling for heavy penalties against terrorists, and Senator Bayard sought a resolution of regret and sympathy. The House as a whole demanded information on the United States' involvement. Although leading Irish-Americans held a public protest in Washington and although Edmunds's bill died in committee, the power of Ireland's sympathizers grew much weaker.

Although the pork dispute was rooted in genuine economic grievance, because it could affect American markets in times of depression, the Irish issue was transparently political. To his credit, Blaine, while in office, softpedaled the dispute. Frelinghuysen, on the other hand, abandoned his usual caution, going out of his way to take a strident position and one that did little to ease tensions. The most effective and thoughtful American statesman involved in the dispute, James Russell Lowell, was often the most ignored, and all of the American principals were fortunate that Britain, for reasons that were not connected with United States pressure, desired to end the quarrel.

The Arthur government not only engaged in controversies with Germany and Britain but with African countries as well. Diplomatic and consular officials had been continually pushing for a more aggressive commercial policy. Frederick A. Mathews, American consul at Tangiers, warned that British and French steamship lines had severely cut into American trade, and similar complaints came from places as diverse as Egypt, the Canary Islands, Liberia, and Sierra Leone. Frelinghuysen not only wanted to crack the European carrying trade; he also looked to the day when commerce with the Boers of South Africa would increase many fold. The secretary of state had more reason to look with satisfaction on the east coast of Africa. The United States already dominated the commerce of the area, with the exception of the island of Zanzibar; and almost half of Zanzibar's trade was with America.

The attention of the administration was particularly focused on the west coast of Africa, especially on the Republic of Liberia. For over a quarter of a century, Liberia had been involved in a boundary dispute with the British colony of Sierra Leone, one concerning a narrow strip of land that stretched over twenty miles of coast and reached forty-five miles inland. On March 20, 1882, a British gunboat flotilla appeared in Monrovia, there to enforce the claims of its ward. The American Colonization Society, which represented Liberia in Washington, asked the State Department to come to Liberia's defense. The American minister resident in Monrovia concurred, reporting that the British were pressing Liberia to give up valuable territory to which the British had no right. Bancroft Davis, acting as secretary while Frelinghuysen was ill, informed the British Foreign Office that the United States would view "with positive disfavor the compulsory alienation of territory."[21] Besides, he added, there were other ways of compensating British claimants. Frelinghuysen's own solution for Liberia's boundary dispute was simple: persuade both the Congress and the American Colonization Society to buy off the British claims and thus bloc further British expansion there.

The solution, however, was not all that easy. Lowell reported from London that the Liberians had originally seized the disputed area. In addition, so the American minister concluded, Liberia would not be able effectively to manage more territory; a boundary on the Mano River would be the best compromise. If either country refused to allow the United States to mediate the quarrel on such a basis, the United States should withdraw its offer and leave the hapless Liberians to their own resources. Frelinghuysen soon concurred, but by that time, both parties had made such a settlement themselves. The United States had been saved the embarrassment of twisting the arm of its African ward.

Although Madagascar did not possess the traditional ties that Liberia did, it drew more public attention during the Arthur administration. And once the commercial treaty of 1881 had been signed, Consul Robinson was well on his way to becoming the leading adviser of the Hovas. Anxious to maximize his influence, he encouraged Queen Ranavalona's government to secure control of the entire island and to do so quickly. The Sakalavas offered surprising resistance, and the French increased their pressure.

Despite the new and imminent threat, Robinson still wanted the Hovas to hold out. In July 1882, Madagascar sent a delegation to Europe and the United States, and the State Department allowed Robinson to accompany them. Assistant Secretary of State Alvey A. Adee warned Robinson against being overtly partisan, reminding him that delicate negotiations were pending over European restrictions on American goods.

From the first, the expedition met with little success. In Paris, the French demanded a protectorate over all Madagascar as well as special privileges on the west coast. When the Hova diplomats refused to accept such exorbitant terms, the French virtually expelled them. In London, Lord Granville denied that France had any right to establish a protectorate, but claimed that, in light of tensions over Egypt, he did not wish to injure Britain's relations with France further.

By now, even Washington was becoming aware of Madagascar's predicament. On January 2, 1883, it was the topic of Arthur's cabinet meeting. The cabinet refused to heed Robinson's pleas for American military assistance. The United States, it maintained, lacked sufficient force, would be participating without England's material support, and might risk the pork negotiations with France. At the same time, Arthur's cabinet called for immediate ratification of the 1881 treaty, and soon the Senate complied.

Early in March, the Hova mission arrived in the United States. Although on the surface the visit was made in order to ratify the commercial treaty, in reality it was an effort to get American arms. Delegates first met with President Arthur; then they conferred with various merchants, manufacturers, missionary groups, and politicians. The Hovas promoted such native products as hides, copal gum, and spices while seeking munitions and cotton goods. Frelinghuysen told them that he supported their cause, but he stressed that the United States could do little more for them. The *Nation* put the issue more bluntly: "the people of the United States want as little of foreign policy as possible."[22]

The Hova mission had no chance of moderating the French, who, on June 13, bombarded and occupied Tamatave, the nation's leading coastal city. The Hova forces abandoned the ports to the French but waged guerilla warfare in the interior. For many months, both sides faced a stalemate: the French, shelling the western ports, hoped to starve out the Hovas; the Hovas continued to dominate an almost impenetrable hinterland.

Misreading the commercial treaty of 1881, the Hovas continued to seek United States aid. Robinson, who had arrived in Tamatave early in May, urged the State Department to press arbitration with the French. Frelinghuysen flatly refused. Nothing in the 1881 treaty, he said, in what was obviously a tortured construction, should be interpreted as recognizing Hova sovereignty over the whole island. Rather, the treaty merely expressed America's hope that the Hova government would eventually be able to establish total control. Any effort at promoting arbitration, the secretary maintained, would place the United States in the position of being an interested party.

In July, Secretary of the Navy Chandler ordered the flagship of the South Atlantic Squadron to western Madagascar, giving it orders to protect American commercial interests. And late in the fall, Chandler had Lieutenant Mason A. Shufeldt, son of Commodore (now Admiral) Shufeldt, explore Madagascar's interior. Aside from these two actions, however, the United States did nothing.

Despite the fact that Washington avoided any intervention, the two warring parties soon came to terms. In 1885, France forced a treaty upon the Hovas that gave the former an indemnity of ten million francs, the port of Diego Suarez on the northern tip of the island, and control of Madagascar's foreign relations. As a result of the disturbances, United States trade had fallen by nearly 80 percent, and both the British and the French were capturing American textile markets there.

Frelinghuysen had wisely refused to involve the limited resources of the United States in a region where its interests were marginal and unclear. It would be stupid, he believed, to take action that might involve European commercial retaliation. The United States was sending infinitely more agricultural and manufacturing goods to Europe than to Africa; new commitments, for the present, had to remain limited.

To realize that the United States had failed in most of its objectives is by no means to cast a blanket indictment upon its diplomacy. Blaine's legacy was at best ambivalent. Then, Frelinghuysen boorishly irritated relations with the British, entering into a situation that has later led to charges of "moral imperialism."[23] More often than not, however, Arthur's secretary of state was sensibly cautious. He ignored popular demands for retaliation in the pork dispute, and he turned down Consul Robinson's request to aid the Hovas.

America was not able to secure the commercial access it desired because it possessed no leverage. Even in dealing with the non-Western world, the United States lacked the military means to enforce any policies. Commercial retaliation, as Frelinghuysen well knew, would only backfire, resulting in the exclusion of still more goods. The nation, to be sure, was in an uneasy predicament, and one that might bode ill for the future.

9

★ ★ ★ ★ ★

TO FAR-FLUNG SHORES

If the United States desired to be a major commercial power, a stronger navy would obviously be needed. The condition of the United States Navy was indeed poor. One historian has labeled it "a disgrace to the nation"; another has dismissed it as "a flotilla of death-traps and defenseless antiques."[1] Within fifteen years of the Civil War, it had declined from being the world's strongest to one of the weakest.

There were several reasons for such feebleness. Among them were a general focus upon continental expansion, reliance upon Europe alone to maintain global equilibrium, a Congress that was responsive to economy-minded constituents, and the comforting thought that the country had no colonies to defend and only domestic markets to foster.

Building up America's strength would not be easy. The standing army of twenty-five thousand men was poorly financed and lacked serious direction. Formally, its job involved manning coastal fortifications, maintaining West Point, and "policing" Indians. Informally, it bore the task of supporting a monotonous garrison life on neglected and worthless seacoast forts, as well as a lonely and dangerous existence on the frontier.

Given this general context, it was hardly surprising that the navy was so weak. A public ethos, rooted as far back as Jefferson's time, had defined the navy's task in the most limited of terms: to protect American merchant vessels, raid enemy commerce, and defend the coastline. Given such minimal duties, cruisers and gunboats—not battleships—had sufficed. Party sentiments invariably weakened the navy's strength, because any reformist steps taken by industrially based Republicans would be stifled when agrarian-minded Democrats gained control of the House. Then, when the Republicans regained power, they would vote against whatever expansion the Democrats desired. And even had the Congress been less partisan, it lacked the technical knowledge needed for adequate modernization.

All these factors could not help but take their toll, and by 1881, every major European power and several Latin American ones possessed navies superior to that of the United States. The United States Navy did not possess a single up-to-date warship, and of its two hundred craft, not one carried a high-powered cannon. Although Britain and France were rapidly constructing steel navies, thirty-three of the thirty-seven United States ships of the first, second, and third rank were made entirely of wood; they boasted "full-sail power." In addition, the nation owned thirteen single-turreted ironclad monitors, but these were much too unseaworthy to maneuver effectively. Even though such craft made for snappy exercises and ably displayed the flag, they could offer little comfort in combat. Shipbuilder John Roach was hardly exaggerating when he said, "The mention of our navy only excites a smile." Captain Alfred Thayer Mahan, stationed at the New York Navy Yard, agreed: "We have not six ships that would be kept at sea in war by any maritime power."[2]

Handling this decrepit establishment were some of the most incompetent personnel ever to swab a deck. Nearly forty-five hundred workers were employed in nine navy yards and five naval stations, a complex that cost $54 million a year to maintain. Yet, despite such generous staffing and allocations, the Navy Department was not able to repair harbor fortifications, eliminate overlapping bureaus, enforce discipline, or boost sagging morale. In addition, the navy had a disproportionate number of officers, one, in fact, for every five seamen. Such politically minded officers as Robley D. ("Fighting Bob") Evans acted insubordinately towards the secretary of the navy, and a few brashly began to treat ships under their supervision as if they were private yachts. When a leaking ship, the *Ashuelot*, was sunk at Amoy in February 1883 and eleven seamen were lost, the drunken commander was never punished. Political hacks tended to be shunted into the Navy Department; at times, even the secretary himself was unqualified. For example, Hayes's secretary, Richard W. Thompson, had supposedly expressed surprise that ships were hollow!

By the 1880s, a small, conscious elite of officers and technicians was beginning to demand reform. Fear was a primary motive—fear of defeat by Chile (the most frequently cited of all powers), Germany, Britain, and even China; fear that export trade would be lost unless it was protected (commented Commodore Shufeldt in 1878, *"It is a question of starving millions"*); fear of unguarded American interests in such far-flung outposts as Samoa or the Congo.[3] The *New York Herald* went so far as to warn that the Turkish fleet could mortify the United States; Lieutenant Commander Henry H. Gorringe, writing in the prestigious *North American Review*, envisioned a naval war with Spain ahead, one that would be triggered by revolt in Cuba. Prestige was almost as important a motive, because the integrity of the Monroe Doctrine, Blaine's aggressive pronouncements, and American control of an isthmian canal all depended upon seapower. Given such sentiments, it was little wonder that Admiral David D. Porter desired a navy that would be strong enough to "take the initiative," that Garfield's Secretary Hunt wanted one capable of "active and aggressive warfare," and that Congressman Kasson—borrowing the terminology of Germany's Iron Chancellor—asserted that modern history could be reduced to "Blut und Eisen."[4]

There was, of course, opposition. Some Americans believed that the United States had fought its last major war. Others, particularly those in the interior, found battleships an unsuitable weapon for a pristine republic. Still others claimed that the supposed vulnerability of the nation's coastlines had been greatly exaggerated.

President Arthur would eventually receive praise for having founded the modern navy, but it was a Garfield appointee who started the initial reformist steps. For the post of secretary of the navy, Garfield had chosen Judge William H. Hunt, a tall, goateed attorney from New Orleans. Hunt was a southern Unionist, famous because of his four marriages. He possessed a strong personal interest in the navy. During the Civil War, he had opened his home to the forces of Admiral David C. Farragut, and one of his sons had served as a northern naval officer.

Hunt's appointment was primarily political, for the president wanted a "safe" southerner in the cabinet. Yet the new secretary, who took the job extremely seriously, soon found himself appalled by the decrepit condition of the navy. He appointed able advisers, and he established a planning board to survey the navy's needs. Headed by the respected Rear Admiral John Rodgers, the board made two basic recommendations: It called for the construction of sixty-eight ships, and it insisted that a large number of these be made of steel. Though steel cost more than wood or iron, its weight and endurance made it preferable for new craft. Believing war unlikely, the board stressed the need for cruisers and smaller ships that could protect commerce and defend American coasts.

When Arthur became president, he strongly endorsed Hunt's program. In his annual message of 1881, he denied that the nation was afraid of "danger from abroad"; however, the country had to be ever ready to defend its harbors and protect its citizens. Undoubtedly Arthur's previous experience as collector of the Port of New York had encouraged him to mention what he called "the highways of commerce, the varied interests of our foreign trade" in his plea for bolstering the navy. Similarly, there is little doubt that his role in Civil War mobilization had helped him to assert with firmness: "We must be prepared to enforce any policy which we think wise to adopt."[5] The House Committee on Naval Affairs, releasing its own lengthy study, called for "wise and energetic action." To delay any longer, it said, would "be not only folly but even crime."[6]

In order to fulfill such visions, in April 1882, Arthur replaced Hunt—whom he made minister to Russia—with William E. Chandler, the able if ruthless party organizer from New Hampshire and one of the few Half-Breeds among the president's new appointees. Chandler, a small, wiry man, had been naval solicitor and judge advocate under Lincoln; he had also helped to devise the scheme that ensured Hayes's victory in 1876 and had served as Blaine's floor manager at the 1880 convention. Garfield had nominated him for the post of solicitor general, but he had been rejected by a Senate coalition of southerners, who had found him too problack, and certain conservative Republicans, who considered him unqualified. A year later, the Senate backtracked, confirming him for the navy post by a vote of sixteen to twelve.

Although his public reputation remained that of a wheeler-dealer par excellence, Chandler did a superior job. Once in office, he manifested unusual executive ability: he was at once businesslike, energetic, and accessible, and he possessed the knack of getting quickly to the heart of a matter. The secretary found that most of the navy's task still lay in coastal defense and commerce, but he was not above envisioning occasional offensive functions. The United States, Chandler claimed, possessed "natural, justifiable and necessary ascendency in the affairs of the American hemisphere"; hence the nation required a navy that would be "capable on brief notice of being expanded into invincible squadrons."[7]

Given such dreams, reforms were not long in coming. Chandler reduced the officer corps by over four hundred men, organized the much-needed Naval War College at Newport, Rhode Island, and established the Office of Naval Intelligence. In addition, he closed down superfluous navy yards at Pensacola, Florida, and New London, Connecticut; oversaw plans for erecting gun foundries; and established an eight-hour day in naval-construction facilities. The secretary was less successful when it came to installing a merit system for promotions or to requiring a fixed amount of sea service in order to qualify for advancement or to keeping ships from congregating in such attractive ports as Yokohama.

Yet the secretary's most important action lay in his appointment of a new naval advisory board, headed by Commodore Robert W. Shufeldt.

The officer-diplomat concurred with the emphasis that the Rodgers Board had placed upon the protection of commerce, but he saw that larger craft would eventually be needed. Realizing that Congress would never vote for sixty-eight ships, the new board scaled the number down considerably. In December 1882, it recommended the commissioning of three new armor-plated cruisers and one dispatch boat (or "clipper"), as well as the completion of four partially constructed double-turreted monitors. True, such ships could not yet compete with first-rate European craft; however, as Kenneth J. Hagan has noted, their anticipated speed, endurance, and armament made them ideal for one task: namely, that of protecting distant commercial interests "where the danger usually came from unarmed native populations fitfully contesting western encroachments on their customs and lands."[8]

The lame-duck Congress accepted all these recommendations, and on March 3, 1883, Arthur signed the bill. Two of the cruisers were later named the *Atlanta* and the *Boston*, the largest craft was called the *Chicago*, and the dispatch boat was christened the *Dolphin*; in the popular mind, they soon became known as the "ABCD ships." The new law prohibited the repair of any vessel if the expense exceeded 20 percent of its cost; therefore, many old wooden ships were junked. Chandler was delighted with this particular provision, later boasting: "I think that I did my best work in destroying the old Navy."[9]

Chandler was not impeccable in all ways. He violated his own reformist beliefs in honesty and efficiency by his highly partisan use of shipyards. For example, during the campaign of 1882, he gave Mahone a free hand in the Norfolk yards, although a year later, the Virginia boss promised Chandler that he would not seek any more favors.

As if Chandler's overt politicking were not enough, it soon became known that all four ABCD contracts had been awarded to John Roach of Chester, Pennsylvania. A figure out of Horatio Alger, Roach had immigrated to the United States as a penniless, semiliterate Ulsterman, first working as a hod carrier and earning a quarter a day. By 1870, however, he had become a leading producer of steam engines and heavy machinery. He was a generous contributor to the Republican party, and he was a favorite of Grant's secretary of the navy, George M. Robeson. In addition, he had often used his close friend Chandler as his lobbyist in Washington.

Fortunately, both Chandler and Roach were honest. Furthermore, Roach's Chester plant was the most modern shipyard in America, indeed the only one that had steel works and a rolling mill. In vying for the ABCD contracts, Roach had submitted the lowest bids. The stocky sixty-seven-year-old shipbuilder had, in fact, saved the government over $30,000.

Nevertheless, all of this did not prevent the Democrats from moving quickly to his jugular. When it was learned that Roach had suggested the civilian marine architect and the engineer—two highly qualified people—who served on Shufeldt's board, the planning board was dubbed "the Roach board." Democrats went so far as to accuse the Arthur administration of promoting a strong navy in order to stir up international turmoil and thereby promote the shipbuilder's fortunes. The president addressed himself to such criticism in his third message to Congress, responding that he did not intend for the new navy "to cope with that of the other great powers of the world."[10] Had Chandler been able to divide the contracts among several firms, he would have saved himself and his chief executive much grief.

Chandler's embarrassment was compounded by unforeseen delays in construction. High-quality steel took painfully long to produce, the weather was bad, a fire damaged much of the Chester yard, and the Shufeldt board had been careless in preparing blueprints. The *Dolphin* alone was subjected to fifty changes, twenty-three of which involved the ripping out of completed work.

Other criticisms were more inevitable. Traditionalists attacked ships possessing only two-thirds sail power, while reformers found it absurd to have any sails at all. Security-minded Americans noted that the new unarmed vessels could not, for so much as a single minute, stand up against British or Italian ironclads, while budget-minded people recognized that the navy could have bought better ships from the British themselves.

In 1883, Chandler, undismayed by such criticism, recommended that seven additional cruisers and four gunboats be built, but his proposals quickly ran into trouble. With a Democratic House and a Senate barely Republican, Chandler and Roach were again subject to personal attack. For example, Democratic Congressman Abram S. Hewitt of New York accused Chandler of pocketing the profits from the government's sale of condemned ships, thereby forcing the secretary to submit evidence that confirmed his own innocence. Other Democrats, however, joined the Republicans in demanding a larger navy. Morgan of Alabama, for example, spoke in terms of creating four separate fleets: one for each ocean bordering the United States, as well as one for the Gulf of Mexico and one for the Great Lakes. In February 1884, the Senate passed Chandler's proposal, only to see it shelved by the House. Congress had allocated funds for the completion of the ABCD ships; it had also blocked further naval construction.

The very last annual message of President Arthur again returned to the factor of naval defense: "The long peace that has lulled us into a sense of fancied security may at any time be disturbed."[11] This time, Congress appropriated $1,895,000 for two cruisers and two gunboats, and the president, on his final day in office, signed the bill into law.

Chandler did not rest content with constructing new steamships; he called for coaling stations and naval bases as well. In his 1883 report, he asked for fifteen of these posts, in such locations as the Caribbean, Brazil, the Straits of Magellan, Central America, Fernando Po, and the Coastal island of Korea. This chain of outposts, as Robert Seager II has noted, would not only have given the United States control of the entire hemisphere; it would have made American bases part of "a complete circle girding the earth."[12]

At first, Samoa appeared a good prospect. In 1878, the Samoans had given to the United States commercial and naval privileges at Pago Pago. When the death of Samoa's king raised fears of civil war, the United States played the leading role in settling the dispute. The American consul—one Thomas M. Dawson—advised the State Department that the Samoan population would probably accept becoming an outright protectorate of the United States. Only by such a step, Dawson said, could political stability on the islands be assured and the constant conniving of the British and Germans be ended. Chandler kept wanting the Pago Pago station put "on a firm basis" but found the area as yet too remote for further commitment.

Venezuela presented a second opportunity. By the beginning of 1883, it had entrusted the solution of its two most important diplomatic problems—a boundary dispute with British Guiana and a heavy debt to France—to the United States. In October of that year, Venezuela's president, desperate for United States backing, offered a comprehensive alliance. Venezuela would open all ports and rivers to United States trade while becoming its "moral protectorate." Frelinghuysen, fearing that his nation would become involved in Venezuela's civil disturbances, countered with a proposal of his own: Venezuela would allow United States ships to enter its ports and waters, provide special guarantees for American life and property, and probably abolish export duties. In return, the United States would offer similar concessions, as well as pledge its good offices in future disputes. This time, it was Venezuela's turn to defer action: it allowed its boundary controversy with Britain to remain unsolved, and it was forced to concede priority to the French claims. The United States had again turned down suggestions for a protectorate and naval bases.

Then there was the case of Haiti. The regime of Lysius Salomon, Haiti's autocratic president, had been facing a series of revolts. When, in March 1883, a more serious rebellion broke out, one that lasted for the rest of the year, Salomon first agreed to cede the island of Tortuga to the United States as a naval base; then he suggested Môle St. Nicolas. Salomon's price was steep: he asked for money, two warships, two gunboats, a guarantee that Haiti would remain independent, and the use of the United States' good offices in any dispute between Haiti and any other foreign country. Frelinghuysen again rejected Salomon's offer, maintaining that such territories entailed responsibilities that were beyond the existing naval strength.

Though the impact of Chandler's naval policy should not be exaggerated, the failure to gain coaling stations was not his only disappointment. The secretary, as well as Roach and Blaine, could not secure support, either from the public or from Congress, for a merchant marine. In 1880, only 17.0 percent and, in 1882, only 15.5 percent of the nation's foreign carrying trade was handled by American ships. In February 1881, the *Nation* reported that not a single ironclad vessel carried the flag of the United States. Arthur continually pushed for domestic shipping, declaring in 1882 that "the ocean highways are already monopolized by our formidable competitors."[13] On January 18, 1883, the House passed an innocuous shipping bill, which allowed craft that had been built abroad to carry United States registry. However, it eliminated provisions, just adopted the previous day by the Committee of the Whole, that would have permitted all ships and shipbuilding materials to enter duty free.

Furthermore, neither Chandler nor his allies could alter all of the navy's traditionalism. Much of its brass strongly opposed giving up sails, and the service's top-ranking officer insisted that new cruisers should "have enough sail power . . . to go around the world without touching their coal."[14]

Most important of all, it would take years before the ABCD ships would prove their worth, even more years before Chester Alan Arthur's contribution would receive just recognition from historians. By March 1885, when the president left office, only the dispatch vessel *Dolphin* had been completed, and this ship needed to have modifications after its trial run. Cleveland's secretary of the navy, William C. Whitney, conducted a vicious political vendetta against Roach. He refused to pay additional installments until the *Dolphin* had passed further tests, a situation that drove Roach—who lacked a reserve of working capital—into both bankruptcy and a nervous breakdown. Whitney's own report of the state of the navy ignored Chandler's reorganization, patronized the advisory board, and emphasized abuses in purchasing and the continual need for repairs.

On the one hand, it could be said that the "new navy" of the Arthur administration never progressed beyond three cruisers and a dispatch boat. As it was not until the 1890s that America's first battleships were constructed,

Chandler's successor was not far wrong in declaring that "we have nothing which deserves to be called a Navy."[15] The United States did not have the desire, much less the technology or facilities, to rival the fleets of Europe. By 1889, naval coaling stations were limited to Honolulu, Samoa, and Michilingue in Lower California.

On the other hand, the origins of the modern American navy can be found in the Arthur administration, and for this achievement the president himself deserves much credit. Such origins, in fact, go far beyond the ABC cruisers. They reveal a maturing ideology, one that linked national honor to prosperous trade and both to naval protection. The ideological seeds of what Walter LaFeber has called "the new empire" were emerging long before the theories of Admiral Mahan were publicized.

Even before Arthur nominated Chandler to be secretary of the navy, one naval personage had been extremely active in American policy-making. This was Commodore Shufeldt, who had finally received Blaine's instructions authorizing him to negotiate with Korea. From late March to the middle of April 1882, Shufeldt and China's Li Hung-chang had worked on an agreement. The final document, called the Treaty of Chemulpo, dealt almost entirely with commerce. By its terms, diplomatic and consular offices would be exchanged, the United States would receive most-favored-nation treatment and extraterritorial rights, and both powers would pledge their good offices if Korea were to become involved in a dispute. Li's primary concern was with America's recognition of Chinese suzerainty, not greater trade for Korea. He did agree to drop a phrase that would have committed the United States to recognize Korea's dependency upon China. However, the Korean king sent President Arthur a letter affirming that China controlled the peninsula. Indeed, the text of the message read, in part: "The King of Korea acknowledges that Korea is a tributary of China; but in regard to both internal administration and foreign intercourse it enjoys complete independence."[16] Such vagueness would permit all parties to make their own interpretation. They were not slow in so doing.

When Frelinghuysen received the king's letter, he ignored it. "As far as we are concerned," said the secretary in March 1883, "Corea is an independent sovereign power."[17] Frelinghuysen could not help noting that for many years, the Chinese government had not assumed any responsibility for Korea's activities, and he found it a bit late to start now. Yet, while considering Korea an independent nation, the United States never did intend to support such a status by force. And if either China or Korea faced threats from Russia and Japan, it would have to stand alone. China, on its part, acted as if Korea's dependency status had not been altered in any way.

In the United States, the Senate approved the agreement, doing so in January 1883; but it still expressed skepticism, noting that Korea's status remained ambivalent. Despite Shufeldt's doubts concerning Korean trade, Arthur, in his third annual message to Congress, given on December 4, 1883, stressed Korea's commercial potential. Korea, he said, "needs the implements and products which the United States are ready to supply. We seek no monopoly of its commerce and no advantages over other nations, but as the Chosenese, in reaching for a higher civilization, have confided in this Republic, we can not regard with indifference any encroachment on their rights."[18] Britain, France, Germany, and other European powers, suspecting that the Koreans could actually open their own doors, negotiated treaties patterned on the American model.

It was one thing to sign an accord acknowledging Korea's independence; it was quite a different thing to see this independence become a reality. The United States or the Korean monarchy might have thought that the Treaty of Chemulpo would signify the end of Korea's subserviency, but if so, they were sadly mistaken. The agreement, as one historian notes, "set Korea adrift on an ocean of intrigue which it was quite helpless to control."[19]

From July 1882, China intervened in Korea in a manner that had not been used since the first half of the seventeenth century. As Li told John Russell Young, United States minister to China, "I am King of Korea whenever I think the interests of China require me to assert that prerogative."[20] In an obvious effort to nullify the most-favored-nation provisions of Shufeldt's treaty, Li promulgated trade regulations by which the Kingdom of Korea would grant China privileges that other treaty powers could not claim. Under the new rules, the Americans were forbidden, but the Chinese were permitted, to trade at four points in the interior, to travel inside Korea, and to transport native produce from one port to another. Fearing that the Open Door was suddenly being closed, Frelinghuysen tersely remarked: "To this the United States cannot consent."[21]

Despite China's obvious domination, the United States continued to treat Korea as an independent nation. In February 1883, Frelinghuysen appointed Lucius H. Foote as minister plenipotentiary, the highest rank in the foreign service. Foote, a prosperous California lawyer, had been an active Republican, adjutant general of California, and—during most of the War of the Pacific—consul general at Valparaiso. "Seoul," as Tyler Dennett once noted, "was the most slippery spot in which any American diplomat ever had to keep his feet," and Foote quickly discovered this fact.[22] Immediately upon arriving, he learned that the Korean government was trading only with China and Japan. The king of Korea, however, feared both powers and was anxious to check them. He liked Foote from their first meeting, consulted with him about various Western innovations, and encouraged United States commerce.

In July 1883, the Korean king made a more overt bid at securing American support. He sent a mission to the United States, instructing it to confer with President Arthur, observe American institutions, and perhaps arrange for a loan and for advisers. Ten officials of the highest rank were chosen. The Korean delegation visited factories in Massachusetts, telegraph offices and fire departments in New York City, the Brooklyn Navy Yard, and military training grounds at West Point. Before leaving Washington, it was given a farewell audience with the president. Frelinghuysen assured the group that he would send them competent civil and military advisers.

One such adviser was Ensign George Clayton Foulk, who, on his way to serve as naval attaché in Seoul, accompanied the returning Koreans. Foulk had served on two cruises with the Asiatic Squadron; he greatly respected Oriental institutions; and he already knew both Japanese and Chinese. Handsome and intelligent and possessing a quick mind, Foulk had been brought to the personal attention of President Arthur. He learned the Korean language soon after his arrival, served as the unofficial chargé for nearly two years, and became America's primary diplomatic representative there.

Arriving at Seoul on June 7, 1884, Foulk sided with the modernizing, pro-Japanese element, led by Kim Ok Kiun, a position that made Li and Korea's pro-Chinese party suspicious. Soon American steamers—laden with petroleum, machinery, rifles, and notions—were entering Korea. Hostilities between the French and the Chinese, which broke out at the end of August, distracted China's attention from Korea, and by the fall, Chinese influence there was definitely in decline.

Yet Kim wanted more power and therefore planned a coup. On December 4, 1884, acting with his pro-Japanese progressives, he used the occasion of a state banquet to seize control. Within two days, the revolt had failed. Korean mobs attacked Japanese subjects living in Seoul and drove the Japanese guard out of the country. Kim and his allies fled, and the king quickly restored the old order. He then asked Foote to mediate between Korea and Japan, and Foote did help to arrange a settlement. As a result of the abortive coup, China was forced to recognize Japan's complete equality in Korea. The United States was far less fortunate. Foote's influence and rank were reduced as American influence diminished rapidly. All diplomatic duties were left in attaché Foulk's hands, an indication that the United States was no longer going to seek power in Korea.

Although merchants and missionaries would continue to enter the nation, in 1887, Secretary of State Thomas F. Bayard would claim that henceforth the United States would not pursue further controversy in the area.

Rather, it would restrict its activity to "the protection of American citizens and their commerce."[23] Early dreams of becoming a power in East Asia were over.

If the setback in Korea were not enough to sober America's vision of becoming a major force in the Orient, rebuffs over Indochina surely should have been convincing. France had been involved in Indochina since Louis XIV had promoted missionary activities there, and by 1870, France had made Cochin China virtually a protectorate. In 1882, the French seized Hanoi and Hué; a year later, by the Treaty of Hué, they established two more protectorates, those over Annam and Tonkin. As China had long claimed suzerainty over both areas, it was furious. Li sought American mediation but learned that the United States would only arbitrate if asked by both sides. Levi P. Morton, America's minister to Paris, sounded out the French Foreign Office, but without success.

France imposed a settlement in May 1884, but in less than a month, fighting had broken out again. Once more the Chinese requested the United States to negotiate, and once more the French blocked these efforts. The French soon gained the upper hand militarily, destroying most of the Chinese war fleet as well as such Chinese fortifications as Foochow. By early September, the regime of France's imperialist premier Jules Ferry, who believed that his nation had achieved enough of a victory, once more considered American mediation. Frelinghuysen suggested that China pay a nominal indemnity of five million francs (Ferry had suggested eighty million), agree to temporary French occupation of two Formosan ports, and accept certain unspecified commercial privileges. China rejected the proposals, and so the United States efforts ended.

Only in the following year was the British inspector general of the Chinese customs system, Sir Robert Hart, able to bring both sides together. The Treaty of Tientsin, signed on May 11, 1884, omitted any mention of an indemnity, but it did commit the Chinese to evacuate the province of Tonkin, recognize French suzerainty over Annam, and permit French merchants to trade on the Indochina frontier. Within two months, China was forced to confirm French protectorates over Annam and Tonkin and also over Cambodia. As in the case of Korea, both the American public and its policy makers were not ready to commit their nation to wide-sweeping policies. The American impact on Indochina was a small one indeed.

As yet, the United States was poorly equipped to act as a power in Asia. Because it lacked any real instruments of military force and because it was aware that immediate commercial opportunities were few, it was limited to using rhetoric and making symbolic gestures. It soon realized, for example, that China could violate Shufeldt's treaty at will and that France could dismiss America's offer of good offices with impunity. At one point, although it endorsed Japan's efforts to end extraterritorial inroads on Japan's sovereignty, it refused to press the European powers.

Gilded Age diplomacy might serve as prelude to John Hay's Open Door notes and Theodore Roosevelt's mediation in northeast Asia, but these policies lay well in the future. For the present, its Asian policy revealed the United States as a nation still in the midst of diplomatic adolescence.

The United States was less reluctant to become involved in the Congo controversy, a dispute that concerned a half-dozen European powers vying for the heart of the African continent. The French relied upon the explorations of the Italian-born Count Savorgnan de Brazza to gain treaty rights north of the Congo River. Portugal sought to control the south bank, and in January 1880, there was strong likelihood that Portugal and Britain—both of which were fearful of a French monopoly—would make an agreement that would shut all other nations out of the Congo valley. The Belgians possessed the best claim, using the explorations of Henry M. Stanley, a Welshman mistakenly thought to be an American citizen, to establish trading stations for what was commonly known as the African International Association.

The African International Association was headed by King Leopold II. Leopold had been an imperialist even before he had assumed the Belgian throne in 1865, but he had not been able to rally his people behind the cause. He feared that his European rivals would close the mouth of the Congo, thereby ruining his secret plans to establish a trading company in its rich valley. Hence, couching his greed under the guise of philanthropy and the Open Door, he called for internationalization of the river and recognition of his organization.

Such a program had some supporters. For example, Stanley, then the greatest living African explorer, was wont to boast of the Congo's potential wealth. In addition, so he claimed, if each female Congolese bought a single Sunday dress, over 320 million yards of cotton sheeting would be purchased. Most businessmen in the United States, however, did not share Stanley's enthusiasm for the region; they focused instead upon agricultural exports to a famished Europe and upon less risky enterprises in America's South and West.

Stanley was not Leopold's only promoter. The Belgian king found a staunch supporter in Henry S. Sanford. A prominent land and business promoter in both the United States and Latin America, Sanford had been Lincoln's minister to Belgium, from where he had directed the federal secret service in Europe. Listed among his friends were such influential policy makers as Arthur, Grant, and Chandler. A member of the executive committee of Leopold's organization since its founding, Sanford declared in December 1882 that the Congo area could provide "for relief from the overproduction which now threatens us in some of our manufactures."[24] He was a genuine idealist, who sincerely believed in Leopold's altruism, but he had a personal stake in the matter as well. By the 1870s, he was in desperate economic straits, and he hoped that an investment underwritten by Leopold would prove lucrative.

Yet by the middle of 1883, Sanford was ready to launch a full-scale campaign, one that would involve United States recognition of Leopold's association. The association, so Leopold promised, would admit American products to the Congo area duty-free. Frelinghuysen responded positively, declaring that he favored making all river posts neutral. One of Sanford's suggestions—which involved the supervision of all the association's stations by a high-ranking American naval officer—met with much less enthusiasm from the administration; Chandler was singularly indifferent. Admiral Shufeldt, who headed the Naval Advisory Board, had claimed in June 1879, after personally visiting the Congo, that trade there could only pander "to the lowest tastes of the savages, by selling to them the worst grades of rum and gin."[25]

Sanford arrived in Washington from Brussels late in November, carrying with him Leopold's secret codes. Frelinghuysen soon told Sanford that United States recognition depended upon additional proof that the new stations would be self-sustaining. Arthur, in his annual message, was far more encouraging. He said, "It may become advisable for us to cooperate with other commercial powers in promoting the rights of trade and residence in the Kongo Valley free from the interference or political control of any one nation." In referring to Leopold's "philanthropic" group, the president noted that "the rich and populous valley of the Kongo" would offer free commerce to the United States. Indeed, he said with almost unmatched naïveté, that the association "does not aim at permanent political control, but seeks the neutrality of the valley. The United States can not be indifferent to this work nor to the interests of their citizens involved in it."[26] Despite the fact that the statement was a vague one, it represented Sanford's first victory. The president of the United States had now gone on record as opposing European colonialism in Central Africa.

By the beginning of 1884, Sanford's propaganda was starting to pay off. Banquets, interviews, planted newspaper stories—all these the American branch of Leopold's society used to good effect. The Congo, so Sanford claimed, would end up as independent as Liberia, because the association's trusteeship would only be temporary.

In January 1884, the association gained a powerful defender. This was John T. Morgan, a strong imperialist and chairman of the Senate Foreign Relations Committee. Morgan asserted that Leopold's group was firmly established in the Congo valley, that it possessed solid claims, and that it would encourage self-government for both settlers and the indigenous population. The Congo, he continued, not only offered rich resources but also provided a market for American surpluses and for southern cotton in particular. The short, pugnacious Alabaman assumed leadership in the Senate, introducing a resolution in February 1884 to recognize the association. Morgan stressed equal commercial access (trade in the Congo valley, he claimed, reached over £2 million a year), but he had more of an eye on avoiding racial confrontation at home by sending blacks overseas.

On April 10, the Senate passed Morgan's resolution, and within two weeks, Frelinghuysen issued a declaration of formal recognition, the first nation to do so. France and Britain followed almost immediately. Frelinghuysen thought that the association would offer the best hope for ending the slave trade, assuring the Open Door for American goods, and paving the way for self-rule.

In one sense, Frelinghuysen's move was quite daring. The United States had intervened in Africa while Portugal was claiming the lower Congo; France was staking out the northern area; Germany was establishing protectorates in Southwest Africa, Togoland, and the Cameroons; and Britain was negotiating a treaty with Portugal that would involve joint control of navigation on the Congo. James L. Roark writes, "While the American declaration did not recognize specific frontiers, it was clearly interference in the affairs of the Old World."[27] United States recognition had greatly enhanced the international status of the Congo and, with it, the status of King Leopold II.

Acting in the fear that German commerce would be banned from the area, in 1884, Bismarck called a general conference on Congo claims. The meeting, which commenced on November 15 in Berlin with the Iron Chancellor presiding, limited itself to three topics: free trade in the Congo; free navigation of the Congo and Niger rivers; and procedures for the establishment of future African colonies. In accepting Bismarck's invitation, Frelinghuysen stressed that the United States reserved the right to reject any conclusions that might be made by the conference. The United States, he said, could only sanction unrestricted free trade and the type of neutral political control that he thought the association represented. But despite the secretary's caution, the United States—for the first time in its history—was participating in a conference established in order to consider the fate of a territory outside the Western Hemisphere.

John A. Kasson, American minister to Germany and a leading Stalwart expansionist, took the lead, doing so with little interference from Frelinghuysen. A personal friend of Sanford's, Kasson was well acquainted with the speculator's plans and had visited Sanford's Belgian chateau on his way to Berlin. Kasson appointed Sanford and Stanley as associate members of the American delegation, in which capacity they acted as unofficial agents for Leopold. During the conference, Stanley attempted to foster trade between Britain and the Congo, and he tried to have minister Morton, in Paris, protest against exclusive French claims. Stanley's efforts to secure a railroad monopoly for the association met with failure. Without the contribution of Sanford in particular, the establishment of Leopold's Congo state might have been far more difficult. Yet as Lysle E. Meyer notes, Sanford saw his actions "as in the best interests of all trading nations, including his own."[28] Frelinghuysen's own agent for the Congo, Amazon explorer Willard P. Tisdel, distrusted Sanford's motives. Tisdel, who was a friend of Senator Morgan's, cautioned both the senator and the secretary not to rely on Sanford. The warning went unheeded.

In Kasson's first address to the conference, he betrayed his innocence by noting the "high and philanthropic European patronage" of the association, which was "dictated by the principles of civilization and humanity."[29] Although he claimed to realize that other delegates saw him as a mere mouthpiece for Leopold, he maintained that the association was the only alternative to chaos. During the meetings, the American delegation continually stressed the Open Door, turning the most technical questions over boundaries into demands for commercial freedom.

During the conference, Kasson urged a more visible American presence. Early in December, at the minister's prompting, Navy Secretary Chandler sent the warship *Kearsarge* to the mouth of the Congo, there to keep an eye on European maneuvering. Chandler and Kasson sought a coaling station and commercial post on the river, but Frelinghuysen objected. Such requests, the secretary argued, violated America's long-standing renunciation of any territorial claims.

At the final session, held on February 26, 1885, the assembly formally recognized Leopold's association, henceforth to be called the Congo Free State. American delegates gladly backed provisions that pledged religious freedom, free trade, and navigation on the Congo and Niger rivers. They endorsed the condemnation of the slave trade and were thankful that the body made provisions for mediation by a third power. Leopold had gained Europe's acquiescence in association control of some 900,000 square miles; Bismarck had stabilized a volatile area, while blocking English control and safeguarding German interests; and Frelinghuysen and Kasson had seen general endorsement of the Open Door.

The administration's problems, however, were just beginning, for the treaty was hotly debated in the United States. Defenders claimed that the Berlin Conference contributed to both peace and humanitarianism. In his last annual message, President Arthur referred to "the rich prospective trade of the Kongo Valley," and the business press emphasized the tempting commercial prospects there.[30] Nonetheless, Half-Breeds and Democrats offered a variety of protests. Both Blaine and Congressman Perry Belmont (Dem., N.Y.) suggested that such participation could give Europe the right to call a conference on Latin America. Other opponents suspected Leopold's real motives, called Frelinghuysen the dupe of Sanford, feared involvement in any possible African war, and doubted whether Central Africa would ever provide a good market. And if markets ever should become lucrative, they would best be gained, not through European conferences, but by revising the nation's tariff and currency laws.

Frelinghuysen attempted to defend his diplomacy, doing so in reports to the House and Senate Foreign Relations committees. He denied that the Berlin Conference threatened the Monroe Doctrine: Latin American nations had long governed themselves, whereas Africa remained very much an open continent. He defended United States participation, reminding Congress that it had spurned his efforts to advance American commerce through reciprocity arrangements, naval appropriations, and provisions for modernizing the consular and diplomatic service.

Congress was still not convinced. Even the Republicans on the House Foreign Affairs Committee claimed that no prospect for commercial advantage justified "entangling alliances" with the Old World. The treaty did not reach the Senate Foreign Relations Committee until a few days before the session ended, and the administration did not submit the Berlin convention until Arthur's last day in office. Incoming President Cleveland claimed that the United States was in no position to help in enforcing neutrality in the Congo. Despite the prodding of Morgan's Foreign Relations Committee, he never did submit the treaty to Congress.

In almost an anticlimax, Arthur's special agent in the Congo, Willard P. Tisdel, eventually reported that Americans should not "want anything to do with Central Africa."[31] The Congo basin, he reported, was unsuited to agriculture; the people were too poor to buy American imports; the climate was too unhealthy for safety. In addition, major commercial cities at the river's mouth were already under the control of European companies.

Seldom had American diplomacy been so naïve. The United States had the misfortune of watching its diplomats exploited by one of the most ruthless and expediential of Europe's rulers. In concurring with the Berlin agreement, Frelinghuysen—usually more cautious—was mistaking rhetoric for reality. By 1885, both Europe and the United States were beginning to learn something of the truth concerning Leopold's venture: organizational breakdown in the Congo Association; falsified reports; privation, illness, and death among association employees; and bloody massacres of the Congolese. Within a year, Leopold ended the charade and proclaimed personal sovereignty over the Congo Free State. American dreams of absolute free trade and an end to the slave trade remained unfulfilled. Democratic tutelage of the Congolese was yet more distant. And by 1890, even the faithful Sanford was disillusioned. In short, the noble dream of Arthur and Frelinghuysen had turned out to be something of a nightmare, and the United States, if the truth be known, had been party to a swindle.

If Frelinghuysen's policies met with indifferent success in Europe and with setbacks in Africa, they were even more of a failure in the Near East. Most of the area from the Dardanelles to the Euphrates was controlled by the Ottoman Empire, a ramshackle domain that gave much local autonomy to various rulers. As was the case in Africa, most United States contacts had centered on missions; also as in Africa, visions of wider interests were, as yet, doomed to failure. Here, as elsewhere, the nation was by no means ready for long-term commitments.

The Ottoman Empire sought neither American goods nor American involvements, and it made its hostility known at every turn. It levied punitive taxes on foreign-owned real estate, hindered the storing of American petroleum, placed a duty—indeed, an illegal one—on American alcohol, and denounced a commercial treaty that had been made in 1862. As if such economic restrictions were not enough, the empire remained apathetic when Turkish bandits and mobs attacked American missionaries. After one notorious murder had gone unpunished for close to a year, Secretary Blaine demanded punishment and an indemnity. The Turks, masters of procrastination, effectively used delaying tactics; and the United States minister to Turkey, General Lew Wallace, was continually being stalled. Then, during the summer of 1883, two American missionaries were knifed by a band of Kurds. This time, the United States retaliated by sending the Mediterranean squadron to Turkish ports, although the show of force could not budge the Turkish government.

Perhaps the United States contained its outrage against the Turks because it wanted to play a greater role in Egypt, an area nominally under the control of the Turkish sultan. When, early in 1882, an Egyptian nationalist leader named Ahmed Arabi became the khedive's minister of war, Britain and France jointly sent a fleet to Alexandria to cow him. As a result, some fifty Europeans were killed in antiforeign riots. The British, this time acting alone, demanded that Arabi be deposed and sought to gain outright control.

On July 4, the sultan called in Wallace to request that the United States mediate. At first, Frelinghuysen was most enthusiastic. Immediate Turkish capitulation to British demands, so both he and Wallace believed, would prevent a full-scale British invasion. Their hope was a futile one, because neither the sultan at Constantinople nor the khedive at Alexandria any longer commanded Egypt. The British squadron at Alexandria opened fire a week later. After routing the Egyptians at Tel el Kébir, British troops proceeded to occupy the country. The United States had been given its usual rebuff.

10

★ ★ ★ ★ ★

TRADE AND TARIFFS

Such remote involvements could not restore a sagging economy. Garfield's assassination in July 1881 had marked the first break in the nation's prosperity. Prices suddenly dropped, then rose, then fluctuated for weeks as bulletins were released on the president's condition. The stock market went into decline and remained so for a year. In September, as Garfield lay dying, drought wiped out all prospects for normal crops. By the end of the year, corn, cotton, wheat, and pork products had fallen behind the production level of 1880.

During the new year, 1881, there were 477 work stoppages, involving 130,000 laborers and creating fears that the class struggles of the Old World would soon be reproduced in the New. The striking laborer had little protection. In 1881, the Knights of Labor had yet to prove itself, while the new Federation of Organized Trades and Labor Unions (later called the American Federation of Labor) was almost stillborn. Organized labor, as yet, could not make many real threats.

Arthur's accession to the presidency occasioned little economic improvement. Railroad building, which reached its peak in 1882, soon became inert. And when railroads canceled orders for steel rails, iron and steel prices were forced down. Iron workers began a series of strikes, and for more than three months, over 100,000 men were out of work. Wages in general stopped rising and at times even declined. At the end of 1883, industry had remained weak, while many farmers were barely making a living. In 1884, the closing of the brokerage house of Grant and Ward created a financial panic in which more than one business in ten failed and in which foreign investors started to withdraw gold. Although the slump was not as grave as those of the 1870s, 1890s, or 1930s, it was more than a mere recession.

Various reasons were given for this decline, ranging from protective tariffs to bad loans. Undoubtedly the recovery of European agriculture was a factor, for it cut off much of America's export market. With Russia again supplying commodities and with the Suez Canal making Indian and Australian grain more accessible to western Europe, United States crops might well be excluded with impunity. Businessmen feared budding surpluses as much as farmers did, and many writers addressed themselves to the need for greater exports. In the words of David M. Pletcher, publicists were "suggesting as potential markets nearly every part of the world except the polar icecaps."[1]

Americans would find market expansion uphill work, for Europeans, in particular the British, dominated most international trade. In 1881, for example, the British sale of cotton goods to Latin America and the Far East exceeded that of the United States by thirteen to one, and British exports of iron and steel undoubtedly surpassed American exports a hundred to one.

Such challenges heightened American wants. From the Worthy Master of the Mississippi Grange, who asserted that "the farmers are imbued with a money-making spirit," to Senator Morgan, who claimed that "our home market is not equal to the demands," farmers and their spokesmen were looking for widening opportunities. Congressman Kasson of Iowa declared, "We must turn our eyes abroad, or they will soon look inward upon discontent."[2] Undoubtedly, agrarian unrest helped the Democrats capture the House in 1882. Business journals such as the New York *Commercial Bulletin* and *Bradstreet's* often stressed foreign markets, and their comments were nothing if not candid. According to the New York City Chamber of Commerce, "Our sole resource is to open new markets to our people." And to reformer Carl Schurz, "The more limited the market is, the more easily it will be glutted."[3]

There was hardly a policy maker who did not address himself to the issue. Blaine asked, "What are we going to do with this surplus?" then predicted that Latin America would seek United States goods for the "next hundred years." "Fail to give our farmers and manufacturers the open markets of the world," warned Treasury Secretary Windom, "and there will be a giant glut at home, prices will go down, and prosperity will diminish." In his report for 1884, Windom's successor, Hugh McCulloch, agreed: "Unless we can share in the trade which is monopolized by European nations, the depression now severely felt will continue, and may become more disastrous." By 1885, Arthur was claiming that "the most effective means of increasing our foreign trade and thus relieving the depression" was "one of the gravest problems" the nation faced.⁴ Frelinghuysen, the most vocal and persistent of American leaders, envisioned an integrated system in which the United States would export manufactured goods and investment capital to nonindustrialized regions and, in return, would gain the raw materials needed to supply its own factories.

One must be wary, however, of overstating the market factor. Secretary Blaine, for example, often pressed the cause of increased exports. "If the commercial empire that legitimately belongs to us is to be ours," he once said, "we must not lie idle and witness its transfer to others."⁵ Yet most of his diplomatic activity—as we have seen—centered far more upon such factors as security and prestige. Blaine himself said that it was the domestic market, not the foreign one, that had created the nation's prosperity.

Much of the United States, even in time of depression, still had an insular focus, with many Americans wanting to keep trade, capital, and troops at home. Congress and the public might well have shared a consensus on such issues as hemispheric preeminence and a canal on the isthmus, but the best means for maintaining this presence was much disputed. Though tariff reformer David A. Wells sought low tariffs and new markets, labor commissioner Carroll D. Wright denied that either device could relieve the surplus. To say that many voices in the nation, including some highly placed ones, were seeking foreign markets is one thing; to claim that such demands had little opposition, still more that they determined American policy, is quite different. Anxieties concerning overproduction were still far fewer than they would become in the nineties.

It remains questionable how much business itself sought either foreign annexation or investment opportunities for surplus capital. The promotion of export trade was still more likely to come from government offices than from corporations. From 1877 to 1881, exports accounted for 8.2 percent of the gross national product, and from 1882 to 1886, the percentage went down to 6.6. Hard times are hardly conducive to increases in production, much less to commercial expansion. Until the 1890s, the majority of United States manufacturers had the most casual of interest in exports. Although a few businesses, such as Standard Oil, were beginning to distribute their products overseas, American commercial representatives were often poorly trained and inefficient. They lacked effective organization and knowledge of foreign banking arrangements, and they still suffered from a relatively poor communications system.

To compare national behavior with national rhetoric, one should first examine the tariff debates. The tariff, as one historian has described it, was "that great touchstone of American economic policy during the decades after Appomattox"; it always remained one of the most hotly contested issues of the Gilded Age.[6] To low-tariff spokesmen, increased trade would lead to prosperity; high tariffs, on the other hand, would artificially raise prices and subsidize incompetent industries. Reduced tariffs, so such partisans asserted, would aid farmers in particular: they would permit the husbandman to buy manufactured goods more cheaply, while giving his own products access to a world market. Protectionists, however, claimed that only the tariff kept the wages of American workers high. Without it, they argued, cheaply made British goods would flood American markets. In fact, the Anglophobia of the protectionists was rapidly becoming a new "bloody shirt." In addition, so they claimed, farmers were more likely to find customers among well-paid American wage earners than among increasingly competitive foreign markets.

The debate was compounded by the fact that the interests of producers of raw materials were often opposed to those of manufacturers. The same set of duties acted to shelter one group while ruining another. Sometimes a compromise might be found, as when domestic wool growers and textile producers both sought protection. At other times, interests clashed, as when shippers sought to purchase foreign craft, while shipbuilders demanded tariffs and government subsidies.

Nevertheless, despite the obvious complications ensuing from the tariff issue, an increasing number of Americans wanted reform. Garfield's assassination postponed discussion for several months, forcing both protectionists and reformers to place their hopes on the new incumbent. Protectionists realized that change was inevitable, but they wanted loyal tariff supporters to direct any revision. In fact, it was the arch protectionist, William D. ("Pig-Iron") Kelley (Rep., Pa.), who revived an old proposal calling for a special tariff commission.

Arthur himself endorsed the idea, although, as his latest biographer notes, his own position was little in doubt. In his first annual message, the president asked Congress for a moderate tariff revision. "Important changes," he stressed, "should be made with caution."[7] The treasury had long shown an embarrassingly high surplus, a condition that presented a major financial problem whenever money was in short supply. The surplus, which drew over $100 million annually, reached $145 million in 1882. Furthermore, discrepancies in duties made administration of the tariff both irrational and difficult.

The Stalwarts had long been high-tariff men; Ulysses S. Grant and Edwin D. Morgan soon assumed leadership in the New York Association for the Protection of American Industry. However, Kelley's bill for a tariff commission passed both houses, largely by party vote, and on May 15, 1882, Arthur signed it. Acting at the president's request, Senator Justin S.

Morrill (Rep., Vt.), chairman of the Senate Finance Committee, drew up a list of candidates. The majority were Republican protectionists, since, Morrill said, "the country and Congress are overwhelmingly that way."[8] John L. Hayes, secretary of the National Association of Wool Manufacturers, was appointed president; among the other members were lobbyists from the wool, sugar, and iron industries.

The commission first met for a week in Washington; next held a month of hearings at a resort on the north Jersey shore; then spent nearly three months traveling around the country. In the course of its investigations, it called 604 witnesses (including a young Atlanta attorney named Woodrow Wilson) and took some 2,625 pages of testimony.

The responses of many spokesmen were predictable. Producers of raw materials sought protection; manufacturers favored having no duty on raw materials but tariffs on their finished products. And certain dilemmas became all too apparent. In Louisiana, for instance, sugar planters wanted high rates on raw sugar; sugar refiners, a reduction on raw sugar only; and sugar importers, a general lowering.

To almost everyone's surprise, the commission called for a substantial reduction in duties. Indeed, it went so far as to say that such a move had been demanded by "the best conservative opinion of the country."[9] The proposed lowering averaged between 20 and 25 percent but in some cases reached 50 percent. Furthermore, the free list was considerably enlarged. Revealing its manufacturing bias, the commission focused upon reducing the duties on raw materials. Hence congressmen from areas that produced such materials—for example, those from the sheep-raising regions of the Middle West—were far from enthusiastic.

In November 1882, the Democrats captured the House by a comfortable margin, and soon they threatened a more radical revision than most Republicans desired. The recession, with its falling prices and rising unemployment, had already taken its toll. Realizing that the lame-duck session would leave them little time, such protectionists as Senators Hoar and Frye started to press for reform. Even Morrill remarked: "I suppose that if the Bible has to be revised from time to time, the tariff may have to be."[10]

Arthur's second annual message reached Congress on the same day that the commission's report was released. Here the president sought an enlargement of the free list and a substantial reduction of duties on such items as cotton, iron, steel, sugar, molasses, silk, wool, and woolen goods. He made no specific recommendations, declaring that Congress would fix the exact rates. Since the cause of tariff reform, like that of civil-service reform, might gain votes in 1884, Republicans voiced little opposition to general reduction.

Protectionists soon converged on Washington, seeking higher duties than the commission had thought advisable. Given the protectionists' power and given the high-tariff sentiment still remaining in Congress, the commission's proposals were rapidly distorted beyond recognition. The Senate Finance Committee reported a high-tariff bill, although the full Senate amended it so as to meet commission recommendations more closely. Only one Republican opposed it; nine of twenty-seven Democrats supported it. It still had to face the House, where it met with the coldest of receptions. The House Ways and Means Committee, dominated by high protectionists, drafted its own, more protectionist bill, one that proposed reductions of only about 10 percent. Kelley, who had proposed that there be a commission in the first place, went so far as to claim that the Senate bill would both ruin Pennsylvania's economy and kill the Republican party.

With only a few days remaining before the Democrats would assume control of the House, Representative Thomas B. Reed (Rep., Me.) appointed a joint committee, full of protectionists, to revise the Senate schedules. House Democrats protested against the packing by refusing to answer the roll call, and the Senate Democrats boycotted the two seats that had been allotted them. On March 2, after deliberating for just one day, the joint committee offered its own upward revision of the Senate bill, according to which some rates went even higher than those proposed by the House. Yet, realizing that time was pressing, Senate Republicans rallied behind the revision almost to a man. On that very midnight, the Senate passed the measure by one vote, and on the next day, the House followed by a tally of 152 to 116. Moments before the constitutional hour for adjournment, Arthur signed the bill, doing so without comment.

After all the jockeying, Congress had only reduced duties on an average of 1.47 percent. The legislative monstrosity was so illogical that the bill soon became known as the Mongrel Tariff. In some cases, duties on raw materials were increased; in others, those on manufactured goods were decreased. One type of steel had three different rates set in three different places, and the measure throughout possessed more dangling modifiers and convoluted jargon than an undergraduate term paper.

The bill backfired, winning few supporters for the GOP. Many industries expressed their displeasure. The National Association of Wool Manufacturers might thank Senator Morrill for reducing wool duties, but wool growers in Ohio looked on with dismay when their Senator John Sherman focused most of his attention upon the protection of pig iron. The American Iron and Steel Association in turn, noting a moderate reduction of duties on pig iron, regretted that all duties were not raised. Louisiana sugar planters complained about the slight reduction in rates, while refiners objected because they were not lowered further. *Appletons' Annual Cyclopaedia*, not intentionally given to understatement, commented that "there was ample evidence that the result was satisfactory to no considerable class of citizens."[11]

The new tariff made little impact upon the economy. The United States continued on its road to depression, and in 1885, a government report claimed that about a million people, or 7.5 percent of the labor force, was unemployed. Protection, as Paul S. Holbo notes, was a "heated, partisan issue," one that revealed many producers to be "less concerned with opening doors abroad than with closing doors to foreign competition for the massive domestic market."[12]

Few Americans, however, blamed Arthur for the fiasco. The president had appointed a commission that had taken its task seriously; he had personally endorsed downward revision. But Congress very much held the whip hand, and Arthur's influence over the lame-duck session could only be minimal.

During the economic crisis that began in 1881, many sectors of the economy had looked for markets overseas. If, however, the congressional alignment over the Mongrel Tariff reflected underlying economic concerns within the United States, advocates of the Open Door were relatively powerless. Congressman Joseph G. Cannon (Rep., Ill.), who claimed that America need not seek overseas markets for many years, could undoubtedly rally more supporters than could Congressman Abram S. Hewitt, who thought that foreign purchasers were essential to the nation's prosperity. And even had the alternative of foreign markets been the dominant one, it was doubtful that a country lacking a strong navy or merchant marine could have taken the most advantage of it. It was equally doubtful whether foreign discrimination could have been successfully resisted.

The fate of the tariff did teach the Arthur administration one thing: if American commerce were to be expanded and if the surplus were to be reduced, the executive branch would have to take the initiative. Here Frelinghuysen took charge, pressing on a variety of fronts. He sought to expand the diplomatic and consular services, distribute port and harbor information to United States ships, and create an integrated financial structure, which would be headed by a parent intercontinental bank in New York. (American bankers themselves were not yet prepared to back the third proposal.) Part of the secretary's hemispheric system included a common coinage and a consultative council, the latter point coming far closer to Blaine's vision than his successor cared to admit.

It was reciprocity, however, that served as the linchpin of Frelinghuysen's system. Retaliation would be self-defeating, and free trade was totally infeasible; but reciprocal trade, if executed with effectiveness, might grant free entry for many foreign raw materials while providing fresh markets for American manufactured goods. The fact that the industrialized nations were beginning to shut out United States products only drove the point home. The future of the country, so such policy makers as Frelinghuysen believed, undoubtedly lay with nations that still lacked significant industrial development.

Reciprocity appeared to create the best of all possible worlds. Not only could it be used to amend the tariff without significantly altering American protection, but it possibly possessed other benefits as well: it could alleviate much overproduction, stabilize the economy, deprive the Democrats of a campaign issue, dispose of the dollar surplus, minimize congressional tampering, expand Washington's political influence overseas, and further the efforts to dominate an isthmian canal. In addition, it might enable the United States to exercise the necessary control over various groups of people outside this country without assuming the responsibilities connected with direct rule.

President Arthur realized the importance of reciprocity. In his last annual message, he claimed that "countries of the American continent and the adjacent islands are for the United States the natural marts of supply and demand."[13] While admitting that overproduction had no single cure, he took his cue from Frelinghuysen and outlined an intricate customs union for the hemisphere. Among his specific proposals were a subsidized consular service, a congressionally financed merchant marine, an inter-American monetary union, and reciprocity treaties containing the conditional form of the most-favored-nation.

Arthur faced an extremely difficult task. Despite its proximity to South America, the United States, by 1883, conducted only 18.9 percent of its trade there. If, as one trade enthusiast has said, the hemisphere was "a new 'West & South,'" it remained an untapped frontier.[14] In the Caribbean and in Central America, the picture was more favorable. Trade ratios reached above 50 percent, and United States investments were proportionately high. American investment in railroads, for example, concentrated upon nations that were closer to the United States, and due to former President Grant and United States minister John Watson Foster, Mexico in particular received much attention.

There were, of course, good reasons for much of the failure. Capitalists were reluctant to invest in countries where there were unstable regimes. The Indian and mestizo population was too poor to supply many buyers. Some Americans realized that they had only themselves to blame for dishonest measurements, inferior products, stringent credit terms, and ignorance of the Spanish and Portuguese languages. The United States did not always need the raw materials that some Latin American countries produced, a factor making exchange quite difficult. Chile, for example, would buy British, rather than United States, textiles, because Britain would be able to purchase Chilean copper in return.

Attempting to expand business opportunities, in 1884, Frelinghuysen recommended that a special commission visit Latin America. When Congress voted the funds, the president appointed one of Grant's personal friends to head it; the other two members were equally obscure. In the summer of 1884, although Arthur had already lost the presidential nomination, the commission began its work. It first interviewed American merchants on the east and west coasts and on the Gulf of Mexico as well; then it traveled to the Caribbean countries, Mexico, and Central America. Even after Cleveland had been inaugurated, it continued its journey. The commission proceeded down the west coast of South America and then returned by way of the Plata Basin and Brazil. Arriving home at the end of 1885, it presented a glowing report to the new president. The commissioners endorsed the recent reciprocity treaties; in addition, they recommended a hemispheric conference to discuss commerce, banking facilities, and a common currency. All their proposals, however, were adversely reported from committee, and Congress took no action on them.

Frelinghuysen was not about to leave potential United States profits in the hands of any commission. As early as 1882, he began to negotiate reciprocal treaties. He concentrated on the Caribbean, undoubtedly for two reasons: focus on this area might aid in alleviating domestic surpluses; it could help to counter de Lesseps's isthmian efforts and give the British second thoughts about continuing the Clayton-Bulwer Treaty.

As Mexico held the greatest attraction for American trade and investment, it was Frelinghuysen's first and primary target. In November 1880, the Mexican government, probably acting in the hope that it could prod the new administration, announced that it would terminate its fifty-year-old commercial treaty with the United States. Because Blaine had alienated the Mexicans over the Guatemala-boundary issue, it took the incentive of Frelinghuysen to seek a new agreement. Late in 1882, Frelinghuysen appointed Grant, who was then head of a group of railroad promoters, and William Henry Trescot as commissioners.

Negotiating at Grant's Washington home in January 1883, the diplomats drafted a treaty, one that involved exchanging United States manufactured goods for Mexican foodstuffs and raw materials. The United States agreed to admit twenty-eight categories of goods duty free, including beef, barley, sugar, coffee, fruit, henequen and istle fibers, uncured hides, and leaf tobacco. In return, Mexico put on her free list such manufactured items as agricultural tools, locomotives, rails, steam engines, sewing machines, and wire.

Within the United States, the agreement was hotly debated. Frelinghuysen was delighted with the treaty, believing, as did Trescot, that Mexico had sacrificed more potential revenue than had the United States. The *Chicago Tribune* spoke in terms of an "almost virgin outlet for extension of the market of our overproducing civilization."[15] Grant personally promoted what he had just negotiated, pointing with alarm to European penetration of Mexico and predicting a great commercial bonanza.

Some groups in the United States objected, however, that the treaty would subsidize a number of vested interests, including foreign planters, St. Louis sugar refineries, and the railroad interests of Jay Gould and Collis P. Huntington, two men who had backed Grant's railroad venture. Louisiana business interests were ambivalent: they welcomed increased trade with Mexico but feared that the Mexican sugar industry would capture markets currently belonging to the South. Certain critics, pointing to a riot in Mexico City in December 1883, claimed that Mexico was near bankruptcy; it could neither preserve its own peace nor protect United States property.

Many Mexicans in turn opposed reciprocity. Such an agreement, they feared, might lead to annexation, ruin Mexican industry, bolster a corrupt and unstable government, and violate unconditional most-favored-nation commitments which it had made to such nations as Germany. Matías Romero, the Mexican treasury minister who negotiated the agreement, tried to reassure Frelinghuysen. Mexico, he pledged, would abide by the conditional interpretation of the most-favored-nation policy, a United States practice that granted favors to third parties only in return for special compensation. Yet in March 1883, Romero was forced to admit that his government had overruled him.

Even before the Congress convened in 1884, the treaty was in trouble. The Democratic House, led by Speaker John G. Carlisle of Kentucky and by William R. Morrison of Illinois, chairman of the Ways and Means Committee, had no mind to commit itself to any trade program that would exclude a general tariff reduction. In addition, the House did not want the opposition party to receive praise. Nor did it seek to tie the hands of any possible Democratic president-elect. Then high-tariff partisans had their own objection. They feared that the agreement might, in the words of Tom E. Terrill, signify a break in the "vitally needed dike" of protection.[16] Senator Morrill, who led this opposition, claimed that the administration would lose too much revenue, had made too many concessions to Mexico, and had violated Congress's prerogative of introducing trade legislation.

On March 11, 1884, the Senate ratified the treaty, doing so by a vote of forty-one to twenty. Party alignments were often blurred. Senators from tobacco and sugar states, fearing that Mexico would destroy their markets, fought the agreement. The battle was not yet won, however, as administration supporters allowed the opposition to attach a crippling amendment, one that gave the House responsibility for passing any implementing legislation. The Mexican Congress, ignoring the protests of its own nationalists, approved the treaty two months later.

Such implementing legislation was soon stalled. In June 1884, the House Ways and Means Committee reported one bill favorably, but it never reached a full vote in the House itself. Opponents found reinforcement in a Treasury Department report on Mexico, released in January 1885, that described the labyrinth of Mexico's customs service, its impoverished Indian population, and the despotic nature of its government. And once Cleveland had assumed the presidency, he buried the entire issue.

Long before the Senate considered the Mexican treaty, Frelinghuysen was ardently seeking a reciprocity treaty with Spain, one that would concern, not the Iberian Peninsula, but the Spanish possessions of Puerto Rico and Cuba. The United States had been conducting a lively trade with Cuba in particular, investing in its sugar plantations and iron mines. Indeed, by 1881, the United States was engaged in almost seven times the commerce in Cuba that Spain was; sugar planters in both Cuba and Puerto Rico were virtually acting as American agents. Cuba, fearful that Europe's development of beet sugar would deprive it of the market there, sought salvation in a reciprocity agreement with the United States.

In February 1883, Arthur sent John W. Foster to Madrid, where he was to negotiate regarding trade with the two Spanish possessions. Foster, who has recently been called "one of the few first-class diplomats whom the patronage system had produced during the 1870's," had campaigned for Grant in 1872.[17] Later in the decade, he had served as minister to Mexico, conducting diplomacy during the border troubles. For a variety of reasons, the administration urged haste in completing the negotiations: Cuba's economy, dependent upon an increasingly depressed United States, was failing; filibustering expeditions, launched by Cuban rebels from Key West, were embarrassing the United States; the American consul at Havana, Grant's protégé Adam Badeau, had assailed Frelinghuysen's policy as vacillating and dishonorable; it was rumored—quite inaccurately, in fact—that Spain would soon sell Cuba to Germany; and, above all, Arthur's government was approaching its end. In the summer of 1884, Foster warned Spain that its refusal to negotiate might bring dire consequences, including United States reciprocity treaties with other Caribbean rivals, an increase in claims against Spain made by naturalized Cuban-Americans, and growing rebellion within Cuba.

In November 1884, after several months of dickering, the diplomats signed the treaty. If ratified, it would eliminate all economic barriers to Cuba and Puerto Rico. The United States would extend its free list to thirty-two categories of Cuban and Puerto Rican agricultural products, including the all-important crop of sugar. In exchange, the two Spanish colonies would admit such United States manufactured goods as cast iron and machinery. Spain also would accept the conditional form of most-favored-nation treatment on behalf of her two wards and would clear up doubtful points concerning the security of American property in Cuba.

Foster realized that his treaty had planted the seeds of an informal empire. On October 26, he wrote to Postmaster General Gresham that his agreement would be "the most perfect reciprocal treaty our Government has ever made," one that would "result in giving us the almost complete commercial monopoly of the commerce in Cuba." Stressing the value of free sugar and increased markets, he added, "It will be annexing Cuba in the most desirable way." Other American policy makers were equally jubilant. Frelinghuysen spoke of the "immediate benefit to our citizens, our trade, and our vessels." Arthur maintained that trade would be "scarcely less intimate than the commercial movement between our domestic ports."[18]

As in the case of the Mexican agreement, however, special interests quickly organized the opposition. From Samuel Gompers of the Federation of Organized Trade and Labor Unions (and, perhaps more significantly, the Cigar Makers International Union) to John L. Hayes of the National Association of Wool Manufacturers, many parochial voices made their disapproval known. New York sugar refiners and Louisiana sugar planters were alarmed over Cuban competition. Blaine, who was seeking the presidential nomination, turned against Arthur's entire reciprocity program. And protectionists saw the whole United States commercial system at stake. True, farming and shipbuilding interests backed the treaty, but the president needed more support.

By the middle of February 1885, the strong coalition of politicians and interest groups had destroyed all chances for ratification. Just before he left office, Arthur was able to remove tobacco from the free list and obtain a token tariff on Cuban sugar, but even this action could not salvage the agreement. Cleveland withdrew the treaty and a pending treaty with Santo Domingo as well.

The Dominican agreement had its genesis early in 1883, when the United States consul there had made efforts to undercut French influence. The Dominican Republic soon proposed reciprocity to Washington, seeing it as one means of reviving a depressed sugar industry. On December 4,

1884, a treaty was signed. Under its terms, the United States would agree to place twenty-nine Dominican products on the free list, including tobacco and certain forms of sugar. The Dominican Republic in turn promised to admit sixty-eight American products duty-free; to lower tariffs on such crucial items as cotton, wool, and linen textiles by 25 percent; and to make the American dollar the Dominican Republic's unit of currency for international trade. Although the treaty was more favorable to the United States than either the Mexican or the Spanish agreement had been, it never reached the Senate.

Reciprocity efforts centered not only on Mexico, Cuba, Puerto Rico, and Santo Domingo but on other areas of the world as well. Hawaii had been part of the commercial orbit of the United States since 1875, when the Grant administration had negotiated a reciprocal treaty there. By its terms, the United States agreed to abolish duties on such crucial items as unrefined sugar; Hawaii agreed to admit a long list of American products, including cotton manufactures, hardware, and clothing. By 1880, more than 70 percent of all Hawaii's imports came from the United States, and within three years, Americans had invested so heavily in Hawaii's sugar plantations that two-thirds of them passed into American hands. In addition, 95 percent of all Hawaiian commerce was carried by American vessels, and the United States usually served as the creditor nation. As Pletcher notes, "Hawaii had become an economic satellite of the United States."[19]

Hawaii soon came to be treated as an American preserve. Britain and France tried to claim unconditional most favored-nation privileges based on earlier treaties, but they soon learned that Hawaii recognized United States privileges as exclusive. The Senate Foreign Relations Committee commented that the islands "may be said to be properly within the area of the physical and political geography of the United States."[20]

A British effort to promote immigration of East Indian coolies and thereby to extend Britain's own influence met with a reply from Blaine that the islands belonged in the sphere of the United States. In writing to General James M. Comly, United States minister to Hawaii, Blaine realized that increased sugar production had caused an acute labor shortage. Hence he called for a "Hawaiian homestead act," by which "labor trained in the rice swamps and cane fields of the Southern States" could supply the new manpower. Hawaii, he said, might be as remote politically from United States control as was China, but economically it was practically part of an "American zollverein." Arthur too claimed that foreign immigration to Hawaii might "impair the native sovereignty and independence, in which the United States was among the first to testify a lively interest."[21]

President Garfield feared that King Kalakaua might sell the islands to a European power; Blaine, that the Hawaiian ruler planned to organize a Polynesian confederacy allied to China. The secretary continually stressed the interdependence of Hawaii and the United States, in particular the West Coast. "Under no circumstances," he wrote on December 1, 1881, "can the United States permit any change in the territorial control . . . which would cut it adrift from the American system" to which it, like Cuba, "indispensably" belonged.[22]

Opposition to the 1875 treaty, however, continued throughout the early 1880s. The agreement, so American critics claimed, lacked genuine reciprocity, drained the public treasury, and might well lead to formal annexation. In all these attacks, not surprisingly, domestic sugar interests were particularly vocal.

Arthur strongly sought the renewal of the 1875 treaty, and in his second and third annual messages, he asked Congress to act decisively. Frelinghuysen and Treasury Secretary Folger admitted that the agreement had weaknesses, but both men wanted it amended, not abrogated. Like Blaine, Frelinghuysen believed that Hawaii belonged in an American commonwealth and that, were the United States to start establishing protectorates, Hawaii would obviously be the first choice. The Senate Committee on Finance, acting under Morrill's influence, criticized the treaty, but the Senate and House committees on foreign relations endorsed its renewal.

The deadlock had not been resolved by December 6, 1884, when Frelinghuysen and the Hawaiian minister signed an agreement extending the 1875 agreement. Morrill again spoke in opposition, declaring that American power in the Pacific could not withstand "the slightest aggression, . . . which a modern gunboat, or a few Old World guineas, might extinguish in forty minutes."[23] And although Morrill was able to unify the protectionists, the Democrats were too divided to support the treaty unanimously: Bayard, for example, backed extension, while Morrison opposed it. Only in 1887 did the Senate approve the renewal of the treaty (which contained a naval lease on Pearl Harbor), and in just over a decade the United States would annex the islands.

Reciprocity was an idea whose time had not come. With the exception of the belated Hawaiian agreement, it steadily lost out to parochial and partisan interests. Even much of the business press did not share the administration's solution for America's surplus. The *Commercial and Financial Chronicle*, for example, went so far as to deny that overproduction had caused the depression of the eighties; rather, economic stagnation was rooted in lack of investment and the slow exchange of money. *Banker's*

Magazine concurred: "We need not be very much concerned in the country concerning the extension of our trade."[24]

The timing of Arthur's reciprocal agreements was anything but fortuitous. Most treaties came before the Senate after the Republican standard-bearer, James G. Blaine, had made the high tariff a keynote of his campaign and after the Democrats had captured the presidency. Frelinghuysen waited several weeks before responding to congressional inquiries, and Arthur did not push for the agreements. As in the case of the Nicaraguan canal arrangement, the treaties were negotiated prior to the development of a merchant marine and a navy. And in some cases where policy makers were considering reciprocity—Canada, El Salvador, Colombia, and Venezuela, for example—it was the State Department that did not follow through.

Trade remained relatively insignificant, particularly with nations outside of Europe. In 1884, exports totaled just 7.1 percent of the gross national product, and in 1885, only 11.7 percent of United States exports went to Asia and Latin America, an actual reduction from 1875 of 0.8 percent. Even as late as 1900, the United States traded little with the non-West: Great Britain remained its best customer.

Pletcher makes the point well: the expansionist commercial policies of Garfield and Arthur had simply collapsed.[25] Even Blaine could not have been more unsuccessful. When judged by behavior, not rhetoric, the results were poor indeed. Foreign policy was still determined by party politics and local economic interests, and this condition would continue as long as policy makers did not perceive that the nation was in danger. Moreover, the bulk of the American public still saw security in continental terms and commerce in protectionist ones; it was, as yet, unwilling to have the United States act as an aggressive world power.

Only in future years would the United States follow through on policies advanced during this time. Reciprocity would eventually come into its own, because President McKinley would find it an apt vehicle for extending American commerce while preserving much protectionism. In time, the United States would modernize its consular services, build the isthmian canal, annex Hawaii, hold Pan-American conferences, and mediate disputes in Asia. It was simply a case of the policy makers, particularly Frelinghuysen, being ahead of both the public and Congress, and it would take some years before either would catch up.

11

★ ★ ★ ★ ★

THE SUMMING UP

Much of the failure of Arthur's foreign policy was rooted in more general problems—namely, his illness and a divided party, two circumstances that were bound to make his bid for reelection half-hearted. The president did receive acclaim from a variety of sources: the New York business community, the *Chicago Tribune*, the *Nation*, George William Curtis, Mark Twain, and the Reverend Henry Ward Beecher, who claimed that the presidential candidate should be jovial, "big-bellied and big-chested." Yet many Americans, as one New Jersey Republican noted, simply saw the period as "a kind of lapse between one man who was elected and another who is going to be elected."[1]

Arthur, the machine man *par excellence*, was now isolated, so much so that his latest biographer calls him "virtually a President without a party."[2] He had not won the Half-Breeds over, having given them only token patronage. At the same time, his general apathy towards spoils lost him the backing of many Stalwarts. Grant endorsed Logan, Platt backed Blaine, and Conkling kept an aloof silence. The Independents, recalling Mahone's antics one minute, the star-route affair the next, returned to Edmunds. Indeed, Republicans of all sorts and conditions, remembering the results of the 1882 congressional elections, saw the president as a weak vote getter. There was little public demand for a second term, and certainly Arthur had never been a man able to inspire great masses.

Although he realized that the GOP would not turn to him, Arthur would not bow out. As Thomas C. Reeves notes, retreat would "raise suspicion about his health, cast doubt upon his competence to handle the burdens of the presidency, and carry with it the implication of cowardice—of a record as President that could not bear scrutiny, of a personal fear of defeat at the convention or at the polls."[3] He told a young supporter that he would not seek reelection; he ordered his leading lieutenant, William E. Chandler, to keep away from the forthcoming nominating convention; and he turned down several deals over patronage. Of all his associates, only Frelinghuysen knew about Arthur's true physical condition.

At the Chicago convention, the Arthur forces, led by Postmaster General Hatton, never had a chance. Walter Q. Gresham has used the analogy of an army without a commander. The Arthur and Edmunds groups could not even unite in stopping Blaine, who, by the fourth ballot, was clearly the victor. Arthur pledged "earnest and cordial support," and within two weeks, he told Conger that he had, at most, a few more years to live.

During the bitter campaign between Blaine and Democratic nominee Grover Cleveland, neither Arthur nor his cabinet gave Blaine and his running mate, "Black Jack" Logan, any support. The president would not meet with the Republican National Committee, and the New York Stalwarts, who dominated the state committee and who were led by Arthur men, concentrated on local contests. Conkling, when asked to campaign for Blaine, replied, "I don't engage in criminal practice."[4] Cleveland won the closest election in the nation's history—that is, as far as his margin in the electoral college was concerned. Arthur regretted that the party had been defeated, but his grief went no further.

The lame-duck president spent his final ailing days in office on such ceremonial matters as dedicating the Washington Monument. His last official act was to nominate Ulysses S. Grant as a general on the retired list, thereby giving a bankrupt and dying man some means of subsistence. Before leaving the White House, he had declined a Stalwart invitation to become senator from New York. On November 18, 1886, Chester Alan Arthur died of the disease from which he had suffered for so long.

Of the two men who occupied the White House from 1881 to 1885, Garfield—as a president—remains more of a mystery. We know that he saw the office of chief executive primarily in administrative terms and that his great battle was over keeping the power of appointment in his own hands. By winning a victory over the Stalwarts, he enhanced both the power and prestige of his office. As a man, he was intelligent, sensitive, and alert, and his knowledge of how government worked was unmatched. Long before Woodrow Wilson made his mark, it was James Abram Garfield who was "the scholar in politics." His advocacy of education as the solution to

Negro hardship was simplistic, but it surely was an essential step in advancement for blacks. And his flirtation with the Virginia Readjusters showed a needed flexibility, one that aided both his party and a segment of the defeated South.

The Garfield record, however, is ambivalent. He often lacked judgment at crucial points, as can be seen by his replacement of Merritt. Whether he totally had his bearings after the Robertson fight remains problematic, for he was assassinated within two months. Blaine's chaotic diplomacy would have undoubtedly proven embarrassing, and one can only wonder if the president would have curbed the power of his secretary of state. Given Garfield's rigid adherence to laissez faire and hard money, his ability to cope with a declining economy remains in doubt. To grow in office, he would have needed far more wise and diverse counsel than Half-Breeds alone could offer.

Arthur was one of the nation's great political surprises, for few expected a man of his limitations to do a commendable job. Yet, despite his poor health, he attempted to govern competently, and he was successful to a degree that has not been acknowledged by his fellow politicians, the press, the great mass of his countrymen—and, most of all, historians. True, he could be vindictive, as can be seen in his treatment of Silas Burt. And equally true, his ideology, as rigid as that of Garfield, left him unable to deal with a failing economy. But some of his appointments were superior; Frelinghuysen, in particular, showed a real grasp of his nation's economic distress and offered a positive program to alleviate it. Arthur demonstrated genuine courage in his major vetoes and in his endorsement of the findings of the tariff commission. He conscientiously tried to administer the new civil-service program and to prosecute the star-route cases when, in both instances, he could have imposed impediments. He realized the need for naval reform, and he promoted its cause. He was by no means fully sensitive to the condition of black Americans, but his southern strategy won substantial endorsement from Negroes. If his stress on Indian severalty was less wise, it was the solution advocated by leading reformers. His state papers were often far-sighted, showing a grasp of such issues as consular reform, commercial agreements, currency policy, and presidential disability.

True, Arthur initiated little new legislation and was not an active leader, but he conducted the office with dignity and restraint. By twentieth-century standards, he would be evaluated a weak president. In a sense, such a judgment is unfair, for he seldom had to confront directly the massive problems created by the burgeoning technological revolution. By the standards of his time, which stressed administrative competency, he was most adequate. If the presidency as an institution did not gain much power, it did not lose much either. Few of his successors would find the conditions of their rule so fortunate.

NOTES

CHAPTER 1

1. James Bryce, *The American Commonwealth,* 3 vols. (London: Macmillan, 1888), 3:559.
2. Eric F. Goldman, *Rendezvous with Destiny: A History of Modern American Reform* (New York: Knopf, 1952), chap. 5.
3. Edward Chase Kirkland, *Dream and Thought in the Business Community, 1860–1900* (Ithaca, N.Y.: Cornell University Press, 1956), p. 14.
4. Oliver Wendell Holmes, *The Common Law* (Boston: Little, Brown, 1881), p. 10.
5. Santayana is cited in the introduction to *The Genteel Tradition: Nine Essays by George Santayana,* ed. Douglas L. Wilson (Cambridge, Mass.: Harvard University Press, 1967), p. 14.
6. Richard J. Jensen, *The Winning of the Midwest: A Social Analysis of Midwestern Politics, 1888–1896* (Chicago: University of Chicago Press, 1971), p. 3.
7. Ibid., p. 11.
8. Robert D. Marcus, *Grand Old Party: Political Structure in the Gilded Age, 1880–1896* (New York: Oxford University Press, 1971), p. 58.
9. Bryce, *American Commonwealth,* 2:292.
10. John G. Sproat, *"The Best Men": Liberal Reformers in the Gilded Age* (New York: Oxford University Press, 1968), p. 46.
11. Leonard D. White, *The Republican Era, 1869–1901: A Study in Administrative History* (New York: Macmillan, 1958), p. 1.
12. Bryce, *American Commonwealth,* 2:20.
13. Morton Keller, *Affairs of State: Public Life in Late Nineteenth Century America* (Cambridge, Mass.: Belknap Press of Harvard University Press, 1977), p. 114.
14. Loren P. Beth, *The Development of the American Constitution, 1877–1917* (New York: Harper & Row, 1971), p. 4.
15. Garfield cited by White in *Republican Era,* p. 4.
16. Woodrow Wilson, *Congressional Government* (originally published in 1885; republished, New York: Meridian, 1956), pp. 49, 181.
17. White, *Republican Era,* p. 48.
18. Hoar cited by John A. Garraty in *The New Commonwealth, 1877–1890* (New York: Harper & Row, 1968), p. 231.
19. Conkling cited by H. Wayne Morgan in *From Hayes to McKinley: National Party Politics, 1877–1896* (Syracuse, N.Y.: Syracuse University Press, 1969), p. 33.
20. Garfield cited by Allan Peskin in *Garfield* (Kent, Ohio: Kent State University Press, 1978), pp. 452–453.
21. Marcus, *Grand Old Party,* p. 36.

22. Blaine cited by Peskin in *Garfield*, p. 396.
23. Wilson, *Congressional Government*, p. 196.
24. Bryce, *American Commonwealth*, 3:533.
25. Wilson, *Congressional Government*, p. 173; Bryce, *American Commonwealth*, 1:104–105.
26. Robert H. Wiebe, *The Search for Order, 1877–1920* (New York: Hill & Wang, 1967), p. 36.
27. Bryce, *American Commonwealth*, 2:550.

CHAPTER 2

1. Morgan, *From Hayes to McKinley*, p. 57.
2. Marcus, *Grand Old Party*, p. 35.
3. Garfield cited by Thomas C. Reeves in *Gentleman Boss: The Life of Chester Alan Arthur* (New York: Knopf, 1975), p. 168.
4. Conkling cited by Peskin in *Garfield*, p. 465.
5. Reeves, *Gentleman Boss*, p. 179.
6. Arthur and Conkling cited in ibid., p. 180.
7. *Nation* 30 (1880): 445.
8. Reeves, *Gentleman Boss*, p. 164.
9. Garfield cited by Peskin in *Garfield*, pp. 44, 79.
10. Garfield cited in ibid., pp. 153, 125, 244.
11. Ibid., p. 262.
12. Garfield cited in ibid., p. 373.
13. Garfield cited in ibid., p. 262.
14. Garfield cited in ibid., p. 419.
15. Thomas Donaldson cited by Margaret Leech and Harry J. Brown in *The Garfield Orbit* (New York: Harper & Row, 1978), p. 171.
16. Garfield cited by Peskin in *Garfield*, p. 454.
17. Ibid., pp. 396, 434.
18. Reeves, *Gentleman Boss*, p. 187.
19. Republican platform and delegates appear in Herbert J. Clancy, *The Presidential Election of 1880* (Chicago: Loyola University Press, 1958), pp. 95–96.
20. Garfield cited by Marcus in *Grand Old Party*, p. 53.
21. Peskin, *Garfield*, p. 489.
22. Garfield cited in ibid., p. 490.
23. Peskin, *Garfield*, p. 491; Reeves, *Gentleman Boss*, p. 194.
24. Jensen, *Winning of the Midwest*, p. 32.

25. Garfield cited by Reeves in *Gentleman Boss*, p. 202.
26. Garfield cited in ibid.
27. *Nation* 31 (1880): 258.
28. Hancock exchange cited by Morgan in *From Hayes to McKinley*, p. 119.
29. Garfield cited by Theodore Clarke Smith in *The Life and Letters of James Abram Garfield*, 2 vols. (New Haven, Conn.: Yale University Press, 1925), 2:1043.
30. Schurz and Morgan cited by Morgan in *From Hayes to McKinley*, p. 121.
31. Garfield cited by Smith in *Life and Letters*, 2:1047.
32. Garfield cited by Reeves in *Gentleman Boss*, p. 163.
33. Peskin, *Garfield*, p. 396.
34. Conkling cited by Smith in *Life and Letters*, 2:1057–1058.
35. Blaine cited in ibid., 2:1059.
36. Blaine cited by Peskin in *Garfield*, p. 524.
37. *New York Times*, January 18, 1881.
38. Blaine cited by Smith in *Life and Letters*, 2:1078.
39. Garfield cited in ibid., 2:1082–1083.
40. Reid cited in ibid., 2:1092.
41. Morgan, *From Hayes to McKinley*, p. 127.
42. Garfield cited by Smith in *Life and Letters*, 2:1098.

CHAPTER 3

1. Garfield cited by Peskin in *Garfield*, p. 544.
2. Garfield cited in ibid., p. 564.
3. Hay cited by Allan Peskin in "President Garfield and the Rating Game: An Evaluation of a Brief Administration," *South Atlantic Quarterly* 76 (1976): 96.
4. Garfield cited by Peskin in *Garfield*, p. 551, and by Smith in *Life and Letters*, 2:1152.
5. Ari Hoogenboom, "The Pendleton Act and the Civil Service," *American Historical Review* 64 (1959): 302.
6. Compare Ari Hoogenboom, "Spoilsmen and Reformers: Civil Service Reform and Public Morality," in *The Gilded Age: A Reappraisal*, ed. H. Wayne Morgan (Syracuse, N.Y.: Syracuse University Press, 1963), pp. 69–72, with Reeves, *Gentleman Boss*, pp. 45–46, 63–66. Garfield cited by Smith in *Life and Letters*,

2:1151-1152.

7. Irwin Unger, *The Greenback Era: A Social and Political History of American Finance, 1865-1879* (Princeton, N.J.: Princeton University Press, 1964).

8. Godkin cited by Sproat in *"Best Men,"* p. 185.

9. Dorman B. Eaton, "Political Assessments," *North American Review* 135 (1882): 209.

10. Morgan, *From Hayes to McKinley,* p. 105.

11. Blaine cited by Smith in *Life and Letters,* 2:1060.

12. Peskin, *Garfield,* p. 551.

13. Garfield cited by Smith in *Life and Letters,* 2:1104.

14. Blaine cited by Peskin in *Garfield,* p. 554.

15. Conkling cited by Peskin in *Garfield,* p. 561; Grant cited by Smith in *Life and Letters,* 2:1134.

16. *Nation* 32 (May 19, 1881): 342.

17. Garfield cited by Smith in *Life and Letters,* 2:1109, and by Peskin in *Garfield,* p. 564.

18. Reid cited by Reeves in *Gentleman Boss,* p. 225.

19. Garfield cited by Smith in *Life and Letters,* 2:1111.

20. Reeves, *Gentleman Boss,* p. 226.

21. Conkling cited in ibid., p. 228.

22. *Chicago Tribune* cited by William Lester Ketchersid in "The Maturing of the Presidency, 1877-1889" (Ph.D. diss., University of Georgia, 1977), p. 50.

23. Garfield cited by Smith in *Life and Letters,* 2:1127.

24. Garfield cited by Peskin in *Garfield,* p. 570.

25. Garfield cited by Smith in *Life and Letters,* 2:1135.

26. Hayes cited in *Nation* 32 (June 9, 1881): 397.

27. Morgan, *From Hayes to McKinley,* p. 135.

28. Garfield cited by Smith in *Life and Letters,* 2:1136.

29. Garfield cited in ibid., 2:1157.

30. Garfield cited by Morgan in *From Hayes to McKinley,* p. 157.

31. Garfield cited in ibid., p. 24; Peskin, *Garfield,* p. 493; and Stanley P. Hirshson, *Farewell to the Bloody Shirt: Northern Republicans & the Southern Negro, 1877-1893* (Bloomington: Indiana University Press, 1962), pp. 79, 81.

32. Garfield cited by Peskin in *Garfield,* pp. 253, 304, and by Robert Irving Cottom, Jr., in "To Be among the First: The Early Career of James A. Garfield, 1831-1868" (Ph.D. diss., Johns Hopkins University, 1975), p. 269.

33. Garfield cited by Peskin in *Garfield,* p. 332, and by Vincent P. De Santis in "President Garfield and the Solid South," *North Carolina Historical Review* 36 (1959): 453-454.

34. Garfield cited by Hirshson in *Farewell,* p. 92.

35. *New York Age* cited by De Santis in "President Garfield," p. 452.

36. Garfield's inaugural address, March 4, 1881, in *A Compilation of the Messages and Papers of the Presidents, 1789-1897,* ed. James D. Richardson, 10 vols. (Washington, D.C.: Government Printing Office, 1896-1907), 8:8-9. Hereinafter, volumes of this set will be cited as *Messages and Papers.*

37. Garfield cited by Allan Peskin in "President Garfield and the Southern Question: The Making of a Policy That Never Was," *Southern Quarterly* 16 (1978): 386.

38. Garfield cited by Peskin in *Garfield,* p. 412.

39. C. Vann Woodward, *Origins of the New South, 1877-1913* (Baton Rouge: Louisiana State University Press, 1951), p. 96.

40. Carl N. Degler, *The Other South: Southern Dissenters in the Nineteenth Century* (New York: Harper & Row, 1974), p. 270.

41. Garfield cited by De Santis in "President Garfield," p. 458, and by Hirshson in *Farewell,* p. 95.

42. Garfield cited by De Santis in "President Garfield," p. 460.

43. Garfield cited by Hirshson in *Farewell,* p. 97.

44. Lincoln cited by John S. Goff in *Robert Todd Lincoln: A Man in His Own Right* (Norman: University of Oklahoma Press, 1969), p. 120.

45. Godkin, Hayes, and Foster cited by Reeves in *Gentleman Boss,* pp. 241, 245.

46. Bayard cited in ibid., p. 242.

47. Harrison and Reeves in ibid.

48. Arthur's inaugural address, September 22, 1881, in *Messages and Papers,* 8:33.

49. Adams cited by Harold D. Cater, comp., *Henry Adams and His Friends* (Boston: Houghton Mifflin, 1947), pp. 115–116, 111.

CHAPTER 4

1. For examples of this interpretation see Samuel Flagg Bemis, *A Diplomatic History of the United States,* 4th ed. (New York: Holt, Rinehart & Winston, 1955), p. 437; Richard W. Leopold, *The Growth of American Foreign Policy: A History* (New York: Knopf, 1962), p. 13; and Thomas A. Bailey, *A Diplomatic History of the American People,* 9th ed. (Englewood Cliffs, N.J.: Prentice-Hall, 1974), p. 391.
2. For examples of this view see William Appleman Williams, *The Roots of the Modern American Empire* (New York: Random House, 1969); Walter LaFeber, *The New Empire: An Interpretation of American Expansion, 1860–1898* (Ithaca, N.Y.: Cornell University Press for the American Historical Association, 1963); and Howard B. Schonberger, *Transportation to the Seaboard: The "Communication Revolution" and American Foreign Policy, 1860–1900* (Westport, Conn.: Greenwood Press, 1971).
3. David M. Pletcher, *The Awkward Years: American Foreign Relations under Garfield and Arthur* (Columbia: University of Missouri Press, 1962).
4. Garfield cited by Allan Peskin in "Blaine, Garfield and Latin America: A New Look," *Americas* 36 (1979): 87.
5. Hay cited by Pletcher in *Awkward Years,* p. 19.
6. *Appletons' Annual Cyclopaedia and Register of Important Events of the Year 1881* (New York: Appleton, 1882), p. 734.
7. Blaine to H. J. Kilpatrick, June 15, 1881, in U.S., Department of State, *Papers Relating to the Foreign Relations of the United States, 1881* (Washington, D.C.: U.S. Government Printing Office, 1882), p. 133. Hereinafter, volumes of this set will be cited as *Foreign Relations.*
8. Memorandum of conversation between S. A. Hurlbut and Admiral Lynch, August 25, 1881, in ibid., p. 928.
9. Pletcher, *Awkward Years,* p. 51.
10. Blaine to W. H. Trescot, December 1, 1881, in *Foreign Relations,* 1881, p. 146.
11. David Saville Muzzey, *James G. Blaine: A Political Idol of Other Days* (New York: Dodd, Mead, 1934), p. 248.
12. British minister cited by V. G. Kiernan in "Foreign Interests in the War of the Pacific," *Hispanic American Historical Review* 35 (1955): 33.
13. Blaine to P. H. Morgan, June 21, 1881, *Foreign Relations,* 1881, pp. 768–769.
14. Hayes, message to the Senate, March 8, 1880, in *Messages and Papers,* 7:585; Garfield's inaugural address, March 4, 1881, in ibid., 8:11.
15. Blaine to J. R. Lowell, June 24, 1881, *Foreign Relations,* 1881, pp. 538–539.
16. Arthur's first annual message, December 6, 1881, in *Messages and Papers,* 8:41.
17. Pletcher, *Awkward Years,* p. 64.
18. Blaine to J. R. Lowell, November 19, 1881, *Foreign Relations,* 1881, p. 559.
19. Lord Granville to L. S. Sackville-West, January 14 and 7, 1882, *Foreign Relations,* 1882, pp. 313, 303.
20. Garfield's inaugural address, March 4, 1881, in *Messages and Papers,* 8:10.
21. *London Economist,* cited by Edward C. Kirkland in *Industry Comes of Age: Business, Labor, and Public Policy, 1860–1897* (New York: Holt, Rinehart & Winston, 1961), p. 281.
22. Extract from G. Crump's report, December 21, 1880, *Foreign Relations,* 1881, p. 580; Blaine to J. R. Lowell, March 17, 1881, in ibid., p. 516.
23. Morton to F. T. Frelinghuysen, December 26, 1883, *Foreign Relations,* 1884, p. 129.
24. Blaine cited by Pletcher in *Awkward Years,* pp. 239, 241.
25. Ibid., p. 195.
26. Shufeldt cited by Charles Oscar Paullin in *Diplomatic Negotiations of American Naval Officers, 1778–1883* (Baltimore, Md.: Johns Hopkins Press, 1912), p. 302.
27. Shufeldt cited by John William Rollins in "Frederick Theodore Frelinghuysen, 1817–1885: The Politics and Diplomacy of Stewardship" (Ph.D. diss., University of Wisconsin, 1974), p. 402.
28. Robinson cited in ibid., p. 426.
29. Lester D. Langley, "James Gillespie Blaine: The Ideologue as Diplomatist," in *Makers of American Diplomacy: From Benjamin Franklin to Henry Kissinger,*

ed. Frank J. Merli and Theodore A. Wilson (New York: Scribner's 1974); Milton Plesur, *America's Outward Thrust: Approaches to Foreign Affairs, 1865-1890* (De Kalb: Northern Illinois University Press, 1971), p. 234; Edward P. Crapol, *America for Americans: Economic Nationalism and Anglophobia in the Late Nineteenth Century* (Westport, Conn.: Greenwood Press, 1973), p. 68.

30. Garfield cited by Williams in *Roots*, p. 246.
31. Blaine cited by LaFeber in *New Empire*, p. 46.
32. Pletcher, *Awkward Years*, p. xv; John A. Garraty, *The New Commonwealth, 1877-1890* (New York: Harper & Row, 1968), p. 274; Charles S. Campbell, *The Transformation of American Foreign Relations, 1865-1900* (New York: Harper & Row, 1976), pp. 91-92.

CHAPTER 5

1. John J. Ingalls cited by Morgan in *Hayes to McKinley*, p. 141.
2. Conkling follower and customhouse associate cited by Reeves in *Gentleman Boss*, p. 260; Conkling cited by Morgan in *From Hayes to McKinley*, p. 149.
3. Arthur's third annual message, December 4, 1883, in *Messages and Papers*, 8:185.
4. Reeves, *Gentleman Boss*, p. 86.
5. Hayes and Platt cited in ibid., p. 271.
6. *Washington Commercial Advertiser* cited in ibid., p. 273.
7. Arthur cited by Morgan in *From Hayes to McKinley*, p. 148.
8. Clerk cited by Reeves in *Gentleman Boss*, p. 273.
9. Herndon cited in ibid., p. 318.
10. Ibid., p. 367.
11. Arthur's veto message of August 1, 1882, in *Messages and Papers*, 8:120-122.
12. Reid and *New Orleans Times-Democrat* cited by Schonberger in *Transportation*, pp. 109-110.
13. Elmer Clarence Sandmeyer, *The Anti-Chinese Movement in California* (Urbana: University of Illinois Press, 1939), p. 14.
14. Arthur's veto message of April 4, 1882, in *Messages and Papers*, 8:112-118.

15. The bill is cited in *Appletons' Annual Cyclopaedia and Register of Important Events of the Year 1882* (New York: Appleton, 1883), p. 387.
16. Garfield's inaugural address, March 4, 1881, in *Messages and Papers*, 8:11; Arthur's first annual message, December 6, 1881, in ibid., 8:57.
17. Taylor cited in *Nation* 35 (October 12, 1882): 298.
18. The board is cited by Henry G. Waltmann in "The Interior Department, War Department and Indian Policy, 1865-1887" (Ph.D. diss., University of Nebraska, 1962), p. 332.
19. Matthews cited by Keller in *Affairs of State*, p. 460.
20. Loring Benson Priest, *Uncle Sam's Stepchildren: The Reformation of United States Indian Policy, 1865-1887* (New Brunswick, N.J.: Rutgers University Press, 1942), p. 183.
21. White, *Republican Era*, p. 175.
22. Missionary boards cited by Waltmann in "Interior Department," p. 326.
23. Priest, *Uncle Sam's Stepchildren*, p. 145.
24. Garfield cited by Peskin in *Garfield*, p. 298.
25. Arthur's first annual message, December 6, 1881, in *Messages and Papers*, 8:55-56.
26. Teller and Hooker cited by Robert Winston Mardock in *The Reformers and the American Indian* (Columbia: University of Missouri Press, 1971), p. 215.
27. Teller cited by Francis Paul Prucha in *American Indian Policy in Crisis: Christian Reformers and the Indian, 1865-1900* (Norman: University of Oklahoma Press, 1976), pp. 130-131.
28. Teller cited in ibid., p. 240.
29. Arthur's first annual message, December 6, 1881, in *Messages and Papers*, 8:56-57.
30. Mardock, *Reformers*, p. 210.

CHAPTER 6

1. Reeves, *Gentleman Boss*, p. 300.
2. Arthur cited in ibid., p. 299.
3. Arthur's first annual message, December 6, 1881, in *Messages and Papers*, 8:53.
4. Brewster cited by Reeves in *Gentleman Boss*, p. 302.
5. Dorsey cited in ibid., p. 304.

6. Opinions given in Charles E. Rosenberg, *The Trial of the Assassin Guiteau: Psychiatry and Law in the Gilded Age* (Chicago: University of Chicago Press, 1968), pp. ix, xiii.
7. Guiteau cited in ibid., p. 138.
8. Brewster cited by Reeves in *Gentleman Boss*, p. 264.
9. Guiteau cited by Rosenberg in *Trial*, p. 237.
10. Adams cited by Ari Hoogenboom in *Outlawing the Spoils: A History of the Civil Service Reform Movement, 1865-1883* (Urbana: University of Illinois Press, 1961), p. 214; White cited by Reeves in *Gentleman Boss*, p. 241; Morgan, *Hayes to McKinley*, p. 144.
11. Arthur's first annual message, December 6, 1881, in *Messages and Papers*, 8:60-63.
12. Morgan, *From Hayes to McKinley*, pp. 162-163.
13. Hoogenboom, *Outlawing*, p. 219.
14. Morgan cited in ibid., p. 227.
15. Mrs. Adams cited by Hoogenboom in *Outlawing*, p. 236.
16. Ibid., p. 238.
17. Brown cited in ibid., p. 247.
18. Morgan cited by Reeves in *Gentleman Boss*, p. 325.
19. Ibid., pp. 326-327.
20. Curtis and the commission cited in ibid., p. 327.
21. White, *Republican Era*, p. 215.
22. Paul P. Van Riper, *History of the United States Civil Service* (Evanston, Ill.: Row, Peterson, 1958), p. 84.

CHAPTER 7

Much of the material in this chapter was presented by me, although in quite different form, in "The Republican Search for a Southern Strategy: The Arthur Administration" (a paper delivered at the annual meeting of the Organization of American Historians, New York City, April 13, 1978).

1. Twain cited by Woodward in *Origins*, pp. 153, 157.
2. Grady cited by Paul M. Gaston in *The New South Creed: A Study in Southern Mythmaking* (New York: Knopf, 1970), p. 96.
3. Woodward, *Origins*, pp. 184-185.
4. C. Vann Woodward, *The Strange Career of Jim Crow*, 2d rev. ed. (New York: Oxford University Press, 1966), p. 33.
5. Rayford W. Logan, *The Betrayal of the Negro: From Rutherford B. Hayes to Woodrow Wilson*, new, enl. ed. (New York: Collier, 1965), p. 140.
6. Douglass cited by August Meier in *Negro Thought in America, 1880-1915: Racial Ideologies in the Age of Booker T. Washington* (Ann Arbor: University of Michigan Press, 1963), p. 75.
7. Washington cited in ibid., p. 98.
8. Gaston, *New South Creed*, p. 209.
9. Supplementary Civil Rights Act cited by Michael J. Horan in "Political Economy and Sociological Theory as Influences on Judicial Policy-Making: The *Civil Rights Cases* of 1883," *American Journal of Legal History* 16 (1972): 71.
10. Keller, *Affairs of State*, p. 151.
11. Bradley cited by Alfred H. Kelly and Winfred A. Harbison in *The American Constitution: Its Origins and Development*, 3d ed. (New York: Norton, 1965), p. 491.
12. Ingersoll and Sherman cited by Hirshson in *Farewell*, p. 104.
13. Douglass cited by Meier in *Negro Thought*, p. 71.
14. Turner cited in ibid., p. 66.
15. G. T. Luby to W. E. Chandler, May 23, 1882, William E. Chandler Papers, Library of Congress, Washington, D.C.
16. W. E. Chandler to J. G. Blaine, October 2, 1882, Chandler Papers.
17. *National Republican* and Woodward cited by Woodward in *Origins*, p. 102.
18. J. B. Pitkin to W. E. Chandler, June 8, 1882, Chandler Papers.
19. *Nation* 33 (November 17, 1881): 383.
20. G. C. McKee to W. E. Chandler, July 6, 1882, in Willie D. Halsell, ed., "Republican Factionalism in Mississippi, 1882-1884," *Journal of Southern History* 7 (1941): 93, and D. B. Henderson to W. E. Chandler, July 4, 1882, in ibid., p. 92.
21. Hampton cited by William J. Cooper, Jr. in *The Conservative Regime: South Carolina, 1877-1890* (Baltimore, Md.: Johns Hopkins Press, 1968), p. 71.
22. Rebecca Felton cited by Degler in *Other South*, p. 289.
23. J. W. Menard to W. E. Chandler, November 27, 1882, and J. J. Mott to W. E. Chandler, November 18, 1882, Chandler Papers.

24. Albert D. Kirwan, *Revolt of the Red-necks: Mississippi Politics, 1876–1925* (Lexington: University of Kentucky Press, 1951), p. 15.
25. Memorandum, "Pinchback's Denunciation of the Kellogg Ring: Reasons Why Colored Men Should Desert Carpet Baggers," enclosed in G. T. Luby to W. E. Chandler, May 23, 1882, Chandler Papers.
26. *Nation* 38 (March 13, 1884): 223.
27. Douglass cited by Meier in *Negro Thought*, p. 29, and by Hirshson in *Farewell*, p. 122.
28. Logan, *Betrayal*, pp. 56–57.
29. Hirshson, *Farewell*, p. 105.
30. Reeves, *Gentleman Boss*, pp. 311–312; Arthur's third annual message, December 4, 1883, in *Messages and Papers*, 8:188.
31. J. Morgan Kousser, *The Shaping of Southern Politics: Suffrage Restriction and the Establishment of the One-Party South, 1880–1910* (New Haven, Conn.: Yale University Press, 1974), p. 26.
32. Fortune cited by Degler in *Other South*, p. 291; Douglass cited by James M. McPherson in *The Abolitionist Legacy: From Reconstruction to the NAACP* (Princeton, N.J.: Princeton University Press, 1975), p. 131.

CHAPTER 8

1. Russell H. Bastert, "Diplomatic Reversal: Frelinghuysen's Opposition to Blaine's Pan-American Policy in 1882," *Mississippi Valley Historical Review* 42 (1956): 657.
2. Frelinghuysen cited by Rollins in "Frederick Theodore Frelinghuysen," p. 494.
3. Ibid., pp. 274–278, 507.
4. Davis cited by Pletcher in *Awkward Years*, p. 79.
5. Davis cited by Reeves in *Gentleman Boss*, p. 290.
6. Trescot cited by Pletcher in *Awkward Years*, p. 93.
7. Blaine cited in ibid., pp. 83, 42.
8. *Nation* 34 (March 30, 1882): 264.
9. Arthur's second annual message, December 4 1882, in *Messages and Papers*, 8:130.
10. Alice Felt Tyler, *The Foreign Policy of James G. Blaine* (Minneapolis: University of Minnesota Press, 1927), p. 43.
11. Pletcher, *Awkward Years*, p. 278.
12. Arthur's special message to the Senate, December 10. 1884, in *Messages and Papers*, 8:258.
13. Cleveland's first annual message, December 8, 1885, in ibid., 8:328.
14. Armour and *New York Herald* cited by Williams in *Roots*, p. 256.
15. National Livestock Association cited by John L. Gignilliat in "Pigs, Politics, and Protection: The European Boycott of American Pork, 1879–1891," *Agricultural History* 35 (1961): 10.
16. *Chicago Tribune* cited by Williams in *Roots*, p. 257.
17. Congressman William E. Robinson (Dem., N.Y.) cited by Pletcher in *Awkward Years*, p. 241.
18. Frelinghuysen to J. R. Lowell, April 25, 1882, in *Foreign Relations*, 1882, p. 234.
19. Frelinghuysen to J. R. Lowell, September 22, 1882, in ibid., p. 294.
20. Rossa cited in *Nation* 36 (February 1, 1883): 93.
21. Davis cited by Pletcher in *Awkward Years*, p. 226.
22. *Nation* 36 (March 22, 1883): 249.
23. Owen Dudley Edwards, "American Diplomats and Irish Coercion, 1880–1883," *Journal of American Studies* 1 (1967): 215.

CHAPTER 9

1. Pletcher, *Awkward Years*, p. 116; LaFeber, *New Empire*, p. 58.
2. John Roach, "A Militia for the Sea," *North American Review* 133 (1881): 179; A. T. Mahan to S. A. Ashe, December 21, 1882, in Robert Seager II and Doris D. Maguire, eds., *Letters and Papers of Alfred Thayer Mahan*, 3 vols. (Annapolis, Md.: Naval Institute Press, 1975), 1:544.
3. Shufeldt cited by Williams in *Roots*, p. 239.
4. Porter, Hunt, and Kasson cited by Robert Seager II in "Ten Years before Mahan: The Unofficial Case for the New Navy, 1880–1890," *Mississippi Valley Historical Review* 40 (1953): 500, 509, 495.
5. Arthur's first annual message, December

6, 1881, in *Messages and Papers*, 8:51–52.

6. House committee cited by Reeves in *Gentleman Boss*, p. 341.

7. Chandler cited by Seager in "Ten Years," pp. 505–506.

8. Kenneth J. Hagan, *American Gunboat Diplomacy and the Old Navy, 1877–1889* (Westport, Conn.: Greenwood Press, 1973), pp. 40–41.

9. Chandler cited by Reeves in *Gentleman Boss*, p. 342.

10. Arthur's third annual message, December 4, 1883, in *Messages and Papers*, 8:181.

11. Arthur's fourth annual message, December 1, 1884, in ibid., 8:248.

12. Seager, "Ten Years," p. 508.

13. Arthur's second annual message, December 4, 1882, in *Messages and Papers*, 8:140.

14. Admiral David D. Porter cited by Harold and Margaret Sprout in *The Rise of American Naval Power, 1776–1918*, rev. ed. (Princeton, N.J.: Princeton University Press, 1946), p. 195.

15. William H. Whitney cited by Paul S. Holbo in "Economics, Emotion, and Expansion: An Emerging Foreign Policy," in *The Gilded Age: A Reappraisal*, ed. H. Wayne Morgan, rev. and enl. ed. (Syracuse, N.Y.: Syracuse University Press, 1970), p. 212.

16. King's letter cited by Yur-Bok Lee in *Diplomatic Relations between the United States and Korea, 1866–1887* (New York: Humanities Press, 1970), p. 41.

17. Frelinghuysen cited by C. I. Eugene Kim and Han-Kyo Kim in *Korea and the Politics of Imperialism, 1876–1910* (Berkeley and Los Angeles: University of California Press, 1968), p. 26.

18. Arthur's third annual message, December 4, 1883, in *Messages and Papers*, 8:174.

19. Tyler Dennett, *Americans in Eastern Asia* (New York: Macmillan, 1922; reprinted by Barnes & Noble in 1941 and 1963), pp. 461–462.

20. Li cited by Pletcher in *Awkward Years*, p. 211.

21. Frelinghuysen cited by Dennett in *Americans*, p. 474.

22. Tyler Dennett, "Early American Policy in Korea, 1883–7: The Services of Lieutenant George C. Foulk," *Political*

Science Quarterly 38 (1923): 85.

23. Bayard cited by William John Brinker in "Robert W. Shufeldt and the Changing Navy" (Ph.D. diss., Indiana University, 1973), p. 166.

24. Sanford cited by Williams in *Roots*, p. 262.

25. Shufeldt cited by Rollins in "Frederick Theodore Frelinghuysen," p. 476.

26. Arthur's third annual message, December 4, 1883, in *Messages and Papers*, 8:175–176.

27. James L. Roark, "American Expansionism vs. European Imperialism: Henry S. Sanford and the Congo Episode, 1883–1885," *Mid-America* 60 (1978): 31.

28. Lysle E. Meyer, "Henry S. Sanford and the Congo: A Reassessment," *African Historical Studies* 1 (1971): 32.

29. Kasson cited by Pletcher in *Awkward Years*, p. 318.

30. Arthur's fourth annual message, December 1, 1884, in *Messages and Papers*, 8:236.

31. Tisdel cited by Pletcher in *Awkward Years*, p. 345.

CHAPTER 10

1. Pletcher, *Awkward Years*, p. 6.

2. The grange leader, Morgan, and Kasson cited by Williams in *Roots*, pp. 239, 240, 278.

3. New York Chamber of Commerce and Schurz cited in ibid., p. 244.

4. Blaine cited by Tom E. Terrill in *The Tariff, Politics, and American Foreign Policy, 1874–1901* (Westport, Conn.: Greenwood Press, 1973), p. 46; Windom, McCulloch, and Arthur cited by Williams in *Roots*, p. 250.

5. Blaine cited by Terrill in *Tariff*, p. 48.

6. Pletcher, *Awkward Years*, p. 142.

7. Reeves, *Gentleman Boss*, pp. 229–230; Arthur's first annual message, December 6, 1881, in *Messages and Papers*, 8:49.

8. Morrill cited by Pletcher in *Awkward Years*, p. 152.

9. Commission cited in *Appletons' Annual Cyclopaedia and Register of Important Events of the Year 1882* (New York: Appleton, 1883), p. 780.

10. Morrill cited by Reeves in *Gentleman Boss*, p. 329.

11. *Appletons' Annual Cyclopaedia*, 1882,

p. 785.
12. Paul S. Holbo, "Trade and Commerce," in Alexander DeConde, ed., *Encyclopedia of American Foreign Policy: Studies of the Principal Movements and Ideas*, 3 vols. (New York: Charles Scribner's Sons, 1978), 3:953.
13. Arthur's fourth annual message, December 1, 1884, in *Messages and Papers*, 8:251.
14. Pletcher, *Awkward Years*, p. 177.
15. *Chicago Tribune* cited by LaFeber in *New Empire*, p. 51.
16. Terrill, *Tariff*, p. 83.
17. Pletcher, *Awkward Years*, p. 290.
18. Foster cited in ibid., pp. 296–297; Frelinghuysen cited by Reeves in *Gentleman Boss*, p. 407; Arthur's fourth annual message, December 1, 1884, in *Messages and Papers*, 8:239.
19. Pletcher, *Awkward Years*, p. 174.
20. Senate Foreign Relations Committee cited by Reeves in *Gentleman Boss*, p. 410.
21. Blaine to J. M. Comly, December 1,

1881, in *Foreign Relations, 1894, Appendix 2*, pp. 169–170; Arthur's first annual message, December 6, 1881, in *Messages and Papers*, 8:43.
22. Blaine to J. M. Comly, December 1, 1881, in *Foreign Relations*, 1881, p. 638.
23. Morrill cited by Pletcher in *Awkward Years*, p. 336.
24. *Banker's Magazine* cited by Terrill in *Tariff*, p. 85.
25. Pletcher, *Awkward Years*, p. 348.

CHAPTER 11

1. Beecher reference in *Nation* 38 (March 27, 1884): 266; New Jersey Republican cited by Reeves in *Gentleman Boss*, p. 369.
2. Reeves, *Gentleman Boss*, p. 371.
3. Ibid., p. 370.
4. Conkling cited by David M. Jordan in *Roscoe Conkling of New York: Voice in the Senate* (Ithaca, N.Y.: Cornell University Press, 1971), p. 421.

BIBLIOGRAPHICAL ESSAY

GENERAL WORKS

For general surveys that cover far more than the presidencies of Garfield and Arthur see Samuel P. Hays, *The Response to Industrialism, 1885–1914* (Chicago: University of Chicago Press, 1957); Ray Ginger, *The Age of Excess: The United States from 1877 to 1914*, 2d ed. (New York: Macmillan, 1975); Robert H. Wiebe, *The Search for Order, 1877–1920* (New York: Hill & Wang, 1967); John A. Garraty, *The New Commonwealth, 1877–1890* (New York: Harper & Row, 1968); Walter T. K. Nugent, *From Centennial to World War: American Society, 1876–1917* (Indianapolis: Bobbs Merrill, 1977); and David Herbert Donald, *Liberty and Union* (Boston: Little, Brown, 1978). Wiebe in particular, with his suggestive notion of the "distended society," provides many avenues for further research. By far the ablest general bibliography is *The Gilded Age, 1877–1879*, comp. Vincent P. De Santis (Northbrook, Ill.: AHM, 1973). Superior anthologies of scholarly work include *The Gilded Age: A Reappraisal*, ed. H. Wayne Morgan (Syracuse, N.Y.: Syracuse University Press, 1963; revised and enlarged, 1970), and *Victorian America*, ed. Daniel Walker Howe (Philadelphia: University of Pennsylvania Press, 1976).

No serious historian can escape doing primary research in such journals as *Nation, North American Review, Harper's Weekly, Harper's Magazine, Century*, and *Atlantic. Appletons' Annual Cyclopaedia* (New York: Appleton, 1861–1902) remains indispensable, as does *A Compilation of the Messages and Papers of the Presidents, 1789–1897*, ed. James D. Richardson, 10 vols. (Washington, D.C.: U.S. Government Printing Office, 1897–1907).

· CHAPTER 1

Forrest McDonald, Leslie E. Decker, and Thomas P. Govan, in *The Last Best Hope: A History of the United States* (Reading, Mass.: Addison-Wesley, 1972) offer an able if brief account of the technological revolution. For contrasting views on American agriculture see Fred A. Shannon, *The Farmers' Last Frontier: Agriculture, 1860-1897* (New York: Farrar & Rinehart, 1945), and Allan G. Bogue, *From Prairie to Corn Belt: Farming on the Illinois and Iowa Prairies in the Nineteenth Century* (Chicago: University of Chicago Press, 1963). Agrarian protest in the 1880s is best covered in Lawrence Goodwin, *Democratic Promise: The Populist Movement in America* (New York: Oxford University Press, 1976).

Revisionist accounts of business, which often challenge the type of history represented by Matthew Josephson's *The Robber Barons: The Great American Capitalists, 1861-1901* (New York: Harcourt, Brace, 1934), include Edward C. Kirkland's *Industry Comes of Age: Business, Labor, and Public Policy, 1860-1897* (New York: Holt, Rinehart & Winston, 1961) and his "The Robber Barons Revisited," *American Historical Review* 66 (1960): 68-73; and Glenn Porter's *The Rise of Big Business, 1860-1910* (New York: Crowell, 1973). Labor is described by John R. Commons et al. in *History of Labour in the United States*, vol. 2 (New York: Macmillan, 1918) and by Norman J. Ware in *The Labor Movement in the United States, 1860-1895: A Study in Democracy* (New York: Appleton, 1929), although their findings are updated by Melvyn Dubofsky in *Industrialism and the American Worker, 1865-1920* (New York: Crowell, 1975). For modifications of the traditional picture see the various essays of Herbert G. Gutman, including "Work, Culture, and Society in Industrializing America, 1815-1919," *American Historical Review* 78 (1973): 531-588, and "The Worker's Search for Power: Labor in the Gilded Age," in Morgan's *Gilded Age* (1963 ed.), pp. 38-68. Any student of industrial relations should note *Labor and Capital in the Gilded Age*, ed. John A. Garraty (Boston: Little, Brown, 1968), which excerpts testimony given before the Senate Committee upon the Relations between Labor and Capital.

Given the focus of this book, any bibliographical discussion of intellectual trends must be quite selective. Superior introductions to American intellectual history include Eric F. Goldman's *Rendezvous with Destiny: A History of Modern American Reform* (New York: Knopf, 1952); Ralph Henry Gabriel's *The Course of American Democratic Thought*, 2d ed. (New York: Ronald, 1956); and Stow Persons's *American Minds: A History of Ideas* (New York: Holt, Rinehart & Winston, 1958). For a general focus on the Gilded Age see Paul F. Boller, Jr.'s *American Thought in Transition: The Impact of Evolutionary Naturalism, 1865-1900* (Chicago: Rand McNally, 1969) and Howard Mumford Jones's *The Age of Energy: Varieties of American Experience, 1865-1915* (New York: Viking Press, 1971).

On Social Darwinism, superior works include Richard Hofstadter's *Social Darwinism in American Thought*, rev. ed. (Boston: Beacon Press, 1955); Robert Green McCloskey's *American Conservatism in the Age of Enterprise: A Study of William Graham Sumner, Stephen J. Field, and Andrew Carnegie* (Cambridge, Mass.: Harvard University Press, 1951); and Donald Fleming's "Social Darwinism," in *Paths of American Thought*, ed. Arthur M. Schlesinger, Jr., and Morton White (Boston:

Houghton Mifflin, 1963), pp. 123–146. Sidney A. Fine, in *Laissez Faire and the General-Welfare State: A Study of Conflict in American Thought, 1865–1901* (Ann Arbor: University of Michigan Press, 1956), discusses the debate among economists; while Edward Chase Kirkland, in *Dream and Thought in the Business Community, 1860–1900* (Ithaca, N.Y.: Cornell University Press, 1956), ably treats the ideology of American entrepreneurs. For the encounter of American religion with Darwinism, one should note Paul A. Carter's *The Spiritual Crisis of the Gilded Age* (De Kalb: Northern Illinois University Press, 1971); William R. Hutchison's *The Modernist Impulse in American Protestantism* (Cambridge, Mass.: Harvard University Press, 1976); and D. H. Meyer's "American Intellectuals and the Victorian Crisis of Faith," in Howe's *Victorian America*, pp. 59–77.

Many of the essays in Schlesinger and White's *Paths of American Thought* on various aspects of intellectual development are helpful, particularly I. Bernard Cohen's "Science in America: The Nineteenth Century," pp. 167–189, and Eugene V. Rostow's "The Realist Tradition in American Law," pp. 203–218. Oliver Wendell Holmes offered his own views in *The Common Law* (Boston: Little, Brown, 1881). For another treatment of science see Paul F. Boller, Jr.'s "The New Science and American Thought," in Morgan's *Gilded Age* (1970 ed.), pp. 239–257.

As far as literature is concerned, Robert E. Spiller, Willard Thorp, Thomas H. Johnson, Henry Seidel Canby, and Richard M. Ludwig's *Literary History of the United States*, 3d ed., rev. (New York: Macmillan, 1963) remains definitive. Helpful supplementary essays include Robert R. Roberts's "Popular Culture and Public Taste," in Morgan's *Gilded Age* (1970 ed.), pp. 275–288; Robert Falk's "The Writers' Search for Reality," in ibid., pp. 223–237; and Dee Garrison's "Immoral Fiction in the Late Victorian Library," in Howe's *Victorian America*, pp. 141–159. For Santayana's views see *The Genteel Tradition: Nine Essays by George Santayana*, ed. Douglas L. Wilson (Cambridge, Mass.: Harvard University Press, 1967). Lewis Mumford's *The Brown Decades: A Study of the Arts in America, 1865–1895* (New York: Harcourt, Brace, 1931) is still a classic.

Party politics has recently undergone renewed interest, although such works as James Bryce's *The American Commonwealth*, 3 vols. (London: Macmillan, 1888) and Woodrow Wilson's *Congressional Government* (originally published in 1885; republished, New York: Meridian, 1956) are always helpful. Morton Keller's *Affairs of State: Public Life in Late Nineteenth Century America* (Cambridge, Mass.: Belknap Press of Harvard University Press, 1977) shows that works of distinction can be produced in our own times. The best work on the upper chamber is still David J. Rothman's *Politics and Power: The United States Senate, 1869–1901* (Cambridge, Mass.: Harvard University Press, 1966), but a similar work on the House is much needed. Some of Rothman's conclusions are challenged by William G. Shade, Stanley D. Hopper, and Stephen E. Moiles in "Partisanship in the United States Senate: 1869–1901," *Journal of Interdisciplinary History* 4 (1973): 185–205. Leonard D. White's *The Republican Era, 1869–1901: A Study in Administrative History* (New York: Macmillan, 1958) remains an indispensable starting point for the study of so much governmental activity. Loren P. Beth's *The Development of the American Constitution, 1877–1917* (New York: Harper & Row, 1971) covers far more than the title would suggest. H. Wayne Morgan's *From Hayes to McKinley:*

National Party Politics, 1877–1896 (Syracuse, N.Y.: Syracuse University Press, 1969) puts to rest the stereotypes advanced by Matthew Josephson in *The Politicos, 1865–1896* (New York: Harcourt, Brace, 1938) and does so with both wit and grace. Other works that describe the political system include Vincent De Santis's "American Politics in the Gilded Age," *Review of Politics* 25 (1963): 551–561; Albert V. House's "Republicans and Democrats Search for New Identities, 1870–1890," in ibid. 31 (1969): 466–476; John M. Dobson's *Politics in the Gilded Age: A New Perspective on Reform* (New York: Praeger, 1972); and Geoffrey Blodgett's "A New Look at the Gilded Age: Politics in a Cultural Context," in Howe's *Victorian America*, pp. 95–108.

Party structure and ideology have also been subject to fresh research. Robert D. Marcus, in *Grand Old Party: Political Structure in the Gilded Age, 1880–1896* (New York: Oxford University Press, 1971), and Lewis L. Gould, in "The Republican Search for a National Majority," in Morgan's *Gilded Age* (1970 ed.), pp. 171–187, cover the Republicans. William G. Eidson, in "Who Were the Stalwarts?" *Mid-America* 52 (1970): 235–261, revises traditional stereotypes. The Democrats have been subject to less general analysis, although one should note R. Hal Williams's "'Dry Bones and Dead Language': The Democratic Party," in Morgan's *Gilded Age* (1970 ed.), pp. 129–148; and Horace Samuel Merrill's *Bourbon Democracy of the Middle West, 1865–1896* (Baton Rouge: Louisiana State University Press, 1953).

A new type of political history, one stressing ethnic and religious rivalries, can be found in Paul Kleppner's *The Cross of Culture: A Social Analysis of Midwestern Politics, 1850–1900* (New York: Free Press, 1970) and his *Third Electoral System, 1853–1892: Parties, Voters, and Political Cultures* (Chapel Hill: University of North Carolina Press, 1979) and in Richard J. Jensen's *The Winning of the Midwest: Social and Political Conflict, 1888–1896* (Chicago: University of Chicago Press, 1971). The general orientation is debated by James E. Wright in "The Ethnocultural Model of Voting: A Behavioral and Historical Critique," *American Behavioral Scientist* 16 (1973): 653–674; by Allan G. Bogue, Jerome M. Clubb, and William H. Flanigan in "The New Political History," ibid. 21 (1977): 201–220; by Richard L. McCormick in "Ethno-Cultural Interpretations of Nineteenth-Century American Voting Behavior," *Political Science Quarterly* 89 (1974): 351–377; by J. Morgan Kousser in "The 'New Political History': A Methodological Critique," *Reviews in American History* 4 (1976): 1–4; and by Robert Kelley in "Ideology and Political Culture from Jefferson to Nixon," together with comments by Geoffrey Blodgett, Ronald P. Formisano, and Willie Lee Rose, in *American Historical Review* 82 (1977): 531–582.

There are several biographies of prominent politicos, though one wishes for more. David M. Jordan's *Roscoe Conkling of New York: Voice in the Senate* (Ithaca, N.Y.: Cornell University Press, 1971) updates Donald Barr Chidsey's *The Gentleman from New York; A Life of Roscoe Conkling* (New Haven, Conn.: Yale University Press, 1935). Until we have fresh biographies, David Saville Muzzey's *James G. Blaine: A Political Idol of Other Days* (New York: Dodd, Mead, 1934) and William B. Hesseltine's *Ulysses S. Grant, Politician* (New York: Dodd, Mead, 1935) will remain standard. Similarly, modern studies of Gilded Age activities of John Sherman, James A. Logan, and J. Donald Cameron are needed. For Edmunds see

Richard E. Welch, Jr.'s "George Edmunds of Vermont: Republican Half-Breed," *Vermont History* 36 (1968): 64–73.

CHAPTER 2

Of the works cited previously, those most useful for this chapter include Morgan, *From Hayes to McKinley;* Garraty, *New Commonwealth;* Jordan, *Roscoe Conkling;* Chidsey, *Gentleman from New York;* Muzzey, *James G. Blaine;* Marcus, *Grand Old Party;* White, *Republican Era;* and Keller, *Affairs of State.* For a description of the campaign see Herbert J. Clancy's *The Presidential Election of 1880* (Chicago: Loyola University Press, 1958). Material on the Republican convention is also found in Frank B. Evans's "Wharton Barker and the Republican National Convention of 1880," *Pennsylvania History* 27 (1960): 28–43; and in Allan Peskin's "The 'Put-up Job': Wisconsin and the Republican National Convention of 1880," *Wisconsin Magazine of History* 55 (1972): 263–274.

We are fortunate in having a fresh and thorough life of Garfield. Allan Peskin's definitive *Garfield* (Kent, Ohio: Kent State University Press, 1978) supersedes Theodore Clarke Smith's *The Life and Letters of James Abram Garfield,* 2 vols. (New Haven, Conn.: Yale University Press, 1925); Robert Granville Caldwell's *James A. Garfield, Party Chieftain* (New York: Dodd, Mead, 1931); and John M. Taylor's *Garfield of Ohio: The Available Man* (New York: Norton, 1970). Smith is still helpful on all aspects of Garfield's life, but one must use his quotations with care. Also to be noted is A. Peskin's "Garfield and Hayes: Political Leaders of the Gilded Age," *Ohio History* 77 (1968): 111–124, and his "From Log Cabin to Oblivion," *American History Illustrated* 11 (May 1976): 24–34. Margaret Leech and Harry J. Brown's *The Garfield Orbit* (New York: Harper & Row, 1978) focuses on his personal life, particularly on his relations with women, but resists the overt psychoanalytic approach found in Robert Irving Cottom, Jr.'s "To Be among the First: The Early Career of James A. Garfield, 1831–1868" (Ph.D. dissertation, Johns Hopkins University, 1975). Unfortunately, *The Diary of James A. Garfield,* edited by Harry James Brown and Frederick D. Williams, 3 vols. (East Lansing: Michigan State University Press, 1967–1973), does not yet cover his presidency. James D. Norris and Arthur H. Shaffer have edited *Politics and Patronage in the Gilded Age: The Correspondence of James A. Garfield and Charles E. Henry* (Madison: State Historical Society of Wisconsin, 1970), a work that offers revealing correspondence between Garfield and his chief political lieutenant from 1862 to 1881.

For material on the vice-presidential candidate and on his role during the campaign see the definitive work of Thomas C. Reeves: *Gentleman Boss: The Life of Chester Alan Arthur* (New York: Knopf, 1975); "Chester A. Arthur and the Campaign of 1880," *Political Science Quarterly* 84 (1969): 628–637; and "Chester A. Arthur and Campaign Assessments in the Election of 1880," *Historian* 31 (1969): 573–582.

Several other biographies also illuminate these months; they include Harry J. Sievers's *Benjamin Harrison: Hoosier Statesman: From the Civil War to the White House, 1865–1888* (New York: University Publishers, 1959); Leland L. Sage's

William Boyd Allison: A Study in Practical Politics (Iowa City: State Historical Society of Iowa, 1956); Robert McElroy's *Levi Parsons Morton: Banker, Diplomat and Statesman* (New York: Putnam's, 1930); John S. Goff's *Robert Todd Lincoln: A Man in His Own Right* (Norman: University of Oklahoma Press, 1969); and Richard E. Welch, Jr.'s *George Frisbie Hoar and the Half-Breed Republicans* (Cambridge, Mass.: Harvard University Press, 1971). Bingham Duncan's *Whitelaw Reid: Journalist, Politician, Diplomat* (Athens: University of Georgia Press, 1975) supersedes Royal Cortissoz's *The Life of Whitelaw Reid* (New York: Scribner's, 1921).

CHAPTER 3

One can find valuable material on the many aspects of Garfield's presidency in works already cited, particularly in Peskin's *Garfield;* Smith's *Life and Letters;* Reeves's *Gentleman Boss* and his 1969 essays; Morgan's *From Hayes to McKinley;* and Jordan's *Roscoe Conkling.* In *Strands from the Weaving* (New York: Vantage Press, 1959), Lucretia Comer, a granddaughter of James A. Garfield's, offers a memoir of her father, Harry, which includes descriptions of life in the White House during Garfield's presidency.

Other efforts to evaluate the short Garfield presidency can be found in Allan Peskin's "President Garfield and the Rating Game: An Evaluation of a Brief Administration," *South Atlantic Quarterly* 76 (1977): 93–102; and in William Lester Ketchersid's "The Maturing of the Presidency, 1877–1889" (Ph.D. dissertation, University of Georgia, 1977). For excerpts from the papers of Garfield's private secretary see Joseph Stanley-Brown's "My Friend Garfield," *American Heritage* 22 (August 1971): 49–53, 100–101. An interpretation of Conkling's career in light of railroad issues is given in Lee Benson's *Merchants, Farmers, and Railroads: Railroad Regulation and New York Politics, 1850–1887* (Cambridge, Mass.: Harvard University Press, 1955).

No one can discuss the spoils system and its critics without referring to the thorough work of Ari Hoogenboom: *Outlawing the Spoils: A History of the Civil Service Reform Movement, 1865–1883* (Urbana: University of Illinois Press, 1961); "The Pendleton Act and the Civil Service," *American Historical Review* 64 (1959): 301–318; "An Analysis of Civil Service Reformers," *Historian* 23 (1960): 54–78; and "Spoilsmen and Reformers: Civil Service Reform and Public Morality," in Morgan's *Gilded Age* (1963 ed.), pp. 69–90. The best coverage of the post-office scandals is still J. Martin Klotsche's "The Star Route Cases," *Mississippi Valley Historical Review* 22 (1935): 407–418. Historians debate reform in John G. Sproat's *"The Best Men": Liberal Reformers in the Gilded Age* (New York: Oxford University Press, 1968), in Geoffrey Blodgett's "Reform Thought and the Genteel Tradition," in Morgan's *Gilded Age* (1970 ed.), pp. 55–76, and in Blodgett's "New Look." Garfield gives his own views on the spoils system and on other matters in *Garfield-Hinsdale Letters: Correspondence between James Abram Garfield and Burke Aaron Hinsdale,* ed. Mary L. Hinsdale (Ann Arbor: University of Michigan Press, 1949). For the position of an outspoken reformer see *Henry Adams and His Friends,* comp.

Harold D. Cater (Boston: Houghton Mifflin, 1947). Other sources already cited include Reeves's *Gentleman Boss* and his 1969 essays, Dobson's *Politics,* White's *Republican Era,* and Keller's *Affairs of State.*

Economic conditions of southern blacks are described in John Hope Franklin's *From Slavery to Freedom: A History of Negro Americans,* 5th ed. (New York: Knopf, 1978); Rayford W. Logan's *The Betrayal of the Negro: From Rutherford B. Hayes to Woodrow Wilson,* new, enl. ed. (New York: Collier, 1965); August Meier, *Negro Thought in America, 1880-1915: Racial Ideologies in the Age of Booker T. Washington* (Ann Arbor: University of Michigan Press, 1963); and C. Vann Woodward, *Origins of the New South, 1877-1913* (Baton Rouge: Louisiana State University Press, 1951).

Much attention has been given to Garfield's policy towards blacks and the South, with the most thorough treatment being in Allan Peskin's "President Garfield and the Southern Question: The Making of a Policy That Never Was," *Southern Quarterly* 16 (1978): 375-386. Garfield's policy is also discussed in several works by Vincent P. De Santis: *Republicans Face the Southern Question: The New Departure Years, 1877-1897* (Baltimore, Md.: Johns Hopkins Press, 1959); "Republican Efforts to 'Crack' the Democratic South," *Review of Politics* 14 (1952): 244-264; "President Garfield and the Solid South," *North Carolina Historical Review* 36 (1959): 442-465; and "The Republican Party and the Southern Negro, 1877-1897," *Journal of Negro History* 45 (1960): 71-87. Equally helpful is Stanley P. Hirshson's *Farewell to the Bloody Shirt: Northern Republicans & the Southern Negro, 1877-1893* (Bloomington: Indiana University Press, 1962; reprinted in 1968 by Quadrangle Books).

The entire issue of Negro education, a cause that was close to Garfield's heart, is covered by James M. McPherson in *The Abolitionist Legacy: From Reconstruction to the NAACP* (Princeton, N.J.: Princeton University Press, 1975). For material on a man who strongly influenced Garfield on the matter, see Roy F. Dibble's *Albion W. Tourgée* (originally published in 1921; republished, Port Washington, N.Y.: Kennikat, 1968); Otto H. Olsen's *Carpetbagger's Crusade: The Life of Albion Winegar Tourgée* (Baltimore, Md.: Johns Hopkins Press, 1965); John Hope Franklin's preface to Tourgée's *A Fool's Errand* (originally published in 1879; republished, Cambridge, Mass.: Belknap Press of Harvard University Press, 1961); and Tourgée's own *An Appeal to Ceasar* (New York: Fords, Howard & Hulbert, 1884).

The most thorough work on Mahone remains Nelson Morehouse Blake's *William Mahone of Virginia: Soldier and Political Insurgent* (Richmond: Garrett & Massie, 1935). However, one must also consult Raymond H. Pulley's *Old Virginia Restored: An Interpretation of the Progressive Impulse, 1870-1930* (Charlottesville: University Press of Virginia, 1968); Charles E. Wynes's *Race Relations in Virginia, 1870-1902* (Totowa, N.J.: Rowman & Littlefield, 1971); Carl N. Degler's *The Other South: Southern Dissenters in the Nineteenth Century* (New York: Harper & Row, 1974); and James T. Moore's "Black Militancy in Readjuster Virginia, 1879-1883," *Journal of Southern History* 41 (1975): 167-186.

For material on Garfield's assassination see Peskin's *Garfield* and his "Charles

Guiteau of Illinois: President Garfield's Assassin," *Journal of the Illinois State Historical Society* 70 (1977): 130–139.

CHAPTER 4

David M. Pletcher's *The Awkward Years: American Foreign Relations under Garfield and Arthur* (Columbia: University of Missouri Press, 1962) is close to being definitive on all aspects of United States diplomacy. For a wider context, the work of Milton Plesur is most helpful: *America's Outward Thrust: Approaches to Foreign Affairs, 1865–1890* (De Kalb: Northern Illinois University Press, 1971); "Rumblings beneath the Surface: America's Outward Thrust, 1865–1890," in Morgan's *Gilded Age* (1963 ed.), pp. 140–168; and "America Looking Outward: The Years from Hayes to Harrison," *Historian* 22 (1960): 280–295. Still fresher general accounts include Robert L. Beisner's *From the Old Diplomacy to the New, 1865–1900* (New York: Crowell, 1975), Charles S. Campbell's *The Transformation of American Foreign Relations, 1865–1900* (New York: Harper & Row, 1976), and John M. Dobson's *America's Ascent: The United States Becomes a Great Power, 1880–1914* (De Kalb: Northern Illinois University Press, 1978).

Economic factors in foreign policy have been much debated. For stress upon economic aspects see Walter LaFeber's *The New Empire: An Interpretation of American Expansion, 1860–1898* (Ithaca, N.Y.: Cornell University Press for the American Historical Association, 1963), William Appleman Williams's *The Roots of the Modern American Empire: A Study of the Growth and Shaping of Social Consciousness in a Marketplace Society* (New York: Random House, 1969), Edward P. Crapol's *America for Americans: Economic Nationalism and Anglophobia in the Late Nineteenth Century* (Westport, Conn.: Greenwood Press, 1973), Tom E. Terrill's *The Tariff, Politics, and American Foreign Policy, 1874–1901* (Westport, Conn.: Greenwood Press, 1973), and Howard B. Schonberger's *Transportation to the Seaboard: The "Communication Revolution" and American Foreign Policy, 1860–1900* (Westport, Conn.: Greenwood Press, 1971). For more technical general discussion see David E. Novack and Matthew Simon's "Some Dimensions of the American Commercial Invasion of Europe, 1871–1914: An Introductory Essay," *Journal of Economic History* 24 (1964): 591–605; and their "Commercial Responses to the American Export Invasion, 1871–1914: An Essay in Attitudinal History," *Explorations in Entrepreneurial History* n.s. 2 (1966): 122–147; Rendigs Fels's "The American Business Cycle of 1879–1885," *Journal of Political Economy* 60 (1952): 60–75; and William H. Becker's "American Manufacturers and Foreign Markets, 1870–1900: Business Historians and the 'New Determinists,' " *Business History Review* 47 (1973): 466–481. Paul S. Holbo minimizes economic factors in "Economics, Emotion, and Expansion: An Emerging Foreign Policy," in Morgan's *Gilded Age* (1970 ed.), pp. 199–221, as does Robert Zevin in "An Interpretation of American Imperialism," *Journal of Economic History* 32 (1972): 316–360, 385–392, and Marilyn Blatt Young in "American Expansion, 1870–1900: The Far East," in *Towards a New Past: Dissenting Essays in American History*, ed. Barton J. Bernstein (New York: Pantheon, 1968), pp. 176–201. For a debate over much of the recent literature see James A. Field, Jr.'s "American Imperialism: The Worst Chapter in Almost Any Book," together with comments by Walter LaFeber and Robert L. Beisner and reply, in *American Historical Review* 83 (1978): 644–683. Mira Wilkins's *The Emergence of Multinational Enterprise: American Business Abroad from the Colonial Era to 1914* (Cambridge, Mass.: Harvard University Press, 1970) offers the most comprehensive discussion of United States economic activities overseas. Kenneth J. Hagan's *American Gunboat Diplomacy and the Old Navy, 1877–1889* (Westport, Conn.: Greenwood Press, 1973) covers far more than the title suggests, for it is revealing on many aspects of Garfield-Arthur diplomacy.

Studies of Blaine's foreign policy include James B. Lockey's "James Gillespie Blaine," in volume 7 of *The American Secretaries of State and Their Diplomacy*, ed. Samuel Flagg Bemis (New York: Knopf, 1928), pp. 261–297; Alice Felt Tyler's *The Foreign Policy of James G. Blaine* (Minneapolis: University of Minnesota Press, 1927); and Lester D. Langley's "James Gillespie Blaine: The Ideologue as Diplomatist," in *Makers of American Diplomacy: From Benjamin Franklin to Henry Kissinger*, ed. Frank J. Merli and Theodore A. Wilson (New York: Scribner's, 1974), pp. 253–278.

Among the special works that discuss Blaine's Latin American policy are Herbert Millington's *American Diplomacy and the War of the Pacific* (New York: Columbia University Press, 1948); Russell H. Bastert's "A New Approach to the Origins of Blaine's Pan American Policy," *Hispanic American Historical Review* 39 (1959): 375–412; V. G. Kiernan's "Foreign Interests in the War of the Pacific," ibid. 35 (1955): 14–36; Frederick B. Pike's *Chile and the United States, 1880–1962* (Notre Dame, Ind.: University of Notre Dame Press, 1963); and J. Fred Rippy's "Relations of the United States and Guatemala during the Epoch of Justo Rufino Barrios," *Hispanic American Historical Review* 22 (1942): 595–605. For stress upon Garfield as policy maker see Allan Peskin's "Blaine, Garfield and Latin America: A New Look," *Americas* 36 (1979): 79–89.

Specific economic battles are well described by Louis L. Snyder in "The American-German Pork Dispute, 1879–1891," *Journal of Modern History* 17 (1945): 16–28; by John L. Gignilliat in "Pigs, Politics, and Protection: The European Boycott of American Pork, 1879–1891," *Agricultural History* 35 (1961): 3–12; by Morton Rothstein in "America in the International Rivalry for the British Wheat Market, 1860–1914," *Mississippi Valley Historical Review* 47 (1960): 401–418; and by William David Zimmerman in "Live Cattle Export Trade between United States and Great Britain, 1868–1885," *Agricultural History* 36 (1962): 46–52.

Much material on general American-British relations may be found in Martin Duberman's *James Russell Lowell* (Boston: Houghton Mifflin, 1966). For background on the Irish issue see Thomas N. Brown's *Irish-American Nationalism, 1870–1890* (Philadelphia: Lippincott, 1966), and Owen Dudley Edwards's "American Diplomats and Irish Coercion, 1880–1883," *Journal of American Studies*, 1 (1967): 213–232, the latter an essay that in some ways modifies Pletcher.

Older but still helpful accounts of United States involvement in Korea include Charles Oscar Paullin's *Diplomatic Negotiations of American Naval Officers, 1778–1883* (Baltimore, Md.: Johns Hopkins Press, 1912) and Tyler Dennett's *Americans in Eastern Asia* (New York: Macmillan, 1922; reprinted in 1941 and 1963 by Barnes & Noble). For newer studies see Andrew C. Nahm's "Reaction and Response to the Opening of Korea, 1876–1884," in *Studies on Asia, 1965*, ed. Robert K. Sakai (Lincoln: University of Nebraska Press, 1965); C. I. Eugene Kim and Han-Kyo Kim's *Korea and the Politics of Imperialism, 1876–1910* (Berkeley and Los Angeles: University of California Press, 1968); and Yur-Bok Lee's *Diplomatic Relations between the United States and Korea, 1866–1887* (New York: Humanities Press, 1970). Commodore Shufeldt is the subject of two doctoral theses: Frederick C. Drake's "'The Empire of the Seas': A Biography of Robert Wilson Shufeldt, USN" (Cornell University, 1970) and William John Brinker's "Robert W. Shufeldt and the Changing Navy" (Indiana University, 1973).

CHAPTER 5

In Thomas C. Reeves's *Gentleman Boss* we have a fresh and thorough account of the twenty-first president. His book in every way supersedes George Frederick Howe's *Chester A. Arthur: A Quarter-Century of Machine Politics* (New York: Dodd, Mead, 1934). From correcting the date of Arthur's birth to covering the chief executive's knowledge of his fatal illness, Reeves is without equal. Arthur's presidency is discussed seriously by Ketchersid in his "Maturing of the Presidency" and by John S. Goff in "President Arthur's Domestic Legislative Program," *New York Historical Society Quarterly* 44 (1960): 167–177. Lighter treatment is given by Howard Bailey in "Le Grand Chester," *History Teacher* 3 (March 1970): 50–55; and by Edna M. Colman in *White House Gossip: From Andrew Johnson to Calvin Coolidge* (Garden City, N.Y.: Doubleday, Page, 1927). For lively columns by the Washington correspondent of the *Cleveland Leader* see Frank G. Carpenter, *Carp's Washington* (New York: McGraw-Hill, 1960). Reeves's efforts to find Arthur materials are traced in his "The Search for the Chester Alan Arthur Papers," *Wisconsin Magazine of History* 55 (1972): 310–319. Other helpful works include Jordan's *Roscoe Conkling* and Morgan's *From Hayes to McKinley*.

Material on certain of Arthur's policies is spotty. Schonberger, in *Transportation to the Seaboard*, presents additional data on the rivers-and-harbors veto. There is far more on the Chinese immigration issue. Background is offered in Elmer Clarence Sandmeyer's *The Anti-Chinese Movement in California* (Urbana: University of Illinois Press, 1939); Stuart Creighton Miller's *The Unwelcome Immigrant: The American Image of the Chinese, 1785–1882* (Berkeley and Los Angeles: University of California Press, 1969); and Isbella Black's "American Labour and Chinese Immigration," *Past and Present*, no. 25 (July 1963), pp. 59–76. Pletcher's *Awkward Years* is always helpful.

Material on the relation between the federal government and the Mormons is surprisingly scarce. Leonard J. Arrington's *Great Basin Kingdom: An Economic History of the Latter-Day Saints, 1830–1900* (Cambridge, Mass.: Harvard University Press, 1958) covers far more than the title suggests. See also Thomas F. O'Dea's *The Mormons* (Chicago: University of Chicago Press, 1957).

General studies of the Indian include William T. Hagan's *American Indians* (Chicago: University of Chicago Press, 1961) and Wilcomb E. Washburn's *The In-*

dian in America (New York: Harper & Row, 1975). Among the works particularly pertinent to the Indian policy of the Garfield and Arthur administrations are Henry G. Waltmann's "The Interior Department, War Department and Indian Policy, 1865–1887" (Ph.D. dissertation, University of Nebraska, 1962), Henry E. Fritz's *The Movement for Indian Assimilation, 1860–1890* (Philadelphia: University of Pennsylvania Press, 1963), Elmer Ellis's *Henry Moore Teller: Defender of the West* (Caldwell, Idaho: Caxton, 1941), and Robert M. Utley's *Frontier Regulars: The United States Army and the Indians, 1866–1891* (New York: Macmillan, 1973). See also White's *Republican Era* and Goff's *Robert Todd Lincoln.* Robert Winston Mardock, in *The Reformers and the American Indian* (Columbia: University of Missouri Press, 1971); Loring Benson Priest, in *Uncle Sam's Stepchildren: The Reformation of United States Indian Policy, 1865–1887* (New Brunswick, N.J.: Rutgers University Press, 1942); and Francis Paul Prucha, in *American Indian Policy in Crisis: Christian Reformers and the Indian, 1865–1900* (Norman: University of Oklahoma Press, 1976), discuss Indian life as well as reform movements.

Until we have a full-length study of the star-route scandal, Klotsche's "Star Route Cases" will remain standard. Charles E. Rosenberg, in *The Trial of the Assassin Guiteau: Psychiatry and Law in the Gilded Age* (Chicago: University of Chicago Press, 1968), gives a comprehensive discussion of the Guiteau trial.

CHAPTER 6

The sources on civil service cited in chapter 3 remain crucial, particularly Hoogenboom's *Outlawing the Spoils* and his "Pendleton Act," Blodgett's "New Look," and White's *Republican Era.* Paul P. Van Riper, in *History of the United States Civil Service* (Evanston, Ill.: Row, Peterson, 1958), makes perceptive judgments. For a detailed description of a single controversy see Thomas C. Reeves's "Silas Burt and Chester Arthur: A Reformer's View of the Twenty-first President," *New York Historical Society Quarterly,* 54 (1970): 319–337.

CHAPTER 7

A good many books noted in chapter 3 remain helpful for examining southern politics, economics, and race. These include Woodward's *Origins of the New South,* Meier's *Negro Thought,* Franklin's *From Slavery to Freedom,* and De Santis's *Republicans Face the Southern Question.* Other significant works include Paul H. Buck's *The Road to Reunion, 1865–1900* (Boston: Little, Brown, 1937); C. Vann Woodward's *The Strange Career of Jim Crow,* 2d rev. ed. (New York: Oxford University Press, 1966); John Samuel Ezell's *The South since 1865,* 2d ed. (New York: Macmillan, 1975); Paul M. Gaston's *The New South Creed: A Study in Southern Mythmaking* (New York: Knopf, 1970); Robert L. Brandfon's *Cotton Kingdom of the New South: A History of the Yazoo Mississippi Delta from Reconstruction to the Twentieth Century* (Cambridge, Mass.: Harvard University Press, 1967); Howard N. Rabinowitz's *Race Relations in the Urban South, 1865–1890*

(New York: Oxford University Press, 1978); and Louis R. Harlan's *Booker T. Washington: The Making of a Black Leader, 1856-1901* (New York: Oxford University Press, 1972). Sheldon Hackney evaluates a classic in his *"Origins of the New South* in Retrospect," *Journal of Southern History* 38 (1972): 191-216. Valuable bibliographical information is also found in Paul M. Gaston's "The 'New South,'" in *Writing Southern History: Essays in Historiography in Honor of Fletcher M. Green,* ed. Arthur S. Link and Rembert W. Patrick (Baton Rouge: Louisiana State University Press, 1965).

For material on the legal standing of the Negro American and the Civil Rights Cases see Logan's *Betrayal of the Negro;* Keller's *Affairs of State;* Beth's *Development of the American Constitution;* Loren Miller's *The Petitioners: The Story of the Supreme Court of the United States and the Negro* (New York: Pantheon, 1966); Robert J. Harris's *The Quest for Equality: The Constitution, Congress, and the Supreme Court* (Baton Rouge: Louisiana State University Press, 1960); Leslie H. Fishel, Jr.'s "Repercussions of Reconstruction: The Northern Negro, 1870-1883," *Civil War History* 14 (1968): 325-345; Michael J. Horan's "Political Economy and Sociological Theory as Influences on Judicial Policy-Making: The *Civil Rights Cases* of 1883," *American Journal of Legal History* 16 (1972): 71-86; and Valeria W. Weaver's "The Failure of Civil Rights 1875-1883 and Its Repercussions," *Journal of Negro History* 54 (1969): 368-382.

General treatment of Arthur's strategy may be found in De Santis's "Republican Party and the Southern Negro," his *Republicans Face the Southern Question,* and his "President Arthur and the Independent Movements in the South in 1882," *Journal of Southern History* 19 (1953): 346-363; in Reeves's *Gentleman Boss;* in Hirshson's *Farewell to the Bloody Shirt;* in Degler's *Other South;* and in Justus D. Doenecke's "The Republican Search for a Southern Strategy: The Arthur Administration" (a paper delivered at the annual meeting of the Organization of American Historians, New York City, April 13, 1978). For Negro reaction to Arthur's policy see De Santis, "Negro Dissatisfaction with Republican Policy in the South, 1882-1884," *Journal of Negro History* 36 (1951): 148-159; and Elsie M. Lewis, "The Political Mind of the Negro, 1865-1900," *Journal of Southern History* 21 (1955): 189-202. Reeves, in *Gentleman Boss,* challenges Hirshson, in *Farewell to the Bloody Shirt,* on the Negro response. J. Morgan Kousser, in *The Shaping of Southern Politics: Suffrage Restriction and the Establishment of the One-Party South, 1880-1910* (New Haven, Conn.: Yale University Press, 1974), finds De Santis, Logan, and Hirshson all too harsh towards the Republicans, too lenient towards the Democrats.

Specialized references to Virginia may be found in chapter 3. For sharply contrasting pictures of the Danville incident see Allen W. Moger's "The Origins of the Democratic Machine in Virginia," *Journal of Southern History* 8 (1942): 183-209; Walter T. Calhoun's "The Danville Riot and Its Repercussions on the Virginia Election of 1883," in *Studies in the History of the South, 1875-1922* (Greenville, S.C.: East Carolina College Press, 1966), pp. 25-51; and Wynes's *Race Relations in Virginia,* pp. 29-32.

Mississippi is covered by Vernon Lane Wharton in *The Negro in Mississippi, 1865-1890* (Chapel Hill: University of North Carolina Press, 1947), and by Albert

D. Kirwan in *Revolt of the Rednecks: Mississippi Politics, 1876–1925* (Lexington: University of Kentucky Press, 1951). No student of Arthur's strategy in the Magnolia State can neglect the work of Willie D. Halsell: "Democratic Dissensions in Mississippi, 1878–1882," *Journal of Mississippi History* 2 (1940): 123–135; "James R. Chalmers and 'Mahoneism' in Mississippi," *Journal of Southern History* 10 (1944): 37–58; and "The Bourbon Period in Mississippi Politics, 1875–1890," ibid. 11 (1945): 519–537. Halsell has also edited significant correspondence in "Republican Factionalism in Mississippi, 1882–1884," *Journal of Southern History* 7 (1941): 84–101.

There are some detailed studies for other states. For South Carolina see William J. Cooper, Jr.'s *The Conservative Regime: South Carolina, 1877–1890* (Baltimore, Md.; Johns Hopkins Press, 1968) and James W. Patton's "The Republican Party in South Carolina, 1876–1895," in *Essays in Southern History Presented to Joseph Gregoire de Roulhac Hamilton*, ed. Fletcher Melvin Green (Chapel Hill: University of North Carolina Press, 1949), pp. 91–111. One should also consult George B. Tindall's *South Carolina Negroes, 1877–1900* (Columbia: University of South Carolina Press, 1952). For Georgia see Olive Hall Shadgett's *The Republican Party in Georgia, from Reconstruction through 1900* (Athens: University of Georgia Press, 1964); Judson C. Ward, Jr.'s "The Republican Party in Bourbon Georgia, 1872–1900," *Journal of Southern History* 9 (1943): 196–209; Josephine Bone Floyd's "Rebecca Latimer Felton: Political Independent," *Georgia Historical Quarterly* 30 (1946): 14–24; and John E. Talmadge's "The Death Blow to Independentism in Georgia," ibid., 39 (1955): 37–47. Alabama is covered by Allen J. Going in *Bourbon Democracy in Alabama, 1874–1890* (University: University of Alabama Press, 1951); by William Warren Rogers in *The One-Gallused Rebellion: Agrarianism in Alabama, 1865–1896* (Baton Rouge: Louisiana State University Press, 1970); and by Malcolm Cook McMillan in *Constitutional Development in Alabama, 1798–1901: A Study in Politics, the Negro, and Sectionalism* (Chapel Hill: University of North Carolina Press, 1955). Material on North Carolina is offered in William A. Mabry's *The Negro in North Carolina Politics since Reconstruction* (Durham, N.C.: Duke University Press, 1940) and in Frenise A. Logan's *The Negro in North Carolina, 1876–1894* (Chapel Hill: University of North Carolina Press, 1964), both of which cover more than the titles suggest. Louisiana is discussed in William Ivy Hair's *Bourbonism and Agrarian Protest: Louisiana Politics, 1877–1900* (Baton Rouge: Louisiana State University Press, 1969). Verton M. Queener treats dissent in Tennessee in "The East Tennessee Republicans in State and Nation, 1870–1900," *Tennessee Historical Quarterly* 2 (1943): 99–128.

CHAPTER 8

The most able and most thorough treatment of Arthur's secretary of state is by John William Rollins in "Frederick Theodore Frelinghuysen, 1817–1885: The Politics and Diplomacy of Stewardship" (Ph.D. dissertation, University of Wisconsin-Madison, 1974). For a brief coverage see Philip Marshall Brown's "Frederick Theodore Frelinghuysen," in volume 8 of *American Secretaries of State*, pp. 1–43. Pletcher's *Awkward Years* is definitive on almost all aspects of Freling-huysen's administration.

For Latin America see the sources listed in chapter 3 plus Russell H. Bastert's "Diplomatic Reversal: Frelinghuysen's Opposition to Blaine's Pan-American Policy in 1882," *Mississippi Valley Historical Review* 42 (1956): 653–671; and J. Fred Rippy's "Justo Rufino Barrios and the Nicaraguan Canal," *Hispanic American Historical Review* 20 (1940): 190–197.

Material on the pork war and Irish troubles can be found in the works noted in chapter 3. Edward Younger's *John A. Kasson: Politics and Diplomacy from Lincoln to McKinley* (Iowa City: State Historical Society of Iowa, 1955) covers the role of a major American diplomat. For material on Africa and the Near East see Pletcher's *Awkward Years*, Rollins's "Frederick Theodore Frelinghuysen," and Hagan's *American Gunboat Diplomacy*. Garland Downum, in "The Madagascan Mission to the United States in 1883: Diplomacy and Public Relations," *Historian* 39 (1977): 472–489, offers general background as well.

CHAPTER 9

The history of the United States Navy has always attracted able historians. Harold and Margaret Sprout's *The Rise of American Naval Power, 1776–1918*, rev. ed. (Princeton, N.J.: Princeton University Press, 1946) has long been a classic. New monographs include Walter R. Herrick, Jr.'s *The American Naval Revolution* (Baton Rouge: Louisiana State University Press, 1966) and Hagan's *American Gun-boat Diplomacy*. Among the standard sources, already cited, are Pletcher's *Awkward Years*, Plesur's *America's Outward Thrust*, Reeves's *Gentleman Boss*, and White's *Republican Era*.

Major biographies include Leon Burr Richardson's *William E. Chandler, Republican* (New York: Dodd, Mead, 1940), Leonard Alexander Swann's *John Roach, Maritime Entrepreneur: The Years as Naval Contractor, 1862–1886* (Annapolis, Md.: United States Naval Institute, 1965), Drake's "Empire of the Seas," and Brinker's "Robert W. Shufeldt." Students should be familiar with the work of Robert Seager II: "Ten Years before Mahan: The Unofficial Case for the New Navy, 1880–1890," *Mississippi Valley Historical Review* 40 (1953): 491–512, and *Alfred Thayer Mahan: The Man and His Letters* (Annapolis, Md.: Naval Institute Press, 1977). Seager, with Doris D. Maguire, has edited *Letters and Papers of Alfred Thayer Mahan*, 3 vols. (Annapolis, Md.: Naval Institute Press, 1975). William Patrick Connor, Jr., in "Insular Empire: Politics and Strategy of American Policy in the Pacific Ocean, 1870–1900" (Ph.D. dissertation, Emory University, 1976), discusses the issue of Pacific coaling stations. The Haitian story is best treated in Rayford W. Logan's *The Diplomatic Relations of the United States with Haiti, 1776–1891* (Chapel Hill: University of North Carolina Press, 1941).

For Asian policy see the specialized works cited in chapter 4. Pletcher's *Awkward Years* and Rollins's "Frederick Theodore Frelinghuysen" always continue to be helpful. Additional detailed works include Tyler Dennett's "Early American Policy in Korea, 1883-7: The Services of Lieutenant George C. Foulk," *Political*

Science Quarterly 38 (1923): 82–103; T. C. Lin's "Li Hung-Chang: His Korea Policies, 1870–1885," *Chinese Social and Political Science Review* 19 (1935): 202–233; Harold J. Noble's "The Korean Mission to the United States in 1883," *Transactions of the Korea Branch of the Royal Asiatic Society* 18 (1929): 1–21; and Soon C. Hong's "The Kaspin Coupe and Foote: The Role of An American Diplomat," *Koreana Quarterly* 15 (1973): 60–70. Valuable information on Indochina can be found in Henry Blumenthal's *France and the United States: Their Diplomatic Relations, 1789–1914* (Chapel Hill: University of North Carolina Press, 1970).

For a broad picture of United States involvement in Africa see Clarence Clendenen, Robert Collins, and Peter Duignan's *Americans in Africa, 1865–1900* (Stanford, Calif.: Hoover Institution on War, Revolution, and Peace, 1966). Helpful works on the Berlin conference and American participation in it include Sybil E. Crowe's *The Berlin West African Conference, 1884–1885* (originally published in 1942; republished at Westport, Conn.: Negro Universities Press, 1970); Lysle E. Meyer's "Henry S. Sanford and the Congo: A Reassessment," *African Historical Studies* 1 (1971): 19–39; and James L. Roark's "American Expansion vs. European Imperialism: Henry S. Sanford and the Congo Episode, 1883–1885," *Mid-America* 60 (1978): 21–33. James A. Field, Jr.'s *America and the Mediterranean World, 1776–1882* (Princeton, N.J.: Princeton University Press, 1969) remains definitive on its subject.

CHAPTER 10

Much material for this chapter can be found in Pletcher's *Awkward Years*, Reeves's *Gentleman Boss*, Rollins's "Frederick Theodore Frelinghuysen," Crapol's *America for Americans*, Terrill's *Tariff*, LaFeber's *New Empire*, Plesur's *America's Outward Thrust*, Williams's *Roots*, Holbo's "Economics, Emotion, and Expansion," Novack and Simon's "Commercial Responses," Connor's "Insular Empire," and Beisner's *From the Old Diplomacy*. One should also note Paul S. Holbo's "Trade and Commerce," in *Encyclopedia of American Foreign Policy: Studies of the Principal Movements and Ideals*, ed. Alexander DeConde, 3 vols. (New York: Charles Scribner's Sons, 1978), 3:945–960.

For a general discussion of the economy see Samuel Rezneck's "Patterns of Thought and Action in an American Depression, 1882–1886," *American Historical Review* 61 (1956): 284–307; and Fels's "American Business Cycle." The special Hawaiian problem is covered by Donald Rowland in "The United States and the Contract Labor Question in Hawaii, 1862–1900," *Pacific Historical Review* 2 (1933): 249–269; and by Donald M. Dozer in "The Opposition to Hawaiian Reciprocity, 1876–1888," ibid. 14 (1945): 157–183.

CHAPTER 11

Reeves's *Gentleman Boss* is definitive both on the president's departure from office and on his death.

INDEX

211

tion; Temperature
Providence, R.I., 39
Providence Journal, 18
Pueblos, 86
Puerto Rico, 175–176
Pugh, James L., 7, 100
Pusan, 71

Quakers, 7

Radical Republicans, 12, 13, 22, 118
Railroads: development of, 1, 67, 105, 107, 135, 165; and political parties, 9, 10, 25–26; and corruption issue, 14, 18, 97; Garfield on, 23, 24, 26, 28–29, 56; and Mahone, 50; overseas activities of, 59, 62, 63, 160, 172, 173, 174; Arthur on, 77; and Chinese labor, 83; and Indian policy, 85; and Pendleton, 97; and racial integration, 109–110, 112–113; rates in South Carolina, 118. *See also* Crédit Mobilier; Granger cases; Strikes
Ramona (Helen Hunt Jackson), 90
Ranavalona (queen of Madagascar), 73, 141
Randall, Samuel J., 9, 99
Readjuster movement in Virginia. *See* Mahone, William
Realism, in literature and painting, 4
Reciprocal trade: Garfield on, 56, 74; Blaine on, 74; Frelinghuysen on, 161, 171–173; Arthur on, 172; problems concerning, 172–173; and Mexico, 173–175; and Cuba and Puerto Rico, 175–176; and Hawaii, 177–178; debated, 178–179; evaluated, 179
Reconstruction, 6, 22, 25, 47, 49, 56, 108, 110, 117, 118. *See also* South, the
Redeemers, 52, 108, 109. *See also* Bourbons
Red Sea, 66
Reeves, Thomas C., 21, 25, 27, 43, 54, 78, 80–81, 93, 102, 125, 181–182
Reichstag, 69
Reid, Whitelaw, 26, 32, 34, 43, 52, 81, 121. See also *New York Tribune*
Religion, 2–3
Republican Congressional Campaign Committee, 28, 44, 98, 116
Republican National Committee: nature of, 6; and Cameron, 13; and Dorsey, 26–27, 33; and southern strategy, 120; and Mahone forces in 1884, 121; and 1884 campaign, 182
Republicans: political strength of, 5; ideological, geographical, and ethnic components of, 7–10; and early Senate leadership,

12–14; and Hayes administration, 17; pre-convention maneuverings of, in 1880, 17–19; 1880 convention proceedings of, 20–21, 41, 49; platform of, 25–26, 48; 1880 campaign of, 26–30, 96; Garfield appointments of, 30–35, 41–45; and Congress, 44, 51–52, 76; and Garfield's southern strategy, 49–53; Arthur and party politics, 77–78, 99, 102, 181–182; and Star Route Affair, 94–95; and election of 1882, 99; and Negroes, 108–109, 113, 124–125; and Arthur-Chandler southern strategy, 114–125; and 1884 race, 121, 123, 181–182. *See also* Half-Breeds; Parties, political; Radical Republicans; Republican Congressional Campaign Committee; Republican National Committee; Stalwarts; Star Route Affair
Rerdell, Monfort C., 46, 93–94
Rhode Island. *See* Newport, R.I.; Providence, R.I.
Richmond, Va., 50, 106
Riddleberger, Harrison H., 52, 115, 120, 121
Riddleberger Law, 115. *See also* Riddleberger, Harrison H.
Rifles, 63, 155. *See also* Munitions
Riley, James Whitcomb, 4
Rio Grande, 62
Rivers and harbors, 25, 81. *See also* Internal improvements
Roach, John, 146, 149–150, 152
Roark, James L., 159
Robertson, William H., 32, 42–45, 53, 56, 76, 183
Robeson, George M., 149
Robinson, William E., 101
Robinson, William W., 73, 127, 141–142, 143
Rockefeller, John D., 111
Rodgers, John, 147, 149
Roman Catholics, 18, 28
Romanesque revival in architecture, 4
Romero, Matías, 174
Roosevelt, Theodore, xiii, 99, 157
Rosecrans, William S., 22
Rosenberg, Charles E., 95
Rossa, O'Donovan, 139
Rowland, Henry A., 2
Rumania, 68
Russia, 13, 71, 72, 136, 148, 153, 166
Rutgers College, 128

Sackville-West, Lionel S., 139
Saint Louis, Mo., 105, 174
Sakalavas. *See* Madagascar
Salomon, Lysius, 151–152
Samoa, 146, 151, 153